Seeing Red

Seeing Red

ANGER, SENTIMENTALITY,
AND AMERICAN INDIANS

CARI M. CARPENTER

THE OHIO STATE UNIVERSITY PRESS
COLUMBUS

Copyright © 2008 by The Ohio State University.
All rights reserved.

Library of Congress Cataloging-in-Publication Data
Carpenter, Cari M., 1973–
Seeing red : anger, sentimentality, and American Indians / Cari M. Carpenter.
  p. cm.
Includes bibliographical references and index.
ISBN 978-0-8142-1079-6
1. American literature—Indian authors—History and criticism. 2. American literature—Women authors—History and criticism. 3. Callahan, S. Alice, b. 1868—Criticism and interpretation. 4. Johnson, E. Pauline, 1861–1913—Criticism and interpretation. 5. Hopkins, Sarah Winnemucca, 1844?–1891. Life among the Piutes. 6. Indians in literature. 7. Anger in literature. 8. Sentimentalism in literature. 9. Indian women authors—United States—Intellectual life—19th century. 10. Indian women authors—Canada—Intellectual life—19th century. I. Title.
PS153.I52C37 2008
810.9'897—dc22
         2007048957

This book is available in the following editions:
Cloth (ISBN 978-0-8142-1079-6)
CD-ROM (ISBN 978-0-8142-9158-0)
Paper (ISBN: 978-0-8142-5619-0)
Cover design by Melissa Ryan
Text design by Jennifer Shoffey Forsythe
Type set in Adobe Caslon Pro

To my parents,
my biggest fans

A CURSE FROM THE DEPTHS OF WOMANHOOD
IS VERY SALT, AND BITTER, AND GOOD.
—Elizabeth Barrett Browning

I AM MAD
BUT I CHOOSE THIS MADNESS.
—Gloria Anzaldúa

Contents

List of Illustrations / xi
Acknowledgments / xiii

INTRODUCTION
Anger, Sentimentality, and American Indians / 1

CHAPTER 1
Playing Angry: S. Alice Callahan's *Wynema* / 29

CHAPTER 2
"A Woman to Let Alone": E. Pauline Johnson
and the Performance of Anger / 54

CHAPTER 3
Lost (and Gained) in Translation: Language, Anger, and Agency
in Sarah Winnemucca Hopkins's *Life Among the Piutes* / 87

CONCLUSION
An Anger of Their Own / 126

Notes / 141
Bibliography / 151
Index / 165

Illustrations

FIGURE 1

Pauline Johnson, BHS Image #635 ("First English Dinner Dress").
Courtesy of the Brant Museum & Archives. / 64

FIGURE 2

Pauline Johnson ("London, 1895"). Reprinted in Walter McRaye,
Pauline Johnson and Her Friends (Toronto: Ryerson, 1947), frontispiece.
Courtesy of the Newberry Library, Chicago. / 65

Acknowledgments

At West Virginia University I have been fortunate enough to find the collegial and financial support to complete revisions of this manuscript. I am grateful to Eberly College for the Riggle Fellowship, which allowed me invaluable research time in the summer of 2005. I also thank the English Department: Timothy Dow Adams, Gwen Bergner, John Ernest, Lara Farina, Catherine Gouge, Kirk Hazen, Donald Hall, and Timothy Sweet have been particularly helpful in the final transformations of this project. I also extend my thanks to Ellesa High, Bonnie M. Brown, and other members of the Native American Studies Program as well as those affiliated with the Center for Women's Studies. Finally, I am grateful to Sandy Crooms and others at The Ohio State University Press whose diligence and attention have brought this book to its readers.

An earlier version of this book was completed with the support of various divisions of the University of Michigan: Rackham Graduate School; the University Library; Michigan Society of Fellows; Sweetland Writing Center; the Center for Research on Learning and Teaching; the Department of English Language and Literature; and the Women's Studies Program. I am particularly grateful to the staff of Women's Studies (Judy Mackey, Donna Ainsworth, Bonnie Miller, and Roseanne Ernst) who contributed a thousand forms of kindness. My research was aided by an invaluable short-term fellowship at the Newberry Library. While

Acknowledgments

there, I had the opportunity to learn from Bernd C. Peyer and A. LaVonne Brown Ruoff, two scholars who possess an astonishing knowledge of Native American literature.

In my travels I have met a number of individuals who were particularly kind: Harriet Brady, Randy Melendez, and Diane Ferrand (Pyramid Lake High School); Ben Aleck (Pyramid Lake Museum); Georgia Hedrick; Louise Tannheimer; Catherine Fowler (University of Nevada, Reno); Laura Stevens (University of Tulsa); Heidi L. M. Jacobs (University of Windsor); and Sally Zanjani (University of Nevada, Reno). A Lannan seminar at the Newberry Library in the summer of 2003 had an enormous effect on my understanding of the field, thanks in large part to my fellow participants: Ron Carpenter, Brenda Child, Tony Clark, Renee Cramer, Tony Fresquez, P. Jane Hafen, Fred Hoxie, Amelia Katanski, Matt Kreitzer, Katherine Osburn, Malea Powell, Erik Redix, Jeff Shepherd, and Michael Tsosie. A Mellon Postdoctoral Teaching Fellowship at Kalamazoo College afforded me not only the time and resources to revise this manuscript, but the company of generous scholars like Amelia Katanski, Bruce Mills, Amy Smith, Deborah Mix, and Gail Griffin.

My ever-inspiring undergraduate advisor, Katherine Eggert, once told me I would find my graduate student peers the most valuable readers of my work. I thank Chris Matthews, Susanna Ryan, Maureen McDonnell, Sejal Sutaria, and Pavitra Sundar for proving her right.

During graduate school I was blessed with faculty whose astuteness is matched only by their generosity: Janet Hart, Susan Scott Parrish, Anne Ruggles Gere, Julie Ellison, Carroll Smith-Rosenberg, Sandra Gunning, June Howard, and Betty Louise Bell. I appreciate Betty's ability to find that rare balance between giving her students scholarly and professional guidance and granting them the space they need to develop independent projects.

I thank my second parents, Steve and Barb Benjamin, for their unwavering support, and Bonnie Barrios, whose boundless enthusiasm reminds me to cherish my own. I am ever grateful to my parents, Len and Jan Carpenter, whose love and confidence has carried me through everything from my second-grade writing trophy to the last page of this book. They are the only people I know who would happily copy microfilmed, nineteenth-century newspaper articles on my behalf. Finally, I thank Eric Bowen for countless bits of happiness. His constant patience, support, and kindness are beyond words.

The author will donate a portion of the profits from this book to the Indian Land Tenure Foundation.

Introduction

ANGER, SENTIMENTALITY, AND AMERICAN INDIANS

On a February night in 1836, hundreds flocked to the National Theater in Washington, DC, to see George Curtis's *Pocahontas, or The Settlers of Virginia, A National Drama*. An advertisement in the *Globe* earlier that day had promised that the performance would include an impressive display of Indian rituals: "[the Indians] have most liberally offered their services, and will this evening appear and perform their real INDIAN WAR DANCE, exhibiting Hate, Triumph, Revenge, etc., &c., and go through the CEREMONY OF SCALPING."[1] The newspaper noted that Cherokee leader John Ross would appear on stage with nine Indian chiefs. Both this advertisement and the review that followed stressed the authenticity of the war dance, the scalping, and the Indians' "passions," enticing local residents to the stage by presenting the drama as one that was not really staged at all.[2] In the absence of actual Native Americans, the white actors performed the Indians' supposed "Hate" and "Revenge" so successfully that the spectators believed they were watching a Cherokee ritual.

John Ross was in town at the time, but for a far more solemn purpose: to protest the government's American Indian removal policies. On February 15, the *Globe* ran Ross's response to the advertisement:

> [N]either I nor any of my associates of the Cherokee delegation have appeared on the stage. We have been occupied with matters of graver

import than to become the allies of the white men forming the dramatis personae: We have too high a regard for ourselves—too deep a welfare of our people, to be merry-making under our misfortunes.³

Ross's measured response, with his clear dismissal of the antics on stage, is a striking counter to the white actors' manufactured Indian emotions.

This advertisement for Curtis's play demonstrates Anglo-Americans' preoccupation with Indian feelings in the nineteenth century, a preoccupation that tells us far more about whites' own fears and desires than those they professed to enact. The Indian that this audience paid to see was a familiar one: a man who was either fiercely "savage" or admirably stoic. In responding to this performance, Ross was faced with the difficult task of expressing his anger at the production and at Native American removal itself: an anger that had to be sufficiently salient and yet distinct from the "Hate" and "Revenge" on stage.

The task of articulating a legitimate anger in the nineteenth century was doubly challenging for the first published American Indian women writers, who were met not only with these stereotypes of "savage" rage but with social proscriptions against female anger. The negotiations of three early American Indian women—S. Alice Callahan, E. Pauline Johnson, and Sarah Winnemucca—take center stage in this book. These women began writing in a time of great loss. During the nineteenth century, many American Indians were relocated onto reservations that often had little relation to their original homeland. As Robert Warrior notes, Native American land diminished from over 150 million acres between 1880 to 75 million by the turn of the century (*People* 75–76). Native Americans witnessed federal encroachment in other forms as well: in 1871 Congress passed legislation terminating the treaty-making system, and in 1885 the Major Crimes Act gave federal courts jurisdiction over certain crimes if they were committed by American Indians. Scholars have defined this era in terms of dispossession: Vine Deloria, Jr. and Clifford M. Lytle identify Removal and Relocation (1828–87) and Allotment and Assimilation (1887–1928), two periods characterized by the loss and reassignment of land (*American* 6–12). The momentous Dawes Act of 1887 was followed by the Columbian Exposition of 1893, which Shari M. Huhndorf has shown was a contest over the rights to define and perform—in a sense to own—Indianness. And of course the Wounded Knee massacre of 1890 testifies to the tragic consequences of contested possession. Such loss of land, life, and cultural traditions is central to the Native American literature of the period.

But this dispossession is only one side of the story. Its counterpart, indigenous claims to that which is threatened, is just as essential to these narratives. Although we tend to locate American Indian activism in the Civil Rights Movement of the 1960s and 70s, the turn of the century witnessed indigenous protest literature and other forms of political activism, such as the Métis rebellions in Canada. These actions are an important, and often overlooked, element of the late 1800s. A statement from Elizabeth Cook-Lynn's book *Why I Can't Read Wallace Stegner and Other Essays: A Tribal Voice* might well apply to this period: "literature can and does successfully contribute to the politics of possession and dispossession" (40). The first published American Indian women writers used a variety of tactics—what Malea Powell calls "rhetorics of survivance"—to protest such dispossession. One of the most pervasive and intriguing of these, I argue, is sentimentality. Although I maintain that anger is a neglected element of a broad range of sentimental texts, it needs to be recognized as a particularly salient subject in early literature by Native women. Often represented by Anglo-Americans as either savages or stoics—representations intricately associated with constructions of anger—indigenous writers had the difficult task of mounting a respectable protest that was not reduced to such racist stereotypes.

Together, Alice Callahan, Pauline Johnson, and Sarah Winnemucca constitute a case study of indigenous women writers of the 1880s to early 1900s. Rather than pursuing an exhaustive study of early indigenous women writers, I have chosen three whose work is particularly tied to the under-acknowledged connection between anger, sentimentality, and nationhood at a crucial period in Native American history. This case study invites rather than forecloses the examination of these issues in relation to other indigenous writers such as Mourning Dove, who according to Susan K. Bernardin draws from sentimental conventions in order to tell an otherwise forbidden story of miscegenation, or Zitkala-Ša (Gertrude Bonnin), whom I consider briefly in my conclusion. I do not mean to suggest that sentimentality was equally employed by all early American Indian women writers: Narcissa Owen, for example, uses it more sparingly.[4] Instead, I examine the implications of its use for three important authors of the time. I turn now to a closer study of the terms that anchor this project: sentimentality, anger, and nationhood.

SENTIMENTALITY

Regardless of their take on its effectiveness, critics have agreed that sentimentality is identifiable by a particular setting and cast of characters: often the child, slave, or elder on a stage of what Philip A. Fisher calls an "inevitable and fated suffering" (93). This suffering, through which Fisher claims the characters' humanness is earned, is for Jane Tompkins a powerful mode of social commentary rather than, as Ann Douglas had previously argued, an insipid, anti-intellectual collusion between women and male ministers. Tompkins claims that the efficacy of sentimental fiction rests in its ability to forge a connection between the reader and character: a process through which the "other" enters the self metaphorically to become it. The boundaries between the sufferer and the observer are at least momentarily obscured; the reader is not only taught to feel as another does but to (mis)take that feeling as her own. Thus in Harriet Beecher Stowe's *Uncle Tom's Cabin*, the white woman reader recognizes her own maternal devotion in the slave mother's refusal to relinquish her child, and so is more inclined to empathize with, and assist, the enslaved.

Challenging both Tompkins's and Douglas's preoccupation with white, middle-class women as the writers and readers of sentimental fiction, Laura Wexler argues that sentimentality was a vital instrument for the insidious "civilizing" of young Native American women in the boarding schools of the late nineteenth century. Sentimentality, she claims, "was an *externalized* aggression that was sadistic, not masochistic, in flavor. The energies it developed were intended as a tool for the control of others, not merely as aid in the conquest of the self" (15). For Wexler, sentimentality becomes a key tool of nineteenth-century colonization. In a somewhat similar vein, Richard Brodhead argues that the domestic novel of the antebellum era employs sentimentality as a means of discipline. Describing this disciplinary power in terms of maternalism, he contends that such literature is characterized by an intimate and "invisible persuasion" (46). For Brodhead, the disciplinary nature of sentimentality is so potent because of its ostensibly gentle delivery.

Whether sentimentality is construed in terms of sympathetic relations (Tompkins) or manipulative influence (Wexler and Brodhead), anger is thought to stand in its way. As Mary Klages writes, "In sentimental logic, anger stands as the opposite of empathy, leading only to violence and destruction and the complete dissolution of all relation ties. Anger is equated with a lack of self-control, with an inability to step beyond one's own feelings of grievance or wrong and understand another's position" (84–85). Similarly, Fisher claims that while sentimentality was radical at its inception, it was ultimately replaced by the end of the nineteenth century with "strategies of literary naturalism, class struggle, anger, and counterforce"

(92). Placing anger and sentimentality in opposition, however, neglects the complex and often contradictory roles of the former in these texts. And while I am well aware of the racist elements of sentimentality as it was employed in the nineteenth-century United States, I would argue that Wexler overlooks the ability of Native American writers to use the genre to their advantage. Wexler calls Zitkala-Ša's *American Indian Stories* "antisentimental," as if there were no room within sentimentality for the author's engagement (35). In fact, I contend, the American Indian women writers who began publishing in the late nineteenth century incorporated key elements of sentimentality into their texts.[5]

While sentimentality is a vehicle through which Alice Callahan, Pauline Johnson, and Sarah Winnemucca articulate and invoke anger about the dispossession of indigenous peoples, their implementation of sentimentality is not seamless. In drawing from the genre, they invariably contend with its inadequacies as an indigenous discourse: its dependence, for example, on a potentially paternalistic sympathy. I am also uncomfortable with the idea that sentimentality positions American Indians as suffering figures who must earn their humanness through trial. Yet to assume that sentimentality had no use for them, or that it was inevitably a compromising tool, is to ignore early Native women writers' facility with multiple genres in advancing indigenous nationhood. In other words, this study is not meant to fall easily into either the "pro" or "anti" sentimentality camp, but to acknowledge sentimentality as a fraught, yet potentially useful, mode for articulating indigenous anger. The fact that the very tensions these writers faced in using sentimental discourse are replicated in contemporary debates over sentimentality make me all the more determined to avoid any simple conclusions about the genre.

In contending with the various drawbacks to sentimentality, I have found it most useful to acknowledge two versions of the genre: the conventional form and its ironic counterpart. While they share characteristics like direct address and a thematic focus on tears and innocence, the latter form uses sarcasm and irony to critique the categories of "savagery" and "civility" that the conventional version is based upon. Since conventional sentimental language is steeped in sympathy for the less powerful, it can affirm distinctions between racialized groups like the authoritative whites and the helpless Indians. At the beginning of *Wynema*, for example, Alice Callahan can find an authoritative narrative voice only by separating herself from the Native Americans she describes. Later in the novel, as Callahan sutures other scripts onto her original narrative, irony and sarcasm are useful tools for dismantling this very divide between narrator and object. In a few moments toward the end of the book, Callahan's biting language chips away at this distinction in an attempt to affirm indigenous nationhood. Suffering is presented with a razor-sharp edge as the perpetrators of this torment, even the readers themselves, are named. Thus the cozy alliance between, or blurring of, reader and character that characterizes conventional sentimentality is momentarily disrupted, and the text becomes a powerful voice of resistance.

Recent work demonstrates that African American women writers also used sentimentality as a means of accessing and often critiquing the terms of respectability that white women took for granted. As early as the eighteenth century, Joycelyn Moody details in her study of "The Petition of an African Slave, to the Legislature of Massachusetts," author "Belinda" demonstrates that the situation of slaves is one the audience would not allow for themselves, using sentiment to establish their humanity (2; 7). Claudia Tate argues that post-Reconstruction novels written by black women often borrowed from sentimental conventions not only because they were popular, but because they enabled black readers "temporarily to escape oppression and gain access to a collective racial desire for enlarged social opportunity as full-fledged American citizens" (7). Locating the black woman in the sentimental novel, these writers grant her the legitimacy enjoyed by the conventional (white) domestic heroine. Yet we cannot neatly insert Native American women in the place of black writers. While indigenous writers may have implemented sentimentality for some of the same reasons, simply to substitute Native American women in this way would be to neglect the particularities of indigenous people's experience (that they are, for example, an occupied rather than a once-enslaved population) as well as their representations through Anglo-American narratives of nationhood. Any comparison of African American and Native American women writers is further troubled by the fact that Native Americans were not U.S. citizens in the late nineteenth century; indeed, they were not granted federal citizenship until 1924. And we must not forget the unique role of sovereignty in American Indian literature and law. In 1831, Chief Justice John Marshall ruled that tribes occupy a unique legal status as "domestic dependent nations," a term that has laid legal groundwork for Native sovereignty.[6] As Daniel Justice notes, by recognizing Native sovereignty, "the U.S. has acknowledged the fundamental right of Cherokees (and other Indigenous nations) to negotiate in the political arena as more than scattered ethnic or social constituencies, but as national bodies: peoples defined as much by their political relationship to one another as by their kinship ties and genealogies" (22–23). Thus these writers' use of sentimentality to affirm a right to possession becomes a statement of nationhood.

For many scholars of American Indian literature and history, however, sentimentality is an object of suspicion. Lucy Maddox treats "sentimental" as a synonym for "stereotypical" (94), and it is in part the sentimentality of *Wynema* that Craig Womack critiques; as he writes, "even if we place it within the context of the sentimental fiction of the time, it is bad writing" (120). Robert Allen Warrior links sentimentality to assimilation, describing the memoirs of Charles Eastman (Ohiyesa) as "highly sentimental accounts of his childhood in which he portrays Natives as needy for, worthy of, and ready for inclusion in mainstream civilization" (*Tribal* 8). Despite the shortcomings of sentimentality, however, we cannot fully understand the complexities of early Native American women's literature without taking seriously a genre they implemented and manipulated. Indeed, given how sentimentality is intricately linked to ownership, it seems at least in certain forms a viable response to Native dispossession. In disregarding it, we dismiss an important aspect of indigenous resistance.

ANGER

Before delineating my argument about these writers in more specific terms, I need to back up for a moment to clarify what I mean by "anger." I use the word to describe a construct that is more discursive and ideological than psychological. Thus, the following is not so much a project about how anger was *felt* by Native American women in the nineteenth century—a project that would depend on a fallacious assumption that literature neatly communicates the emotions of its author—but instead a study of how anger is defined and understood in certain texts. In Catherine Lutz's words, "The interpretive task, then, is not primarily to fathom somehow 'what they are feeling' inside (Geertz 1976) but rather to translate emotional communications from one idiom, context, language, or sociohistorical mode of understanding into another" (*Unnatural* 8). At the same time, I do not seek to erase the experiential power of anger: for what would anger be if it were separated from any concept of feeling? My task is, then, to investigate how early American Indian women writers *represent* that feeling.

A crucial aspect of anger, psychologist Stephanie Shields has claimed, is entitlement: the sense that one is due something or someone that has been denied or taken away. The degree of entitlement that one is thought to possess relates to one's race and gender; those in "variant" categories are more likely to be judged as inappropriately hostile than those in the "norm." In Shields's words, "What makes anger special? Anger is deeply implicated in the exercise of power. Power is the ability to get what you want; anger is the means to exercise power when faced with the loss of or the threat of losing what you have" (*Speaking* 140). Carolyn G. Heilbrun expresses a similar sentiment in her landmark work, *Writing a Woman's Life:* "If one is not permitted to express anger or even to recognize it within oneself, one is, by simple extension, refused both power and control" (15). In the texts I examine, anger is intimately linked to the possession of self, of land, of nation. To get angry is to position oneself in relation to others; the indignant white woman reformer, for example, identifies herself as the protector of "fragile" Indians. In turn, the angry Indian daughter whom Pauline Johnson describes in the poem "The Cattle Thief" stakes a claim to her father's body.

I choose the term "anger" rather than "rage" or "resistance" in order to mobilize a variety of related though not identical concepts, all of which revolve around an expression of one's rights. As Marilyn Frye has written, "anger is always righteous" (86). Philosopher Angela Bolte distinguishes between anger and rage, noting that rage is more powerful in that it demands attention and is often driven by a profound sense of injustice and self-preservation. I do not limit this book to rage because this affect is not broad enough to accommodate the righteous indignation of Pauline Johnson's "fiery Indian maid" or the Indian reformer. Similarly, to focus only on resistance would be to ignore anger's other incarnations, such as the stereotypical form encouraged by Johnson's predominantly white audience.

Approaching anger as a social construct, I consider how it varies across time and space, exerting tremendous claims on reality in each incarnation. As Catherine Lutz found in her study of a Micronesian community, although the Ifaluk term *song* might be translated into "anger," it refers to a response to a moral transgression specific to Ifaluk culture (*Unnatural* 10). Lutz goes on to illustrate how *song* is evoked when someone is disrespectful of the community, whereas Westerners tend to conceptualize anger as a response to an *individual* injury. In other words, anger is not entirely translatable: it looks and perhaps even feels different across cultures. Linguist Anna Wierzbicka goes a step further, arguing that we cannot impose the word "anger," a linguistic construction particular to certain cultures, on any society. Accordingly, I acknowledge the inherent slipperiness of "anger" and other affect words. Not surprisingly, the meaning of "anger" also differs across Native cultures. In a study of English and Diné (Navajo) speakers, linguist Muriel Saville-Troike found that the "normal" volume of the former was perceived by Diné speakers as an indication of anger or hostility. In turn, Diné speakers express anger through enclitics, or unstressed words attached to the end of another word (like "'em" in English). These enclitics, Saville-Troike notes, are "not recognized as emotion markers by speakers of other languages" (12). In another case, the Muskogee (Creek) definition of "angry" does not include a reference to "madness" or "craziness" that is typically part of English definitions; the two are separate concepts.[7] Since the writers I consider wrote in English, I am most concerned with the English definitions of anger; however, I have tried to remain attentive to various cultural interpretations of this complex affect.

What we might call "anger" went by different names in the nineteenth-century United States, and these different names reveal the particular ideologies at work. In phrenology tracts, anger is most often subsumed within the category "destructiveness," while conduct manuals tend to refer to "ill-temper." Such linguistic ambiguity was initially frustrating as I flipped through the indices of primary documents in hopes of finding a listing for "anger." This linguistic variance is an important tool, however, for tracing the various meanings of anger in the nineteenth century, since words like "ill-temper" signified particular race, gender, and class identities. Likewise, the term "destructiveness" signals the popular conception of anger as an anatomically rooted, potentially dangerous feature of Indians. I have also become aware of the way that anger bleeds into other emotions, defying efforts to isolate it in a kind of literary petri dish. The very roots of the word "anger" suggest its genetic, or at least its generic, relationship to grief: it is related to the Icelandic term "angr" which means sorrow (Davitz 35).[8] This entomological relationship between anger and grief, an emotion often linked to sentimentality, serves as further evidence for anger's underlying connection to the genre.

Historians Carol Zisowitz Stearns and Peter N. Stearns describe an important change in attitudes about anger in the nineteenth-century United States: while child-rearing literature initially emphasized the virtue of anger management in both girls and boys, after 1860 Americans developed a more ambivalent attitude toward anger as an emotion that could (at least for men) characterize a Horatio Algerian assertiveness that was necessary for success in the marketplace. Anger was further complicated by class: middle-class "experts" on child-rearing accused working-class parents of condoning and even encouraging their children's rage (74–75).

Introduction

Although their study is a groundbreaking examination of the subject, Stearns and Stearns do not consider how anger is raced. The ambivalence they uncover in cultural attitudes about male and female anger extends in particular ways, I argue, to American Indian women: Pauline Johnson, for example, delighted in the image of the "fiery Indian maiden" that afforded her a captivated audience. Yet this anger was often eroticized in troubling ways, complicating its capacity for resistance.

This book poses a series of questions that arise from the junction of these early Native American women writers, sentimental conventions, and discourses of anger. Given their need to appeal to a specifically white, middle-class, largely female audience, how did these indigenous writers articulate the anger that underlies their literature—and then provoke it in their white women readers? For if this is protest literature, as A. LaVonne Brown Ruoff has claimed, how do these authors formulate an effective protest against the policies of white leadership given the sanctions against women's anger in the nineteenth century and the construction of anger as evidence of Indian "savagery"?[9] We should also ask whether anger functions as a disruptive force—an impediment to the heroine's self-development—or whether it in fact fosters the affiliation between individuals that is the hallmark of the genre. Wasn't *Uncle Tom's Cabin*, for example, so effective in part because it aroused the anger of white women toward a system that divided mothers from their children? Finally, drawing from June Howard's observation that sentimentality is often dismissed as scripted and thus inauthentic, does the presumed incompatibility of anger and sentimentality stem in part from the perception that the former is unscripted and therefore "authentic" (218)? In turn, how do popular conceptions of sentimentality as excessive—and, accordingly, as fabricated—dovetail with concerns about anger as an excessive affect? How do these constructions of authentic or inauthentic emotions correspond to conceptions of real Indians and real women? I am interested, that is, in the intersection of emotional, racial, and gender performances in these texts: how feeling is crucial to playing Indian—and female.

The concept of "playing Indian"—performing popular inventions of Indianness to achieve personal or national identity—has been explored in detail by scholars such as Philip J. Deloria, Shari Huhndorf, and Rayna Green. Gerald Vizenor offers a sense of how Native Americans might take advantage of these simulations: "the postindian ousts the inventions with humor, new stories, and the simulations of survivance" (*Manifest* 5). Stories like Vizenor's "Almost Browne" enact this survivance in compelling ways. Here, white college students buy blank books from two "almost

Indians," hoping for the real Indianness that the books promise. The joke is on the white students for their hopeless pursuit of the real Indian of their imaginations. To this conversation about authenticity I add anger, a piece that is key to lived and enacted Indianness. Anger is both an element of the enacted Indian (the invention) and a resistance to it. Those who "play Indian" often enact anger, while Native Americans respond to these representations with an anger of their own. The quest to make this anger matter in indigenous terms is the subject of this book.

Scholars of Native American literature and history have considered anger's role as both a stereotype and a resistance tactic. Elizabeth Cook-Lynn notes that her writing originated in anger, but also comments on how it has been used against Native writers: "'stridency' in the native voice is also used to justify editorial intrusion, and comments like 'editors took exception to your tone: far too much anger, sarcasm, and cynicism' are not unusual" (80).[10] The title of Paula Gunn Allen's essay "Angry Women are Building: Issues and Struggles Facing American Indian Women Today" indicates her sense of the political efficacy of explicitly naming Native American women's anger. Others have linked anger to American Indian identities in even more fundamental ways. Describing his complicated position between Pomo and white cultures, Greg Sarris notes that when he took up boxing as a teenager in order to fight non–Native Americans, he was "a good Indian" who embodied "Rejection. Distrust. Anger. Hatred" (93). Sarris's comment indicates his sense, at least at the time, that to be an Indian was to be angry. At the height of the American Indian Movement of the 1960s, an article in *Warpath* declared, "The 'Stoic, Silent Redman' of the past who turned the other cheek to injustice is dead. (He died of frustration and heartbreak.) And in his place is an angry group of Indians" (T. Johnson 22). This statement suggests anger's role as a mark of masculinity, a contrast to a previous and allegedly passive stoicism. This remark seems to reject one racial stereotype—the stoic brave—without acknowledging how this call for an "angry group of Indians" might invoke another. This statement, from a publication with a title that is itself a common allusion to anger, raises the issue yet again of how American Indians might posit an anger that isn't reduced to a stereotype. Others cite "Indian" anger in order to critique it as a stereotype; a sarcastic line in Sherman Alexie's *The Lone Ranger and Tonto Fistfight in Heaven* reads, "The judge was red-faced with anger; he almost looked Indian" (99). To challenge stereotypes of Indians, this line suggests, requires taking on this assumed anger. Certain questions stem from locating this project in Native American studies: what are the implications of making anger a subject of Native American

Introduction

literature? How does one read Native American literature through its lens without simply reifying Euro-American constructions of the "savage" or the "stoic"? Does anger in these early texts tend to be collective rather than individual, as it is for the Ifaluk? It is also important to consider whether anger is represented and understood differently in Native communities. How can we attend to cultural differences without lumping all Native Americans into a single category or oversimplifying their differences from non-Native communities? What are the key distinctions between anger used against versus in the service of American Indians?

These questions are answered in part by acknowledging the indigenous literatures and traditions that these early writers drew from and modified. In this sense I share Craig Womack's, James H. Cox's, and other scholars' emphasis on Native American perspectives, sources, and texts; this is not simply a study of how whites viewed Indians or how American Indians responded to those images. As Kimberly M. Blaeser has reminded us, when theorizing American Indian literature it is critical to identify those "methods and voices that seem to arise out of the literature itself (this as opposed to critical approaches applied from an already established critical language or attempts to make the literature fit already established genres and categories of meaning)" (53–54). Robert A. Williams's study of treaties as legal and literary histories, for example, gives us a sense of how anger was shaped by at least one Native community. He tells of Kiotseaeton, a Mohawk diplomat of the seventeenth century who on his way to a treaty negotiation had to pass a site where his people had been massacred. Turning away with disgust, he hears the voice of his ancestors, who tell him not to be angry (86). Anger is thus understood in terms of its benefit to—or in this case, its harm of—the larger community. Other Native genres include oral literatures, political essays such as those by William Apess and Elias Boudinot, the journalism by Native women that Carol Batker has described, cultural objects like wampum belts and birchbark scrolls, and the mixed genres (self-narrative, remedies for ailments, and tribal history) of Narcissa Owen.[11] As Penelope Kelsey has shown, these genres are closely connected to "conceptions of nation and perhaps suggest the reasons for their continual exclusion from the writing of—and about—the American Renaissance" (152–53). Such genres, especially when named as indigenous, challenge Anglo narrations of the United States. Kelsey identifies Sarah Winnemucca's inclusion of her grandfather's version of a Northern Paiute origin story as a means of legitimating the Paiute nation. Winnemucca also, as David H. Brumble notes, draws from the coup tale and narratives of self-vindication in describing her bravery. Pauline Johnson incorporates the Mohawk matriarch into her magazine stories, and all three writers offer at times the sarcastic treatment of the word "civilized" that William Apess managed years earlier in works such as the "Eulogy on King Philip." We can include sentimentality in this picture not as a detraction from these indigenous traditions, but as a supplement to them. Sentimentality is not simply, that is, a "western" or a "white" literary device; it can also be a powerful tool for indigenous writers.

My study draws not only from Native American studies of anger but feminist accounts as well, many of which originated in the consciousness-raising groups of the 1970s. Such theories regard women's anger as a vital tool for their empowerment. Naomi Scheman, for example, demonstrates how women came to name and even feel their anger in consciousness-raising groups: it does not exist, in other words, before it can be named. In a germinal text on anger, Carol Tavris suggests the efficacy of a female anger that takes a collective form: "Rage, I believe, is essential to the first phase of a social movement. It unifies disparate members of the group against a common enemy; the group becomes defined by its anger" (272). Feminist scholarship has increasingly acknowledged the political value of anger and other affects that Alison Jaggar has termed "outlaw emotions." As Cynthia Burack suggests, this endorsement of anger amends what might well be an ironic reproduction of "a patriarchal horror of enraged women" in traditional feminist analyses, for in expressing anger we call attention to systems of oppression that might otherwise be invisible (112). Similarly, philosophers Lynne McFall and Diana Tietjens Meyers have argued that emotions like bitterness and anger are legitimate when they serve as necessary and ongoing reminders of past (or present) injustice.

A number of women writers have found literature a particularly fruitful canvas for articulations of anger. Deirdre Lashgari's collection *Violence, Silence, and Anger: Women's Writing as Transgression* examines how women writers have used anger in their writing as a form of resistance. Similarly, in her article "Have You Read the One About the Angry Woman Who Laughed?," Gillian Whitlock claims that anger combined with humor can be a potent tool for feminist critique. And Sandra Gilbert and Susan Gubar's groundbreaking study, *The Madwoman in the Attic*, reads Bertha as Jane Eyre's enraged alter-ego: a projection of the fury that a Victorian lady cannot express. Other feminists have noted how grief masks women's anger: Carolyn G. Heilbrun, in the germinal *Writing a Woman's Life*, describes how women seek refuge in depression or madness, while Julia A. Stern has argued that the melancholy of Susanna Rowson's *Charlotte*

Temple (1791) is a guise for women's rage against patriarchal authority. In this configuration, women's anger is not projected onto another individual but cloaked as a more acceptable grief. Similarly, in her study of nineteenth-century white and African American women writers' use of anger, Linda M. Grasso contends that these authors use a variety of masking techniques to articulate an emotion that is taboo. Such studies are useful for their consideration of how anger is employed, represented, and at times masked as a means of resistance.

Critical of scholars' focus on gender to the exclusion of other categories of identity, recent theorists have been attentive to the ways that race, for instance, complicates such interpretations. As Gayatri Spivak has shown, for instance, Gilbert and Gubar do not consider how Bertha is marginalized and demonized in *Jane Eyre* (and in their literary criticism itself). Bertha might be able to live out the anger that Jane can only dream of, but this anger is ultimately associated with the "madwoman's" tragic death. Similarly, Naomi Scheman does not acknowledge that the women she refers to are predominantly white and middle class, and thus more likely to occupy the relatively privileged social position of a housewife. I am not belittling such anger or suggesting that it does not exist, but instead pointing out that we should be cognizant of how such conceptions of anger might ignore women who are not white or economically advantaged. As Grasso has argued, Harriet Wilson's *Our Nig* (1859) shows white women's privileged relationship to anger: for them it affirms their standing in the community, while for black women it is a potential liability. Psychologists Stephanie Shields and Dana Jack both note that previous studies of female anger have been based on white, middle-class women, and so have limited applicability to women who are not located in those categories.

Others have shown how racial stereotypes figure into images of angry (or in some cases stoic) women: Mitsuye Yamada, for example, links her students' irritated declaration that Asian Americans "aren't supposed to get mad" with the difficulties that she encountered when trying to register a complaint against her department. For some women, Yamada's story indicates, anger is a privilege they are denied. Victoria Bomberry similarly notes how the expression of anger is complicated for American Indian women: as a child, she and her peers could only express the anger they felt in the classroom—a notorious site for the oppression of Native children—within the bounds of the schoolyard (27). From an early age, then, these children were taught to hide the anger in which others could indulge.

Anger, Sentimentality, and American Indians

In *Sister Outsider*, Audre Lorde argues that women of color should use their anger as a mode of racial activism and community building:

> Women of Color in america [*sic*] have grown up within a symphony of anger, at being silenced, at being unchosen, at knowing that when we survive, it is in spite of a world that takes for granted our lack of humanness, and which hates our very existence outside of its service. And I say *symphony* rather than *cacophony* because we have had to learn to orchestrate those furies so that they do not tear us apart. (129)

In Lorde's account, anger is not always constructive; she notes its potential dangers and calls on white women to acknowledge and take responsibility for the rage they often direct at women of color. Such scholarship makes clear that anger cannot be construed as a single entity that affects all women in a particular way—just as we cannot speak of "woman" as a single, unified category. Anger is at once a potential obstacle to the solidarity of women of color and its driving force. This book pursues several questions emerging from feminist theories of anger: first, is Native American women's anger inevitably regarded as inappropriately hostile, or do moments exist in this literature when it is deemed legitimate? Do any instances exist in which non-Native anger at indigenous women is *not* destructive or colonialist? Are there certain genres that seem more conducive to the expression of women's anger? Finally, how do femininity, Indianness, and anger intersect in literary representations of the nineteenth century? For these three writers, I argue, sentimentality is a tactic through which anger may be articulated in the defense of an indigenous nationhood. It is not foolproof, however; its success depends on the author's relationship to the nation she narrates and to the genres she is working within.

NATIONHOOD

The first published texts by Native American women require us to reconceptualize nineteenth-century nationhood from indigenous perspectives. Our task, then, is to trace both the construction of these nations and those who affected and were affected by them. The ways that these Native nations might challenge past and present understandings of the United States are often overlooked; even Shari Huhndorf, who offers an important critique of the unquestioned exceptionalism of American studies, speaks of "the nation's" history, inadvertently reinforcing the belief that the nation in question is by default the United States (12). By focusing on these texts, I challenge the contemporary understanding of who was engaged in nationalist projects in the nineteenth-century as well as the very idea of the American nation itself.

A number of scholars in Native American studies, such as Elizabeth Cook Lynn, Robert Warrior, Jace Weaver, and Craig Womack, have placed indigenous nationhood at the center of their historical and literary theory. As anthropologist Audra Simpson asks, "is [indigenous nationhood] some form of historical residue, a marker of colonialism's simultaneous beginning, end or continued life? . . . Is the notion of an Indian or indigenous nationhood merely a vagary of colonialism's living consciousness?" (115). In the pages that follow I borrow from Simpson's answer to these questions, seeing an indigenous nation as "a collectively self-conscious, deliberate, politically expedient formulation and a lived phenomenon" (118). In other words, the individual nations are actively constructed through these texts—they are not simply products of a colonial power. Winnemucca, I argue, is most successful, at least within the pages of her book, at using sentimentality to assert her indigenous nation.

The concept of the nation necessarily invokes the (post)colonial. Cognizant of the particularities of the relationship between Native American nations and the U.S. government, I prefer the terms "internal colonialism" or Jace Weaver's neologism "pericolonialism" (*American* 39) for their more precise reference to an indigenous population that is invaded by a non-Native group. Unlike the classically colonized, a majority group of natives ruled by a smaller, nonindigenous population, American Indians remain colonized; there is no "post" colonialism of which to speak (*People* 10). Even with this distinction in mind, I find some postcolonial theory applicable to early American Indian literature. In his preface to Fanon's *Wretched of the Earth*, for example, Sartre notes that the anger of the colonized toward the colonizer takes a violent form that is essential to "his" selfhood: "The native cures himself of colonial neurosis by thrusting out the settler through force of arms. When his rage boils over, he rediscovers his lost innocence and he comes to know himself in that he himself creates his self" (21). Similarly, in his analysis of Frederick Douglass's work, Ronald T. Takaki argues that the violence resulting from Douglass's rage is at once destructive and empowering. Takaki does not consider whether a female (or feminine) selfhood can also be produced through anger, and if so, what relationship exists between this self and the nation. In focusing on the nation- (and self-) building anger of the man who is colonized, Takaki and Sartre leave others to ask how anger might function for women. Given the intricate association between masculinity and violence, an association not extended to femininity, it would seem that new models need to be developed for understanding anger's significance for a colonized woman of color. In the case of Callahan, Johnson, and Winnemucca, I argue, sentimentality and anger converge to offer these writers one means of asserting self and nationhood.

Although sentimentality and nation-making were once considered distinct (if not mutually exclusive), scholars of nineteenth-century American literatures have begun to question the assumption that nationalism begins where sentimentality leaves off: namely, at the threshold of one's front door. In the essay "Raising Empires Like Children," for example, Karen Sánchez-Eppler argues that the ostensibly innocent Sunday school stories of the nineteenth century were in fact riddled with nationalist and imperialist impulses, combining domestic, sentimental rhetoric with the expansionist ideology of the United States. And as Shirley Samuels contends, it is in sentimental literature that the nation's bodies (the citizens whom white, middle-class women were expected to raise and reform) and the national body converge (3). According to Amy Kaplan, domesticity should be understood as a referent not only of home but of home*land*, and as such, a vital component of nationalism and imperialism. In their capacity as arbiters of the home/nation, white women were instrumental to these projects. In turn, I would argue, early Native American women writers use sentimentality as one means of buttressing their own nationhood. Sentimentality as a means of nation-making is not, in other words, the sole prerogative of white women.

My intent is not to propose a new definition of sentimentality or to track its precise evolution over the course of the nineteenth century but rather to broaden our conception of the genre to include anger—and to think about why contemporary conceptions of sentimentality rarely do so. While Linda Grasso sees anger as an aesthetic or literary mode that replaces "variable" categories like sentimentality (16), I treat anger, which I would argue is just as variable as any literary category, as a system of relations that always communicates power: a mark of the connection (or distance) between self and community that is shaped by race and gender. This relationship between self and community has particular resonance in early Native American literature, not as either individualism or collectivity, but a complex negotiation of both. Given that nineteenth-century

Introduction

"Indian reformers" encouraged Native American individuality in place of "savage tribal life," any simplistic use of either individuality or collectivity should be avoided (Prucha 621).

Although I consider these three writers in order of their success at using sentimentality to affirm indigenous nationhood, this is not meant to be a kind of linear progression from "failure" to "success" at being Native: such a mapping would be far too simplistic, and would reduce the complexity of their tactics. As Maureen Konkle asserts of the Cherokees, including those like Elias Boudinot who have been dismissed as assimilationists, Native struggles "may not qualify as tidy 'successes' over their oppressors, but they certainly are not failures either" (49). Konkle borrows from historian Arif Dirlik, who finds fault with those who see the "victors" only as indigenous individuals who have somehow maintained a "pure" identity outside of Eurocentrism. Such a belief, he argues, denies the reality of modern indigenous experience and resistance: "The effort to overcome Eurocentrism and colonialism does not require denial of an immediate past of which Euro-American colonialism was an integral part but presupposes an identity through a history of which Euro-American domination was very much a reality" (Dirlik 219). Simon Ortiz voiced this sentiment years earlier: "the indigenous peoples of the Americas have taken the languages of the colonialists and used them for their own purposes.... This is the crucial item that has to be understood, that it is entirely possible for a people to retain and maintain their lives through the use of any language" (quoted in Weaver *American* 256–57). Thus someone like Alice Callahan, who has also been charged with betraying her indigenous community through misrepresentation, can be refigured as a writer who employed particular tactics with varying success in response to the colonial context in which she wrote. My intention is not to flatten out differences or preclude critiques of early American Indian writers, but rather to acknowledge their manipulation of available literary forms.

ANGRY SKULLS

Having fleshed out the key terms of my analysis, I turn now to historical constructions of anger in the nineteenth century. One of the most influential was phrenology, a primary vehicle of the racialization and gendering of anger. Phrenologists held that physical attributes such as skull shapes and brain size were crucial indicators of moral, intellectual, and emotional differences between individuals and groups.[12] Temperaments, concepts that originated in the ancient study of humours, designated a constellation of attributes from physical features to personality traits. An individual of a sanguine temperament, for example, was said to be characterized by light or sandy hair, blue eyes, fair skin, a strong pulse, and "correspondingly" strong passions (O. S. Fowler *Practical* 39). Phrenologists' cranial measurements and weighing techniques invariably found that white men were superior to all others, a conclusion that held obvious appeal for many Anglo-Americans. George Combe's *The Constitution of Man* sold 200,000 copies, making it second at the time only to the Bible and *The Pilgrim's Progress* (Colbert 20). Combe's *A System of Phrenology* (first published as *Essays on Phrenology* in 1819) provided measurements of what he called "national skulls," using "national" as we might use the word "racial." Following suit, in 1839, Samuel George Morton published the popular *Crania Americana*, which outlined the differences in the skulls of various "races." Similarly, the brothers Orson and Lorenzo Fowler were a cultural phenomenon: their *Phrenological Almanac* sold 150,000 copies (Colbert 24), and Orson made nearly $75,000 on lectures and phrenological readings by the early 1840s (M. Stern 66).

The figure of the "North American Indian" starred in these phrenological dramas of racial difference. The Fowlers examined the heads of a Cherokee delegation to Congress (23), and Lorenzo Fowler blamed the Seminole War in Florida on Osceola's extreme "inhabitiveness" (M. Stern 46). George Combe's widely advertised works emphasize Indian men's "destructiveness," a phrenological term that closely corresponds to what we now call anger. In *A System of Phrenology*, Combe argues that the skull of the Indian confirms "his" savagery. The Indian's "destructiveness" is said to give "a dark expression to the countenance" (267). Indians are, in short, "*severe, harsh, angry, cruel, fierce, ferocious, savage, brutal, barbarous, atrocious*" (223). This wording suggests that anger *causes* dark skin, which is intricately linked to Indianness. In *The Racial Contract*, Charles W. Mills traces this belief in Native "savagery" to Hobbes, who in his famous treatise on life in nature as "'nasty, brutish, and short'" pointed to the "'savage people in many places of *America*'" (quoted in Mills 64–65). A diagram of a Native American skull later in Combe's book indicates a comparatively large area of destructiveness, which is affirmed by a series of statistics: "scientific" proof of Indian inferiority. *American Phrenological Journal* readings of men like Black Hawk, Osceola, and George Copway also emphasize their destructiveness.[13]

The image of the destructive Native American man existed not only in phrenology tracts but in emerging psychological theories as well. In

Introduction

Emotions and the Will (1859), Alexander Bain views humankind as a continuum from the primitive "savage"—who is like the child in "his" instinctual, unsuppressed emotional display—to the civilized man who has learned to moderate his feelings. Bain paints a rather grim portrait of the former: "There is in the more brutal minds a savage glee in rioting amid scenes of torture and death" (167). Unlike the "civilized," whose minds never "boil up in savage excitement," primitive populations are driven by a desire for revenge (168). They are likened to the "Lower Animals" whom Bain claims demonstrate a "childish wrath" (169). Any anger that Native Americans display is not only dismissed as childish but as an entirely expected aspect of this "inferior" race. Although Bain departs from the phrenologists in his focus on the nature and expression of emotion rather than distinct anatomical differences between races, he still maintains that a significant correlation exists between particular emotions and the groups that express them.

Despite Bain's firm distinction between the "savage" and the "civilized," however, his treatise poses a fine line between the two: it is only through rigorous education that the latter learns to moderate his or her emotions. Emotion is powerful, he suggests, in part because it is so contagious. Warning of the "infection of the passions" he claims that the "violent expression of extreme joy, rage, or astonishment, will induce a disposition to active excitement in the spectator" (211). The sense that a fine line exists between "savagery" and "civility" is related to the popular belief that indigenous groups represented the "infancy of humanity," a position that in the nineteenth century was increasingly regarded in diminutive terms as "arrested development." That is, Native Americans' supposed childishness was seen as a mark not only of innocence but of deficient intelligence.[14] Emotions were associated with various people of color; in *Love and Theft: Blackface Minstrelsy and the American Working Class*, Eric Lott cites polygeneticists' claim that blacks were "intellectually inferior because in thrall to the emotions" (32).[15]

Although such emphasis on Indians' inferior intellects would seem to reinforce a distinction between Native Americans and whites, it also suggested that Anglo-American adults could potentially "regress" to a child-like, "savage" state. The imagined Indian, Roy Harvey Pearce adds, was defined by emotion—by, that is, "fierce and animal-like" passions as opposed to reason (86–87). One does not have to delve far to appreciate that this fear of the savage, the "other," is predicated on a fear of who one might in fact be. As Mills remarks, essential to the Hobbes-inflected racial contract is the fear that "without a sovereign *even Europeans* could descend" to the "savage" state of Native Americans (66). In turn, conduct manuals that claimed to educate the reader in proper emotional display became all the more important: as one notes, "the lurking savage in us ... likes to get the upper hand sometimes."[16] In other words, a white individual's visible anger was construed as a troubling reminder of his or her similarity to Native Americans. Manuals such as Stephen Tracy's *The Mother and her Offspring* (1853) directed readers to restrain their infants' anger while they still could, and children's books like *The Passionate Child* taught their readers the virtues of containing one's displeasure. Childhood was envisioned as a relatively elastic time when one who is given the proper attention can be civilized, a sentiment echoed in calls to "save" Native American children by removing them from their "savage" homes. Such texts demonstrate the minefield these early Native women writers entered when articulating their own anger.

At the same time that people of color were thought to be more emotional than whites, anger was constructed as particularly detrimental to femininity. *The American Lady's Medical Pocketbook* (1833) reported that since women are more liable to passion, they require more restraint: "discontent, peevishness, envy, jealousy and ill nature, embitter life, impair the appetite, render the digestion of the food imperfect, destroy to strength of the body, and tarnish the fairest complexion. They are more fatal to beauty than the small pox was formally; because their ravages are more certain, more disgusting and more permanent" (102). In the nineteenth century, ladies' conduct books went so far as to liken anger to a disease. *The Etiquette for Ladies* (1841) offers a scientific account of the physiological effects of ill-temper: "The changes of the temperament, by abruptly exciting or repressing the regular secretions of the skin, roughen its texture, injure its hue, and often deform it with unseemly, though transitory eruptions" (119–20). These deformities are clearly visible, manifesting themselves in the "livid hues of approaching frenzy" (125). *Woman, and Her Thirty Years' Pilgrimage* (1869) also warns of the physiological affects of anger: "Fear and rage make the heart beat violently, make one gasp for breath, producing a choking sensation in the throat, and take away the voice. Their power over the muscles of respiration is also familiar. It is witnessed in the deep inspiration which precedes a sigh or an expression of surprise" (Bliss 181). Anger influences capillary vessels of the face, making the emotion readily apparent to an observer. These accounts are notable because they describe anger not only as a pathology but a kind of skin color. In both instances, anger is described in clinical terms, a disorder obvious to the trained observer. It was considered particularly pathological in mothers: "Upon her temper, the welfare of her family may be said to turn, because it has the greatest effect in moulding the characters, and in promoting or destroying the happiness of the domestic circle" (Parkes 47). And as several authors warn, the sight of angry face provokes anger in others as if it were infectious.

Given their focus on the visibility of anger, it is not surprising that a contemporary conduct manual recommends that the concerned observer present the angry woman with a mirror so that she may be confronted with her offensive reflection. Forced to see herself as she is seen, a woman would presumably contain her anger and thereby enhance her appearance. *Miss Leslie's Behaviour Book* (1853) similarly warns that an angry woman makes

> herself a frightful spectacle, by turning white with rage, rolling up her eyes, drawing in her lips, gritting her teeth, clenching her hands, and stamping her feet, depend on it, she is not of a nervous, but of a furious temperament. A looking-glass held before her, to let her see what a shocking object she has made herself, would, we think, have an excellent effect. We have seen but few females in this revolting state, and only three of them were ladies—but we have heard of many. (209–10)

This passage presents anger as a vivid, disfiguring force as well as a reliable mark of one's class status: "only" three of such women were ladies. Anger, the author declares, is not only unfeminine; it is entirely uncouth. Likewise, the author of *Woman, and Her Thirty Years' Pilgrimage* claims that the "lower animals" express their emotions through their facial features (Bliss 182). Visible affect thus served as a means of locating individuals into specific, though never entirely stable, social categories. Gail Bederman has argued that in the late nineteenth century, whites differentiated between so-called "savage" and "civilized" groups in part by sex and gender: men and women of the former were said to be strikingly similar, whereas the roles of "civilized" men and women were sharply demarcated: "Savage women were aggressive, carried heavy burdens, and did all sorts of 'masculine' hard labor. Savage men were emotional and lacked a man's ability to restrain their passions. Savage men were creatures of whim who raped women instead of protecting them" (25). In these terms, gender and race were intimately intertwined; to be an Indian woman was to lack white women's emotional delicacy. In turn, white women who were aggressive called their "whiteness" into question.

An image that appeared in an 1846 issue of the *American Phrenological Journal* complicates the link between femininity, anger, and Native

Anger, Sentimentality, and American Indians

American women still further. The article describes a woman of an unidentified race who is driven to anger:

> But when woman is wicked her wickedness is without a parallel. When she swears men cannot conceive oaths as horrid, or imprecations as blasphemous, or terrible, as those which flow from woman as from their own natural fountain. Those, are our witnesses, who have ever heard the daughters of infamy swear. So of her revenge. She rarely takes vengeance into her own hands, except when her domestic feelings have been outraged, or her fair name tarnished, but when she does, her aim is sure and her arrows dipped in poison.[17]

It is from the woman's domestic sentiments that this "savage" anger is said to emerge: a conflation that muddies any simple distinction between femininity, which is usually associated with domesticity, and "savagery," its ostensible opposite. Given that emotion has long been associated with women and people of color, it is not surprising that madness is marked in a woman by the arrows and vengefulness frequently associated with Indians in the nineteenth century. I am intrigued, however, by the idea that femininity might converge "naturally" in Indianness, and that the domestic might be linked not only to anger but to an Indian woman. Such a conflation suggests that anger might have been imagined as a point of connection, rather than distinction, between white and Native American women—especially in the domestic realm. Perhaps in "Indianness" white women found a justified way to be angry.

Just as phrenological readings affirmed whites' beliefs in the destructiveness of Indians, so too did they offer "scientific" explanation for the "the dangerous, vengeful woman" (Colbert 337). As numerous studies have shown, women who were labeled as hysterics in the nineteenth century were frequently described as "savages"; Colombat de l'Isère declares that "Most of the patients utter frightful cries and howls, which can be compared only to those of the wolf" (529). This alleged madness, Elaine Showalter has argued, offered (white) women a certain freedom from the rigid expectations of the female sex. Given the stereotypical association between Indians and madness that I discuss in the first chapter, however, it is questionable whether "madness" could ever be a safe retreat for an American Indian woman. Indeed, all three of the writers I consider represent anger distinct from such madness. Pauline Johnson, for instance, makes a strong case in one short story that the narrator's murder of her former fiancé is entirely justified; the story is after all entitled "A Red

Introduction

Girl's Reasoning" rather than "A Red Girl's Madness." It was in this contested territory, in which whites had long associated anger with the Indian woman, that these early indigenous writers would stage their protest.

My first chapter argues that in Callahan's *Wynema* the anger that is central to the self-development of the white heroine—and in turn the development of the American nation—is denied her Indian counterpart. Here the Indian is figured as a catalyst for the white heroine's rebellion. In this first known novel by an American Indian woman, it is the white reformer who voices a justified protest of the mistreatment of Indians. Like Sarah Winnemucca, Callahan finds in sentimentality a means of articulating anger; but for most of the novel, it is only the anger of the white woman that can be imagined. The fact that the legitimation of the white woman's outrage comes at the cost of the American Indian woman's character suggests the complicated relationship between anger and sentimentality in this early American Indian novel. Native anger is ultimately articulated here, I argue, in the form of a Lakota woman and through the irony and sarcasm that marks unconventional sentimentality. The fact that indigenous anger is available only by breaking away from the main characters and the text's conventional sentimentality indicates this affect's radical disruption of the narratives Callahan lived: she had to sever herself from scripts of temperance and Indian reform in order to voice indigenous anger.

In the second chapter, I study how Pauline Johnson's writing and stage performances are informed by certain racialized and sexualized scripts of female anger. Anger becomes a means of demarcating the main genres—poetry, short stories, and the essays of the *Mother's Magazine*—that Johnson worked within. Stories like "As It Was in the Beginning," a narrative of an indigenous woman's response to the loss of her white lover, illustrate Johnson's fraught attempts to produce an anger that aligns her heroine with white women readers in the sentimental tradition at the same time that it asserts her indigenous identity. She would find a more accessible indigenous anger in her poetry and maternal essays, genres that allowed her either to extend that anger to her white reader or to represent it as safely distinct. Johnson's effort to forge an anger that crosses color lines is a poignant illustration of the possibility for and limits of women's cross-racial alliances.

It is this very alliance between American Indians and whites that Sarah

Winnemucca negotiated in her role as translator for the U.S. government. As I consider in my third chapter, although her position threatened her reputation as a loyal Northern Paiute, in her narrative she combines sentimentality and sarcasm to critique the very system she operates within. Of the three writers, Winnemucca is most effective at using sentimentality to challenge her audience's expectations of "savagery" and "civility" and to affirm her nation. At the end of the chapter, I visit Pyramid Lake, where another Northern Paiute woman confronts similar questions of language, anger, and tribal loyalty (or betrayal) in teaching *Life Among the Piutes*. Framing contemporary debates over Winnemucca in Paiute and non-Indian communities in terms of the nineteenth-century narratives of anger, Indianness, and femininity helps us understand why this author remains a contested figure in one American Indian community—and elucidates a possible relationship between Anglo-American and American Indian women in feminist and anti-racist movements today.

TOUCHING "THE DAZZLING WHIRLWIND OF OUR ANGER"

I cannot imagine writing a book on anger and American literature at this moment in U.S. history without acknowledging its strangely resonant political context. After the colossal terrorist attacks on the United States of September 11, 2001, the intimate relationship between anger and nationhood has become dramatically apparent. Many Arab-Americans have found the public display of patriotic anger increasingly critical to establishing their American citizenship—and, in some cases, their physical well-being. A white man told me that during his post–September 11 taxi ride from the Detroit airport, his Arab-American driver seemed to feel compelled to spend the first fifteen minutes of the drive expressing his rage at the highjackers. And yet Arab-American men's anger must be of a certain kind; that is, it must not resemble the terrorists' rage *toward* the United States. Sex and gender further complicate this phenomenon: the government's focus on Arab-American men as potential terrorists makes Arab identity and masculinity, with its alleged access to anger, a particularly volatile combination in Anglo-Americans' imaginations. In turn, the appearance of female suicide bombers may create unease because it challenges such equations between Arabs, masculinity, and anger.[18]

Yet even before the terrorist attacks, Americans were preoccupied with the provocations and consequences of anger. This is, after all, a time when the lexicon of anger grows larger each day with the invention of terms like "road rage," "air rage," "workplace rage," and even hospital "ward rage."[19] In an attempt to find safe outlets for an anger that is defined as a potentially lethal public threat, schools have implemented anti-bullying programs, and judges often include anger management classes in sentences. This obsession with anger is evident in pop culture; comedian Lewis Black has made a career out of tirades against contemporary American society, and t-shirts and mugs boast tag lines such as "My anger management class really pisses me off!" Anger is often figured as frightening because it is not necessarily visible; it must be tracked and identified before it strikes. Handbooks that detail "suspicious behavior" do not seem far removed from the phrenology tracts of the nineteenth century. And although a number of psychologists have shown that there are few if any differences between women's and men's experience of anger, most continue to believe that women are far more likely than men to hide their anger.[20] So regardless of how anger is actually felt, it continues to be represented in raced and gendered terms.

A century and a half after John Ross lamented the National Theater's performance of Cherokee "Hate, Triumph, Revenge," Muskogee (Creek) writer Joy Harjo dedicated a poem to Anna Mae Pictou Aquash, a young Micmac activist whom she believed was murdered by FBI agents following the Wounded Knee siege of 1973.[21] The poem concludes with the following lines:

> I heard about it in Oklahoma, or New Mexico,
>   how the wind howled and pulled everything down
>   in a righteous anger.
>   (It was the women who told me) and we understood wordlessly
> the ripe meaning of your murder.
>   As I understand ten years later after the slow changing
>   of the seasons
> that we have just begun to touch
>   the dazzling whirlwind of our anger,
> we have just begun to perceive the amazed world the ghost dancers
>   entered
>   crazily, beautifully. (29–40)

Moving from "I" and "me" to the plural "we" and "our," Harjo demonstrates the collective power of an anger that she associates with Native American women. The speaker directs her words to Aquash so that the reader is structurally aligned with the murdered woman. The other women, designated by parentheses that emphasize their sex, sanctify this anger: "(It was the women who told me)." Harjo's poem is a portrait of American Indian women's struggle to articulate a righteous anger often reserved for middle-class, white women. The poem, written in a whirlwind pattern like a dance itself, is not simply a response to these representations or an attempt to define anger in their wake but a form of resistance that is as breathtaking and contagious as the Ghost Dance.

In writing this book, I have been surprised by those who find me not angry enough (too feminine?) to take up the subject. For a woman to write about anger as an intellectual concept is, it seems, to open herself up to personal critique: a reviewer of Linda Grasso's book noted disapprovingly, for instance, that it indicates the author's "unhealthy" preoccupation with what he believes is an unpleasant emotion (Richardson). Such encounters make this project all the more revealing, forcing me to confront questions about who I am and how I appear; how my feelings (or others' interpretations of those feelings) inform my scholarship; and what difference all of this makes in my analysis. As a white woman studying early American Indian literature, I wonder if I can (or should) share the anger represented in this work. Accordingly, one of the major questions that drives this analysis is to whose anger I refer: how can anger be a form of solidarity that respects difference and does not replicate nineteenth-century (and contemporary) white women's paternalistic anger "on behalf of" women of color? My interest in the power of women's anger has led me to act on my belief that the racialization of anger is an understudied and crucial element of consciousness-raising and anti-racist efforts. Even as these texts demonstrate the ways that discourses of anger have been and continue to be used against women of color, they also show how anger might foster their political mobilization.

1

Playing Angry

S. Alice Callahan's
Wynema

I begin with two endings.

But the devoted, romantic love of Hobomok was never forgotten by its object; and his faithful services to the "Yengees" are still remembered with gratitude; though the tender slip which he protected, has since become a mighty tree, and the nations of the earth seek refuge beneath its branches. And the Indians—Chikena's dying prophecy— (Child 150)

But why prolong the book into the future, when the present is so fair? The seer withdraws her gaze and looks once more on the happy families nestling in the villages, near together. There they are, the Caucasian and American, the white and the Indian; and not the meanest, not the most ignorant, not the despised; but the intelligent, happy, beloved wife is
    WYNEMA, A CHILD OF THE FOREST. (Callahan 104)

These closing passages of *Hobomok* (1824) and *Wynema* (1891) are similar not only because they link femininity and Indianness in the form of the "devoted" and "faithful" Hobomok and the "beloved wife"/"child of the forest," but because a commemoration of the title character is also a pronouncement of his or her impending disappearance. In Lydia Maria Child's novel, the alliance between a Wampanoag man and a white woman, which seems to promise an America that is distinct from both England and the Puritan community, is only temporary; the heroine's white lover soon returns to claim her and her son as his own. In turn, Hobomok conveniently fades into the background. In this way, the final passage marks the creation of the American nation that Hobomok's disappearance enables. In Priscilla Wald's words, Hobomok's convenient disappearance "Americanizes those it leaves behind": the Anglos who are his figurative heirs (34).

A similar disappearance is enacted in the final pages of Callahan's novel; the preceding sentences describe the mixed-blood children who, like Hobomok's son, assume Anglofied positions as missionaries of the Indians. In the final paragraph, Callahan interrupts an allusion to the Indians' dismal fate ("And the Indians—Chikena's dying prophecy") in order to return to her Muskogee (Creek) heroine ("WYNEMA, A CHILD OF THE FOREST").[1] By breaking off in mid-sentence, Callahan reminds us of the very "dying prophecy" that she does not repeat: an elderly Lakota woman's prediction that all Indians will soon disappear. Given this bleak projection, the potential for a community of "the Caucasian and American, the white and the Indian" seems precarious at best. The title character, each conclusion suggests, is the United States' noble progenitor who gracefully steps aside to make way for his or her Anglo descendants.

The fact that a nineteenth-century American novel ends with an image of the vanishing Indian is hardly surprising; a number of critics have commented on this trend.[2] What has not been considered, however, is another similarity between Child's *Hobomok* and Callahan's *Wynema:* both present a white heroine whose self-development depends on an anger that is denied the Indian title character. In Child's novel, Mary elopes with Hobomok in what is figured—not unlike the American Revolution—as a justified rebellion against her patriarchal, rigid father.[3] The development of the white heroine of both novels is significant in that it parallels the formation of an American nation that originates in and then disassociates itself from a rebellious anger. The white heroine engages in what I call "playing angry," briefly aligning herself with Indianness in order to enact a rebellion of personal and national consequence. Before attending to Callahan's novel, however, I would like to consider other examples of U.S. nation-making in which anger and Indianness collide. These examples, I suggest, serve as backdrops for the way that the white heroine of *Wynema* ultimately "plays angry."

PLAYING ANGRY

The figure of the Indian has long functioned as a symbol for Anglo-American identity. During the Boston Tea Party, white colonists dressed as warriors protested the taxes that England had levied on the colonies. In Philip J. Deloria's words, "Using Indian identity, misrule, and carnival inversion, Tea Party revolutionaries crossed the boundaries of civilized law in order to attack specific laws that displeased them and to speak to the British from a quintessentially American position" (31). As Deloria details, in the eighteenth century whites dressed as Indians during Maine's land disputes and Pennsylvania's Whiskey Rebellion. Indianness afforded these white men, I would add, a way to "play angry." I use these words not only to evoke Deloria's analysis of the Boston Tea Party and related events but to suggest the temporariness of this performance: the sense that, like play, it is a phase briefly useful but eventually outgrown. Another kind of anger surfaces in narratives of the American Revolution: a "madness" often associated with Indians. An early use of the word "madness" occurs in Samuel Johnson's famous "Taxation Not Tyranny" essay of 1775, which blasts the colonists for an anger he likens to insanity: "The madness of independence has spread from Colony to Colony, till order is lost and government despised, and all is filled with misrule, uproar, violence, and confusion" (quoted in Hardy 120). Here "madness" functions as a derogatory term for what Johnson sees as the colonists' excessive and inappropriate anger. Tory Governor Thomas Hutchinson makes a similar comment on the rebellion: "Where the present disorder will end, . . . I cannot make a probable conjecture; the town is as furious as in the time of the stamp act" (quoted in Drake LIV–LV). Both Johnson and Hutchinson portray the Revolution as a kind of madness that, like the "savage" Indian, threatens violence and anarchy. As Johnson sarcastically declares, "Let us give the Indians arms, and teach them discipline, and encourage them now and then to plunder a Plantation" (quoted in Hardy 130). In appropriating "Indian" anger, the white colonists thus risk association with this "savage" destructiveness.

This concept of rebellion pervades late eighteenth- and early nineteenth-century American literature not only in explicit references to the Revolution but in familial terms as well. According to Werner Sollors, in many of the popular melodramatic plays of the early 1800s, Anglo-Americans associate with Indians in a rebellion against an oppressive father. Such narratives portray a love between a young white couple that is forbidden, most often by the heroine's father. An elderly chief, the stereotypical "dying Indian," then steps in to bless their union. In sanctioning this young love (and anger), the Indian man—the legitimate American—passes this legitimacy onto his adopted white children, symbolically transferring his "Americanness" to them. The couple is rewarded not only with this blessing of their love but also with the inheritance of the Indian's land rights: an inheritance that depends, of course, on the Indian's demise. This demise is famously narrated in *Hobomok*, where the title character seems to endorse his own replacement by whites. In these fictions, the historic genocide and displacement of American Indians is refigured as the Anglo-Americans' justified rebellion against a tyrant of their own. It was with these configurations of anger and Indianness that the first Native American women writers had to contend.

As Deloria demonstrates, the Anglo intrigue with playing Indian did not diminish with the conclusion of the Revolutionary War; it remains, albeit in altered forms, today. In turn, the phenomenon of "playing angry" informs Callahan's later novel, *Wynema*. This text raises questions that I address throughout this book: How are American Indian articulations of anger distinct from "playing angry"? How can they write anger that is not dismissed? What if their narrative is not sufficiently angry or not angry in a particular way? It is this erasure of Creek history and identity that is at the center of Craig Womack's critique of Callahan's novel. The book is "unCreek," he suggests, in part because it is not angry enough; it ignores resistance efforts such as the Red Stick War of 1813–14 or the late-century railroad protests. Although I agree that *Wynema*'s nation-building is fraught at best, I see the book not in terms of Callahan's willful mistreatment or erasure of Creek history but of the narratives and tactics she employed: those of white reformists and missionaries. In drawing from the Indian reform and temperance narratives of these white women, she was largely limited to their scripts of "playing angry": borrowing "Indian" anger in the service of American nation-making.

CLAIMING OUTRAGE

To understand the possibilities Callahan had for imagining anger and Indianness in the last decades of the nineteenth century, we need to turn to another incarnation of "playing angry": the Indian reform that whites engaged in. One of the earliest incarnations of such efforts came in the form of Lydia Sigourney's "Indian poetry," which protested removal policies. In these pieces Sigourney voices her vision of the Native victims of removal: the "noble warriors, venerable patriarchs, grieving mothers, and chaste maidens" (Bennett 59). The movement solidified in 1864, when Lydia Maria Child wrote "An Appeal for the Indians" in response to the Sand Creek Massacre, Colorado soldiers' brutal murder of over 150 Cheyennes and Arapahos. Although she had written earlier pieces—including *Hobomok*—that were sympathetic to American Indians, with the publication of "An Appeal," Child became a leading advocate of the "Indian Cause." As Linda Grasso notes, Child illustrates white women's use of "moral emotionalism," and anger in particular, as a source of empowerment (25). This interest in American Indian affairs was later picked up by Helen Hunt Jackson, who attended a talk by Ponca leader Standing Bear in 1879. There she learned of the U.S. government's appropriation of the Poncas's land and the subsequent starvation of the people. Malea Powell identifies this as a critical moment in Indian reform: "No longer was the Indian simply 'imagined' by the audiences of Eastern reformers; the Indian was present, a presence that signified the absence of thousands of others who had been removed from the arena of daily American life" (403). Despite the presence of actual indigenous people, white women reformers continued to take an active role in dramatizing them. They played angry, in other words, by voicing American Indians in their own terms. Converted from that moment on, Jackson became involved with the Boston Indian Citizenship Association and, later, the Women's National Indian Association (WNIA), writing countless editorials and other accounts in support of American Indians.

One of the mainstays of the Indian reform movement, the WNIA was founded in 1879 by two white women: Mary Bonney and Amelia Quinton. The organization engaged in a host of activities, from sponsoring congressional petitions to sending cloth to the Indian missions with which they were closely affiliated.[4] At its height in the mid-1880s, the WNIA had over 60 auxiliaries in nearly 30 states (Mardock 199). The word "outrage" appears repeatedly in members' writings as both a synonym of the crimes committed against American Indians and the anger that these crimes aroused. This anger is most often associated with the white reformers who have taken up the cause; the Indians' anger is either secondary or nonexistent. At the WNIA conference in Philadelphia in 1884, for example, a Mrs. Crannell of New York read the following poem:

> There comes a murmur on the air
> Of mothers weeping in the West
> O women, rise up in your might

> And let your words be broadcast sown;
> With one great voice, of one accord,
> Demand the red man's lawful right
> To hold possession of his own.[5]

Calling on white women to "demand" property rights for American Indians (and American Indian men in particular), Crannell envisions herself and her colleagues as their indignant spokespeople. As the line "O women, rise up in your might" indicates, the position she envisions for white women is a notably potent one. Buoyed by an active temperance movement and the success of previous abolition work, these women had a linguistic arsenal for imagining themselves as initiators of social change. Rayna Green's analysis of "Wannabee Indians" offers one explanation of the attraction of this performance: "inevitably, and eventually, it draws women, even blacks, into the peculiar boundaries of its performance, offering them a unique opportunity—through playing Indian—of escaping the conventional and often highly restrictive boundaries of their fixed cultural identities based in gender or race" (31). As opposed to the members of the earlier female moral reform societies, whose anger was typically directed at objectionable white men, the anger of these Indian reformers borrowed from white male authority and the legitimate anger that accompanied it.[6] Significantly, Crannell refers to the potential Indian landowner as a male; the "weeping mothers" are not imagined as defenders or possessors of land but those in need of the white women's indignant protection. So while white women were drawn to the authority their reform efforts provided, that authority remained a patriarchal one: they assumed a masculine position in order to secure Native *men's* possessions.

In order to maintain their central role in Indian reform, white women needed to diminish the significance and reality of American Indians' own anger. A WNIA letter that accompanies a congressional petition reads,

> all these committees being composed of patriotic Christian women—permit these to say that into their ears and hearts comes the cry of suffering, undefended, ever-endangered Indian women and children, and that this cry is our appeal to you to secure for them legal protection; that the plea of Indian women for the sacred shield of law is the plea of the sisters, wives, and mothers of this nation for them, the plea of all womanhood, indeed on their behalf to you as legislators and as men. (4)[7]

Here the reformers efface the particularities of American Indian women's experiences in their image of collective "women" that they, of course, represent. In turn, although Anglo-American women's indignation was sanctioned as a moral protest, it was often accompanied by an acknowledgment of white men's authority to accept and act on their "plea." Carol Zisowitz Stearns and Peter N. Stearns contend that although in the late nineteenth century boys were trained in "moral indignation," at the turn of the century women increasingly found outlets for the same emotion "as temperance advocates, feminists, or Progressive reformers" (109). The complex rhetoric of the WNIA supports the claim that the movement offered white women a space for justified anger.

Although the WNIA had few American Indian members, individuals such as Sophia Alice Callahan who were involved in the related temperance movement shared this sense of themselves as spokespersons and reformers for the less privileged. Like many of these women, Callahan attended a respected female institute that prepared her for a teaching career. She later participated in temperance and religious organizations associated with the WNIA: she edited *Our Brother in Red*, a publication of the Methodist school where she taught, she was a member of Muskogee's WCTU, and in 1893 she served as a secretary of the Indian Mission Conference.[8] In at least one scene of *Wynema*, the novel becomes a platform for temperance work: a white girl describes a drunk husband who abuses his wife, and Wynema details the "terrible influence" alcohol has on her community (144). Callahan's regular column on temperance in *Our Brother in Red* suggests her affiliation with the female authority of the organization; she quotes a London publication that declares "American women . . . certainly go ahead at temperance work and advocacy in a way we know nothing of in this country. That may be in part due to the more advanced state of the sex as to public recognition, but is also undoubtedly due to their far superior organization. The W.C.T.U. is a great power in the land."[9] These words indicate Callahan's affiliation with "American women," a specifically gendered and national entity. Methodism, an important constituent of the WNIA and other reform movements of the time, provided her access to this authority.[10]

Callahan's position as a reformer was somewhat complicated, however, by her Creek ancestry. Her father, Samuel Callahan, was one-eighth Creek and active in tribal affairs throughout his life. After serving in the Confederate Congress, he was a clerk in the Muskogee House of Kings, one of the two houses of government. He also served as a justice and a clerk of the Muskogee Supreme Court, a member of the Creek tribal council, and an editor of the *Indian Journal*. He shared his daughter's writing interests as an editor and a writer of several candidates' speeches. Samuel Callahan was closely aligned with a number of Creek leaders including Isparhecher, a full-blood Creek who was elected principal chief in 1895, and for whom Callahan served as a secretary and interpreter. Callahan's skills as an interpreter were such that he was able to translate Isparhecher's wooing words to the white laundress who ultimately became his wife.[11] Isparhecher and his followers established a traditional Creek government to fight the U.S. allotment policies (M. Green *Creeks* 102). The Snakes, as they called themselves, were fundamentalists of the 1890s "favoring a return to traditional ways and rejecting the social, cultural, and economic changes of the colonies or the United States" (Champagne 247). In 1893, the year before Alice's death, leaders of the "Five Civilized Tribes" refused to meet with the commission to discuss allotment, and later rejected it outright (Ruoff "Editor's Introduction" xxxiv). Alice Callahan was undoubtedly privy to these heated discussions of allotment in the years before her death.

Callahan's mother, a white woman, had ambivalent feelings about Creek society; when their home was once raided in her husband's absence, she swore she would never return to Indian Territory (Ruoff "Editor's Introduction" xiv). Such ambivalence was characteristic, historian Angie Debo has shown, of affluent mixed-blood families in the area who had a great deal of influence among American Indians and whites alike. One of Samuel Callahan's obituaries describes this prestigious community:

> This aristocracy was rich and influential. Negro slaves tilled their land and herded their cattle. They controlled Indian politics. They rode in carriages. Pianos and mahogany furniture were brought up the Mississippi and Arkansas rivers in boats to adorn the homes of this class. When their women bought a new dress the whole bolt of cloth was taken to make sure that no other woman secured a similar pattern. (3)[12]

Although the Callahans' class status no doubt fostered Alice's affiliation with the white, middle-class women who formed the WNIA and other reform organizations, such relationships were not without tension. One of the sites where this tension played out was the Harrell Institute, a Methodist school where Callahan taught while writing *Wynema*. Established by a Methodist missionary in 1881, it was authorized by the Creek Council "to hold its sessions not more than one-half mile from the Muskogee depot, where it would not interfere with the rights and privileges of any Creek citizen" (G. Foreman 53). Told from the perspective of a white woman missionary, *Wynema* leaves little space for an exploration of explicit conflict between the missionaries and the Creeks. This erasure is indicative of the narratives Callahan was drawing from, which do not acknowledge such friction.

Although scholars such as Louise Michele Newman have traced white women's involvement in Indian reform, less attention has been given to American Indian women's relationship to the movement. If white women reformers couched reform in terms of their anger on behalf of American Indians, what role was left for indigenous women? In other words, how could American Indian women—already silenced in these accounts—mount their own protests? Given her positions in reform movements as well as the Creek community, Callahan is an intriguing subject for such questions. Unfortunately, her short life left little record; she died of pleurisy at age 26. For such answers we must turn to *Wynema*, her only book-length publication.

Callahan wrote *Wynema* in a period when whites' paternalist attitude toward American Indians was solidified by the momentous Dawes Act, which allotted lands to members of registered Indian nations. Intended in part to replace tribal communities with nuclear family units, the act designated 160 acres of land to each qualifying individual. Members of the WNIA supported allotment as a means of assimilating Indians into Anglo-American society and protecting them from whites' greed, while the Creek nation resisted signing any allotment agreements until 1901.[13] In February of 1882 several founders of WNIA signed a congressional petition that deemed allotment a critical safeguard of Indian women and men. Such efforts positioned white men (and, at times, white women) as the indignant protectors of the Indians, who were often figured as children. Thus a familiar sentimental trope emerged: the protective parent and the helpless child. As "protectors," white women were able to borrow from the masculine authority of white men. Whiteness and masculinity converge, even for white women, in a respectable anger: one that is not ostensibly motivated by a sense of personal entitlement. The complicated representation of allotment that emerges in *Wynema* makes more sense if we understand its standing in the Indian reform literature as well as Creek opposition to that policy.

A protectionist attitude is evident in the publisher's preface to *Wynema*, which notes that although this is the story of an "Indian born and bred"—and thus distinct from whites' accounts of the mistreatment of American Indians—its voice is one of Indians' "inherent weaknesses, of their patient endurance and injustice, oppression and suffering" (ix). In other words, this "real Indian" paints her people as they have been painted by whites: downtrodden individuals who are, because of their helplessness, worthy of the reader's sympathy. Only one clause in this string of descriptors suggests anything other than Indian frailty. Tucked in between the "despair" and the "magnificent results" brought about by white sympathizers is a note of the Indians' "last defiance of governmental authority" (ix). In the context of the passage, this claim is as ineffectual as the American Indians are said to be. Earlier in the preface, Callahan's "protest" is described as "sincere, earnest, and timely," as if to neutralize any of its negative connotations (ix). It is also described as a "plea," a word that places the author in a diminutive relationship to the whites who apparently control the Indians' destiny. And in repeatedly referring to the novel as "this little volume," the publishers dilute any of its potential edge by describing it as a modest, endearing object—a classic move in sentimental literature, where the object is instilled with value (ix). For example, as Gillian Brown claims of *Uncle Tom's Cabin*, "Stowe's sentimental fetishism invests domestic possessions with a sense of empathy between the object and its owner. In this light, sentimental possession and consumerism share a mythology of things in which possessions appear necessary and constitutive supplements to persons" (51). In the first paragraph the publishers defend the novel (and by extension, its author) against potential critics, thus reenacting a defense of the Indians that shores up white personhood.

This particular sentimentality, in which Native Americans are treated as helpless, leaves little room for Callahan as a subject. Her dedication is an aggregate of shifting identities as she seeks a position from which to speak:

> To the Indian tribes of North America who have felt the wrongs and oppression of their pale-faced brothers, I lovingly dedicate this work, praying that it may serve to open the eyes and heart of the world to our afflictions, and thus speedily issue into existence an era of good feeling and just dealing toward us and our more oppressed brothers.

In one sentence she moves from "their" to "our," "us" to "our more oppressed brothers," slipping from the position of the Indian observer of these afflictions, to the Indian victim of them, and finally to the white reformer who expresses her sympathy for her "brothers." These shifts make the object of the dedication unclear—is it the Creek or another nation that is the "more oppressed"? The sentimental voice that she adopts seems to demand oppressed others who are not the speaker herself, a silenced group/object worthy of the reader's sympathy. Drawing from the conventions of Child and other white reformers, Callahan adopts the position of the powerful white reformer who denounces the treatment of Indians—a position occupied by her white heroine. The anger that emerges is ultimately not for the author herself but for her "more oppressed brothers": the children/other/object that need her protection. So while anger exists here, it differs little from that of the white woman reformer who "lovingly" defends those who are more persecuted, and who, as Ruoff notes, calls on the reformist anger of the white reader ("Editor's Introduction" xx).

The opening scene of *Wynema* positions the Indian characters in terms that would be familiar to white readers: a young Indian girl enjoys an idyllic life in her village, unaware of the danger that threatens her Eden-like existence. This scene recalls the opening of Harriet Jacobs's sentimental narrative *Incidents in the Life of a Slave Girl*, in which the narrator as a young girl is ignorant of her slave status. Callahan's characters are portrayed as simple, innocent beings: "Ah, happy, peaceable Indians! Here you may dream of the happy hunting-grounds beyond, little thinking of the rough, white hand that will soon shatter your dream and scatter the dreams" (1). Possessive pronouns immediately position Wynema as an object owned in the sentimental tradition; as the first line reads, "In an obscure place, miles from the nearest trading point, in a tepee, dwelt the parents of *our heroine* when she first saw the light" (1, my emphasis). She is described in diminutive terms as "this little savage . . . the idol of her parents' hearts" (1). The word "idol" is striking for its traditional association with Native Americans and its suggestion of an object of excessive attention. A few pages later, Genevieve describes the title character as "My little Wynema" (9). Adopting a sentimental tone that locates Wynema and her family as subjects of the reader's pity, Callahan creates three positions: the innocent and unsuspecting Indian; the "rough, white hand" that will inevitably be raised against the Indian; and the narrator, a sympathetic white individual who declares her attachment to "our heroine" even as she distinguishes herself from that heroine (1). In a single paragraph, the words "our heroine" and "little savage" coexist without the ironic tone that, I will demonstrate, characterizes the end of the novel.

The direct address typical of sentimental prose targets a variety of subjects, many of whom are treated in paternalistic terms. At one point, the narrator speaks to an Indian reader: "Here is a home like unto the one your forefathers owned before the form of the white man came upon the scene and changed your quiet habitations into places of business and strife" (1). Yet the following sentence refers to the Indian in third

Chapter 1

person: "Here are no churches and school-houses, for the 'heathen is a law unto himself,' and 'ignorance is bliss,' to the savage; but the 'medicine man' tells them of the Indian's heaven behind the great mountain, and points them to the circuitous trail over its side which he tells them has been made by the great warriors of their tribe as they went to the 'happy hunting-ground'" (1–2). One voice that emerges is strikingly condescending, describing the community as "lowly," "dusky," and "primitive" (2). The characters are also referred to in general terms as "the Indians" rather than the Creeks in a replication of the Anglo tendency to lump all nations into an indistinguishable mass. Another familiar image appears in the representation of the overworked Indian woman (17), and Wynema herself is associated with the word "crept"—a word that indicates a certain primitive or infantilized status (19). Even the quotations that Callahan places around phrases like the "heathen is a law unto himself" and "bucks" do little to mount a critique of such stereotypes (1). This belittlement of the Indians is particularly evident when the "'medicine man'" treats Genevieve, who has fallen ill (12). Quotation marks suggest the narrator's distance from and skepticism about the legitimacy of the Creek doctor, which is further implied in the description of his "weird" and ultimately unsuccessful treatment (13). Instead of telling the scene from the perspective of the medicine man whose white patient is ignorant of his healing powers, the narrator shares Genevieve's disbelief. Genevieve describes a traditional Creek dish as "tough and tasteless," words that are not qualified in any way (10), and comments on the "queer noises this savage musician" makes during the busk (20).[14] Genevieve's disparaging tone recalls Louis Owens's description of *The Life and Adventures of Joaquin Murieta* (1854), a book by another biracial author: "It is a novel that stands as fascinating testimony to the conflicts and tensions within the mixedblood author, who moves easily inside the dominant white culture but cannot forget or forgive the denigration by that culture of his indigenous self" (32–33). Indeed, there is little difference in the first half of the book between Genevieve's and the narrator's voices: both are positioned as the adults who watch over wayward, heathen children.

The infantilizing of Wynema is especially pronounced. At one point, Wynema declares of Genevieve, "and I luf her, for she is so good" (19). She is repeatedly described by Gerald and Genevieve as "my little lady" (19) and the "little one" (20). Even when Wynema becomes old enough to join Genevieve as a teacher at the Indian school, she is figured as her devoted assistant, her "little girl" who accompanies her on her trip home (35). Yet early in the novel, Genevieve is also described in diminutive terms; even though she is a grown woman, she is called a "poor little girl" (6) and a "little skeptic" (17). Even when Gerald admits that the phrase "little girl" is "now a *misnomer*," he continues to apply it to Wynema (37). Before the Indian children learn English, Genevieve is entirely dependent on Wynema for her voice; the latter is her trusted interpreter. Later, when Genevieve decides to return to her southern home for a visit, she insists that Wynema come with her since she cannot stand to go alone. This treatment of Genevieve suggests that white womanhood is, within this sentimental economy, at times compromised as well. It also indicates the limits of the white woman reformer: she might have moments of playing angry, but she is still limited by conventional norms of femininity.

From the first page there is a strange juxtaposition of references to Native Americans: the words "bucks" and "heathens" are in quotation marks, suggesting the author's distance from or even critique of them; yet the next paragraph does not quote equally problematic phrases like "the little savage" (1). This juxtaposition exemplifies the heteroglossia that Ruoff describes as well as what I term the competing scripts Callahan inherited: in one line, she is the white narrator viewing the Native American girl as a sentimental object, while in the next she is critical of the stereotypes imposed upon American Indians. Perhaps this indicates the complexity of the reformers themselves, who sought to carve out a distance from certain racist views of Native Americans and yet, in positioning themselves as the "saviors" of the "vulnerable" Indians, employed stereotypes of their own.

This differentiation between the overtly racist view of Native Americans and a perhaps more insidious interpretation of them is most evident in the relationship between Gerald, the white male reformer/missionary, and Genevieve. Gerald educates Genevieve about Creek culture, offering her a more "sympathetic" view of the community. The first description of Gerald emphasizes his sentimental capacity: "possessing a kindly sympathy in face and voice, he easily won the hearts of his dark companions" (2). His influence is presented as the gentle urging of Native Americans from an "uneducated" or "heathen" state. Gerald is described not only as sympathetic but "American," a designation never given to Wynema or her family (15). His sentimentality is also profoundly domestic, as he enters the "tepees" (structures that, as Craig Womack notes, Creeks have never actually lived in): "with a crowd gathered about him, he hold of the love and mercy of the Savior, of the home that awaits the faithful" (2). Domesticity and femininity here take a notably Anglo-American tack as Gerald resolves to speak to Wynema in English, "the mother tongue," rather than Creek, which is of course her actual mother's tongue (3). Wynema is instantly entrenched in sentimental English language; an early conversation with Gerald, in which she begs him to accept her as his student, ends with "her eyes full of grateful tears" (4). Like Sarah Winnemucca, Wynema assumes the position of interpreter, in between the whites and Native Americans. In an early scene she translates Genevieve's explanation of God's love, a translation that has marked effects on the other children: "After this the children seemed to listen to the morning services more seriously and attentively, and before many weeks elapsed were able to join with their teacher in repeating a prayer she taught them" (7). Here Wynema seems to lack Winnemucca's self-consciousness of her complicated position as a potential conduit for conversion and even colonization, a lack that likely fuels Womack's and other critics' frustration with her. And despite Wynema's fluency in English, she is unable to explain customs like the busk to Genevieve; such explanations are left to Gerald, as if he knows more about Creek culture than Wynema does. So while the novel might attempt a neat distinction between "us" (the whites) versus "the foreigners" (the Creeks)—as linked to Gerald's fascination with the "strange, new varieties" of flowers (39)—the sentimental outsider occupies the center of the indigenous community.

A main feature of this centerpiece, as in Winnemucca's narrative, is the school: a site linked to the home in fundamental ways. At the request of Wynema's father, a female (white) teacher is recruited to live with the family: "Let it be a woman, and she may live with us; I want the child to be with her always, for she is so anxious to learn. We will do all we can for the teacher, if she will live among us" (4). In the final line of the chapter Genevieve's arrival is equated with the civilization that is the goal of conventional sentimentality: "Thus came civilization among the Tepee Indians" (5). Here scripture somehow manages to transcend linguistic differences in sentimental terms. The children don't understand "sweet, comforting gospel" like John 14 (6).[15] Yet the "tone went straight to each girl's heart and found lodgment there" (6). The teacher-student relationship is likened to a nuclear family, accomplishing both a religious and a cultural conversion: no longer is the extended family of Creek culture in play. Later in the novel, when Genevieve briefly returns to her southern home, she is described as Wynema's mother; it is she who grants Wynema permission to take candy from Gerald (19). Her maternal position only grows with time; instead of expressing a more realistic trepidation about their daughter's departure with a white person, Wynema's parents give their "hearty approval" for her later visit to Genevieve's home in the South (36).

Playing Angry

It is with Gerald's guidance that Genevieve is able to assume the position of the sentimental narrator. When Genevieve expresses her desire that the Indians quit their "barbaric" dance, Gerald replies, "Do you think, Miss Weir, that if our Indian brother yonder, now full of the enjoyment of the hour, could step into a ball-room, say in Mobile, with its lights and flowers, its gaudily, and if you will allow it, indecently dressed dancers—do you think he would consider us more civilized than he? Of course that is because he is an uncouth savage" (21). Thus the sarcasm that Sarah Winnemucca uses so effectively is here reserved for the white man. With this last note of irony he complicates Genevieve's—and what is often the narrator's—casual use of the word "savage." Gerald is, as Genevieve notes, the perfect "Champion" of the Indian, one on whom they depend for protection from such misrepresentation (22). Yet her response indicates that there is still some work to do: she laughs, granting Native American "superiority" (22) with a lightness that seems more a testimony to her deference toward (and attraction to) Gerald than an earnest belief in indigenous civility.

This deference to the white male reformer is reminiscent of the rhetoric of WNIA, in which a woman's authority is secured through her relationship to the male Indian Rights Association. Gerald imagines himself as the "'father confessor'" who guides (and presumably defends) his less enlightened children (28). This model of the Indian reformer is particularly evident in a scene in which Gerald and Choe Harjo, Wynema's father, discuss the whites' failure to repay the Creeks. In two sentences, Choe goes from speaking of "these poor Indians" to "My people" (30). It is as if the Creeks must be described as racialized others who are the object of his sympathy before Choe can speak as Creek himself. Choe warns Gerald that his people are quite angry, and that he fears violence will follow. For the first time in the novel, a Creek man voices anger at whites—though, significantly, it is another's discontent that he expresses rather than his own. And it is to Gerald that this complaint is made, as if the white man were more prepared to take action. Gerald recalls at length instances of Native American fury: he tells, for example, of an Indian orator who once shared the story of a traitor shot "through and through until there was no flesh to mark a bullet" (32). Even as Gerald emphasizes the speaking skills of this Indian man—likening him to Cicero—it is he, as Womack notes, who speaks the Creek man's words. Choe stands by silently as Gerald describes, and even appropriates, the Indians' "frenzy of emotion" (32) and "warmth and feeling" (31). In this instance of playing angry, Gerald literally voices the Creek man's words, momentarily aligning himself with

Indianness and affirming his ability as a white man to assert himself. If, as I believe, the articulation of anger is aligned with self and national possession, Gerald's speech is of great consequence. Here Gerald voices indigenous suffering most emphatically, playing angry in a way the Native Americans themselves cannot.

An earlier scene suggests that while American Indian anger may be constrained, their grief is not. Genevieve marvels at a Creek widow's grief: "Here was no fashionable grief with its dress of sable hue, its hangings of crepe, and stationery with its inch-wide band of black, such as Madison-Square widows use. Ah! no, here was real, simple, heart-felt grief such as the ignorant and uneducated feel; grief such as Eve felt over the death of her well-beloved son" (24). As opposed to Anglo (and upper-class) women, whose grief is stultified by pretension, the indigenous wife demonstrates a "real" emotion that is likened to the biblical Eve. The task of Gerald and Genevieve is thus to marshal this "natural" feeling for their own devices. Tears stream down the faces of the mourners as they listen to Gerald's sermon, which is given partly in Creek. Here Gerald realizes he can "strengthen" his influence over his "Indian friends" by indulging them in such ceremonies (28). The manipulation of emotion is thus critical to his "civilizing" project.

The final paragraphs of the eighth chapter emphasize the Creeks' growing anger against the delegates who owe them money. As Lisa Tatonetti explains, this section refers to the 1889 scandal in which Creeks were paid only $10,000 out of a two million dollar settlement for a land seizure. Tatonetti notes that the *Muskogee Daily Phoenix* indicates a much more nuanced Creek response to the scandal than Callahan depicts.[16] The Creeks are described as furious: "The wrath of the Indians waxed hotter and hotter, and their secret meetings became more numerous" (33). This recalls the historical murder of William McIntosh, who was killed for selling Native land in the Treaty of Indian Springs in 1825. This reference is immediately followed, however, by a statement that neutralizes the power and complexity of such historic anger: "Not an arm was raised in defence [*sic*] of the poor Indians stripped of their bread-money, notwithstanding the mutterings of dissatisfaction and threats of vengeance heard all along the lines; and thus a great robbery passed into oblivion" (33). This statement suggests the greatest tragedy is not that Creeks have been mistreated, but that no whites are there to defend them in the sentimental tradition. Indeed, as the chapter ends, "But the Indians learned a lesson therefrom, and they were not the only learners" (33). For if they were, this line suggests, oblivion would continue; action is up to the whites who hear of this injustice. Andrea Smith, writing about sexual violence, points to an even more disturbing consequence of this dynamic. Representations of Native American men as perpetrators of violence and Native women as instigators of their own sexual violence persist, so that white men, the actual oppressors, are figured as the rescuer of American Indian women: "Apparently, Native women can only be free while under the dominion of white men, and both Native and white women have to be protected from Indian men, rather than from white men" (23). In the sentimental economy of Callahan's novel, white men are positioned as the sympathetic protectors even though they themselves were historically the perpetrators of violence.

When Genevieve returns to her southern home, Wynema in tow along with her other "Indian relics," she displays the outrage that proves key to her self-development and corresponding protection of the American Indians (42). Her anger is sparked not only by her fiancé's description of her future as his "little girl" and "little wife" but his inability to imagine her as a protector of Indians (47).

> "Your wife, indeed! I have never promised to be such, and please heaven! I never will. My husband must be a man, full-grown—a man capable of giving an opinion, just and honest, without using insult to do so. Good evening! I have no time to spend in arguing about a people who have not the intellect of a dog," and with a curl of her lip, and a toss of the head, she swept from the room, *righteously angry.* (56, my emphasis)

These last two words indicate that Genevieve's anger is expressible and dignified because it is steeped in her moral defense of Indians; it stems not from self-interest but her indignation on behalf of others—an anger that Marilyn Frye notes is often considered more acceptable in women than anger for themselves. Like the representatives of the WNIA, Genevieve relies on an image of Indians who are dependent on whites. Genevieve emerges from this scene a more confident, mature woman who sees herself as a kind of prophet who will return to her "'people, Israel,'" no longer a girl who frets over her role as a missionary (59). Notably, it is here that Callahan voices one of her most poignant feminist critiques, as if in Genevieve's anger and self-development she finds a new confidence herself: "He spoke in the patronizing way men usually adopt when reasoning with women" (55). Maurice must relinquish his hopes of "owning" Genevieve, the quotation marks emphasizing the text's new critique of such possession. Genevieve's heated condemnation of Maurice's racist and sexist beliefs belittles his masculinity and, in the process, suggests her own authority: "Oh, if I pretended to be a man, I'd be a *man*, and not a sniveling coward. If you were a man, I would reason with you, but you do not understand the first principles of logic" (56). Genevieve's characterization of Native Americans as "poor, ignorant, defenseless" (56) indicates that her anger is more about her ability to defend wayward children than the equality of the Native Americans themselves. In other words, Indians become a platform, a catalyst, for her own anger and self-development. Her fiery speech also suggests that it is Gerald's righteous anger—his avowed protection of the vulnerable Indians—that makes him more attractive, more "manly," than Maurice. Indian reform thus proves conducive to the right kind of heterosexual white relations. Following Genevieve's rebellion against the oppressive domesticity of a life with Maurice, she returns to her "own" home, which is located with the Creeks. There she can assume the position of a wife to Gerald and a "mother"/protector of Wynema. With her ignorant views of Creek culture replaced by Gerald's lessons, Genevieve now has more "sophisticated" views on current Anglo-Indian affairs. Genevieve can now become the protector, a position the Native American woman (and man) is denied.

In marked contrast to Genevieve, Wynema does not display the anger that the novel suggests is essential to a woman's development as a protector of others. Although she shares Genevieve's commitment to suffrage, she believes white women's political ascendancy will enhance Native women's power: "we are waiting for our more civilized white sisters to gain their liberty, and thus set an example which we shall not be slow to follow" (45). As opposed to Sarah Winnemucca's narrative, which presents the Northern Paiute political structure as just as or even more egalitarian than that of the United States, Wynema defers to the Anglo example. Like Gerald, it is Robin who seems most able to espouse white women's and indigenous rights, in part by "taking one of the women" (46). And when Genevieve expresses her outrage at her fiancé, Wynema shares none of it—indeed she fears she is its cause. Detailing the dangers of allotment in a heated tone, Genevieve plays the role of the white instructor who must get angry for the less-educated Indian. While Creeks were quite aware of the allotment issue and held a number of positions on the topic, Wynema is oblivious to it, shamefully acknowledging the extent of her ignorance. "What a superficial thinker I am not to have understood this!" she exclaims, telling Genevieve to correct her if she is wrong (52). Here Genevieve assumes Gerald's position as the masculine authority in relation to Wynema. As a catalyst for Genevieve's anger and self-development, Wynema can have little of her own; Genevieve concludes their conversation, "Now go along and enjoy yourself" (53). While Siobhan Senier acknowledges Genevieve's condescension, she suggests that Callahan, in envisioning a predominantly white audience, "may have found Genevieve the safest vehicle for voicing an anti-allotment position" ("Allotment" 427). More broadly, Genevieve is the safest vehicle for female anger in the novel.

The contrast between the mature, angry Genevieve and the appeasing Wynema is highlighted in a following chapter, aptly entitled "Wynema's Mischief." While Genevieve deals Maurice a stunning blow, Wynema—the "witching, mischievous dark-eyed little beauty" flirts with Robin and wishes she were Pocahontas, who "could leap from one tree to another like a squirrel" (60–61). The scripted nature of the scene is emphasized by her own reading of Tennyson as she sits perched in a tree. This scene is a troubling reminder of the superficiality of the title character, especially given Genevieve's simultaneous self-development. When Robin kisses her unexpectedly, Callahan hints that Wynema responds with anger: "She drew herself away, crying reproachfully: 'Oh, Robin!' and fled into the house" (63–64). Yet her irritation soon dissolves into flirtation as she pouts playfully. As with Pauline Johnson's performances, which I consider in the next chapter, a Native woman's anger is represented as a coquettish reproach that white men find attractive: a "no" that doesn't mean no. Earlier, as Wynema waxes eloquently on suffrage, Robin is drawn to her flushed cheeks and sparkling eyes. He soon "became her willing subject, and followed her about everywhere, greatly to her delight and amusement—for Indians are somewhat coquettish" (60). The weight of moral indignation is reserved for the white heroine, who protects the wayward Indian girl by drawing upon a white male paternalism; as Genevieve tells Maurice, "not being content with slandering the poor, ignorant, defenseless Indians, you begin on me" (56). Condemning Maurice's protectionist attitude toward her as belittling and infantilizing, Genevieve chooses the man who teaches *her* to be a protector.

In playing angry, Genevieve temporarily appropriates anger through Indianness—in this case, through the "Indian Cause"—before replacing it with a more contained domesticity. The righteous indignation of the earlier scene with Maurice is ultimately replaced with her deferral to Gerald and other white men reformers; as Gerald reads a threat against the Ghost Dancers, Genevieve declares indignantly that "Some one should answer that" as if she herself cannot (73). Wynema, who also marries and has a child with a white man, has far more difficulty imagining herself as an activist, even for a brief time. As the men prepare to negotiate with a rebellious Lakota leader, she claims, "I should like to go myself if I could be of any service; but I should only be a hindrance" (77). This is an odd statement given that she is fluent in his language. The chapter includes the women's discussion of a potential romance, ending with the merriment of "a marriage bell": a perfect symbol of domestic accord (79). This domesticity is associated with the success of the "civilizing" project, as the culturally inaccurate tepees have been replaced with "neat residences" (34). Accordingly, in the final negotiations between the whites and the Lakotas, Miscona, a chief's wife, appears only at the end to plead with her husband to make peace. Miscona is said to be incapable of understanding his anger; as the narrator laments, "Ah Miscona! Little you knew that the fountain once stirred from its depths can never be quieted" (87). Given that this chapter directly follows a description of Wynema's new role as wife and mother, it only accentuates the sense that while American Indian women might attain domesticity, they are not allowed to "play angry"—a critical component of selfhood as Callahan constructs it.

It would be a mistake, however, to suggest that no space exists in Callahan's novel for an indigenous protest. Chapter 18, entitled "Turmoil with the Indians"—a phrase that de-centers Native Americans—begins with Genevieve's mother commenting that Native Americans only go "on the war-path" with just cause (70). Although this is an endorsement of Native anger, it too is communicated through a white character. Earlier, in response to the treaty scandal, Little Fox declares "fiercely," "I will fight it with my last breath" (57). Most forceful is an editorial by Old Masse Hadjo who writes a brilliantly scathing response to white aggression:

> If our Messiah does come, we will not try to force you into our belief. We will never burn innocent women at the stake, or pull men to pieces with horses because they refuse to join with us in our ghost dances. You white people had a Messiah, and if history is to be believed, nearly every nation has had one. You had twelve apostles; we have only eleven and some of them are already in the military guard-house. We had also a Virgin Mary, but she is also in the guard-house.... The white man's heaven is repulsive to the Indian nature, and if the white man's hell suits you, keep it. I think there will be white rogues enough to fill it. (73–74)

Hadjo's technique of using whites' terms against them resembles Sarah Winnemucca's astute critique of words like "civility" and "savagery"; like her, he employs this ideology in order to reject it. The sentimental phrase that Gerald follows with, "the poor things," seems particularly jarring after

Hadjo's bold words (74). Here the missionary Carl Peterson, a kind of stand-in for Gerald, voices a similar protectionist rhetoric: in his terms they are "My people, the Sioux"; "defenseless"; a "troubled people" for whom he will do everything he can (74).

The elderly Chikena emerges in the final pages to offer a blistering account of whites' massacre of her Lakota community, an account complete with a powerful image of assaulted domesticity: babies dying in their mothers' arms. It is while relating Chikena's story that the narrator voices her most cogent critiques of the whites. Significantly, Chikena appears only after the sentimental novel has been disrupted rather radically by newspaper articles on the dire conditions of the Sisseton and Wahpeton Reservations and a bitter account of Wounded Knee. As opposed to the indiscriminate label of "Indians" that frequents much of the novel, here particular Indian nations are named. While readers usually point to this disruption as an aesthetic fault of the novel, I consider it an opportunity for Callahan to break out of the conventional sentimental narrative and the Indian reform discourse, introducing a more productive indigenous anger. As if to emphasize this shift, the first paragraph of Chapter 21 is in present tense as opposed to the past tense of much of the previous text. The sections on Wounded Knee and Chikena's protest feel disconnected from the rest of the book because they fundamentally are: here are the only occasions when a sustained indigenous anger emerges. Both require a separation, I suggest, not only from the rest of the narrative but from Callahan's own nation and gender—they center on Lakotas and a figure who does not fit neatly into the categories of femininity or masculinity.

Although Womack faults *Wynema* in part for its lack of strategic irony, in describing the murder of Miscona, Callahan expresses a sarcasm and irony that pervades Sarah Winnemucca's *Life Among the Piutes*. Consider, for instance, the biting declaration, "[It was] only an Indian squaw, so it did not matter" (90). This statement is particularly powerful because it is not qualified in any way; Callahan does not end, for example, with "it did not matter to the government." Leaving the statement open, she makes no distinction between the oppressive government or the unsympathetic whites and the white reformers. This elderly Lakota woman is at once to be pitied—"her face dripping with tears"—and admired as the group's fierce defender: "I staid to protect them. But, oh, the bitter, bitter night! The cold wind swept by me and tortured me with its keen, freezing breath; but I drew my blanket more closely about me and defiantly watched my dead" (91). Callahan likens Chikena to "Rizpah of old, on the Gibeah plain" (90). In the Bible, "Rizpah," which means coal or hot stone (and as such a force to be reckoned with), watches over the bodies of her two children for five months to prevent them from being devoured by predators. The scriptural reference is a powerful image of the protector: "And Rizpah the daughter of Aiah took sackcloth and spread it for herself on the rock, from the beginning of the harvest until it rained on them from the sky; and she allowed neither the birds of the sky to rest on them by day nor the beasts of the field by night" (*New American Standard Bible,* 2 Sam. 21.10). Like the daughter of Pauline Johnson's poem "The Cattle Thief," which I consider in the next chapter, Chikena lays claim to the vanquished bodies of her people: she acts, in other words, in defense of the collective. She is maternal, wrapping infants in blankets, and protective—a quality that defines Wildfire's masculinity just a few pages earlier. Chikena, that is, does not sit easily within the rigid masculine and feminine roles that characterize much of the novel. It is because of her transgression of these categories—and the novel's rejection of conventional sentimentality at this point—that she (and Callahan in turn) is able to critique the whites. Indeed, Chikena's commentary is located in a chapter that articulates the Indians' anger about the whites' behavior. Given the previously benign tone, the sentence "But, instead of this, the Indians were slaughtered like cattle, shot down like dogs" is striking (89). In the final paragraph of the chapter quotation marks reappear, this time to expose stereotypes of American Indians: Buffalo Bill's "'showing'" of the Indians (96) and the newspaper's report of the death of "only a few 'Indian bucks'" (92). The distinction between good and bad whites momentarily dissolves, and a forceful American Indian voice is lifted in opposition. As in *Life Among the Piutes,* these moments are effective not despite but because of their unconventional sentimental form; they combine the intimacy of the genre with a stinging critique of its audience. For once, the white reader is not allowed the exalted position of the valiant protector; she is exposed as separate from, and indeed a threat to, the nation that Chikena at least momentarily affirms. Even the final lines, which seem like a testament to Native vanishing, might instead be a reminder of indigenous nationhood. In Siobhan Senier's words,

> the novel's canny parallels between "Caucasian" . . . and "American," "white" . . . and "Indian" move American Indians into a position of primacy in questions of national identity, reversing and stirring up the expected hierarchy. Is this Indian to be included in the national polity through absorption, or to be acknowledged as an enduring, self-determining entity? *Wynema* might well have supplied, or tried to supply, the assimila-

tionist vision Americans sought in 1891. But it also contains the seeds of that vision's undoing. ("Allotment" 436)

This is not to say, however, that the book necessarily ends on an empowering note for American Indians. In the final chapter, conventional sentimentality returns with the domestic setting of the Indians' erasure. Chikena ultimately declares that American Indians are "a people of the past," as if the defiant woman who vows to protect her people were relegated to the vanishing American script (104). The fact that her anger is so fleeting suggests the persuasiveness of this script. As in *Hobomok*, the harmony of the America presented at the end of the novel depends upon the elimination of its "Indianness." In Rayna Green's words, "the living performance of 'playing Indian' by non-Indian peoples depends upon the physical and psychological removal, even the death, of real Indians" (31). This privileging of whiteness is evident in the scene in which the town is given its name. It is called "Wynema" only when Genevieve rejects Wynema's suggestion that it be named "Weir," her surname. This deferral is repeated when Wynema insists on naming her daughter after Genevieve instead of herself. Like Hobomok and Mary's son, the child's Native name is replaced with one that is Anglo. The act of naming, a statement of possession, demonstrates whites' privileged relationship to language; it is as if whites have more power than the Creeks to declare something American Indian. This power is particularly important given the significance of towns, and their names, in Creek culture.[17] Callahan's novel restages a process in which white reformers, professedly securing property rights for American Indians, in fact secure their own self—and national—possession.

The anger the novel raises in critics like Womack is instructive in that it demonstrates our expectations that the first novel by an American Indian woman should represent indigenous cultures in historically accurate terms, or at least undermine stereotypical portraits with an ironic tone. Womack's critique implicitly raises a series of questions: How do we acknowledge the racial and ethnic particularities of an author of color without denying her the artistic liberty that is typically granted white writers? Do we (or should we) hold Callahan more accountable for her representations of American Indians than we would a white woman writer? What if Callahan, through the figure of Genevieve, takes the place of the white woman reformer? Does the author then cease to be angry—and "culturally" Creek? For Womack, it seems that she does. His is not in any way a simplistic definition of "Creekness"—he acknowledges that "defining what a 'Creek perspective' is remains problematic, since there are many

Creeks with many different perspectives"—yet a particular kind of resistance seems critical to his conception of Creek writers (118). He asks, "In what ways does the novel record Creek history, create a sense of place on Creek land, advance Creek culture, or strengthen Creek autonomy? How deeply is it engaged in things Creek?" (120–21). Womack faults Callahan for not writing a historically based novel, but is history what this book is, or should be? Given Callahan's own position in between Anglo and Creek communities, it seems unrealistic to demand of her an anger that is either one or the other. Again, drawing from Arif Dirlik and Maureen Konkle, I would urge us away from such binaries. The fact that there is little room for American Indian anger in *Wynema* says more about Callahan's lack of available narratives, I would argue, than about her failure as a Creek. In the Indian reform context in which Callahan lived and wrote, anger was figured most readily in the form of a white woman.

The image of Chikena weeping in the snow over the bodies of her people symbolizes one form of the intersecting anger and sentimentality that characterize each of the texts I examine. Her angry tears serve as deeds of possession, boundary markers between Lakota and U.S. nations. Yet these tears also have the potential to cross boundaries: in Karen Sánchez-Eppler's words, "as the eyes of readers take in the printed word and blur it with tears" (*Touching* 26). Grief and anger converge, frustrating attempts to keep them apart. The two are so powerful together because they represent both a sharing of feeling (and property) and an assertion of distinct ownership. Psychologists often describe anger as a relationship between an emoter (the one who feels maligned) and a target (the individual or group that the emoter holds responsible for the perceived injustice). Although evaluations of the nature and effect of these relations vary, critics agree that sentimentality refers to or strives for a sense of shared feeling. Anger and sentimentality also mark the value—the potential or actual possession—of someone or something. It is because an object is invested with another's feeling that its appropriation or loss prompts the subject's anger. To get angry, and in turn, to get sentimental, is to assert one's rightful ownership of one's self and nation. It makes sense, then, that anger would be key to nineteenth-century literature by American Indian women, who were staking claims in rather loose earth. In each of these texts, we witness women's attempts to reclaim anger so that it is not madness (and thus beyond their sane, "civilized" control) but a statement of entitlement consistent with and critical to self and nationhood.

With its complicated tangle of genres vying for narrative authority, *Wynema* is a microcosm of the development of Native American women's literature in English. Women like Pauline Johnson would pick up where Callahan left off, finding genres that were more compatible with indigenous anger. Yet Johnson also faced the difficult task of determining when to extend feelings across gendered and racial boundaries and when to claim "a dazzling anger" of her own.

2

"A Woman to Let Alone"[1]

E. Pauline Johnson and the Performance of Anger

> Speak out, brave girl; speak, speak for the nation,
> Of wrongs it has suffered, the woes it hath braved.
> Tell simply the story of sad desolation;
> Of forest crowned heroes who can't be enslaved.
> Speak, speak, for the nation which smiles in its hardships,
> Usurped of its plenty, crushed, dogged and debased.
> For the spirit of freedom swells high with emotion,
> And wild torrents murmur, "we will not be slaves."

This unidentified piece was written by one of E. Pauline Johnson's fans around the turn of the twentieth century.[2] In the author's imagination, Johnson is a courageous "girl" who is called upon to "speak for the nation"—to denounce the atrocities that the "forest crowned heroes" have endured. While she is the voice for these "forest crowned heroes," neither the specific nation nor its oppressor is named. At moments even the identity of this "brave girl" seems uncertain. In the last lines, she is replaced by natural forms: "a spirit of freedom" and a swell of "wild torrents" (7–8). Such ambiguity allows the poem's author (and reader) to associate him- or herself, at least momentarily, with Johnson's protest. Since the nation and the perpetrators' identities are not specified, this "brave girl" (who was in fact at least thirty years old at the time) can be the author's ally or even spokesperson. Johnson and her fan are, in other words, on the same side. So while this poem may at first seem to call for an indigenous voice that is less present in Callahan's *Wynema*, we must consider the degree to which this voice—this protest—is beneficial to an Anglo audience.

"A Woman to Let Alone"

In this chapter I study Johnson's work as a complex negotiation of late nineteenth-century scripts of anger. One was the "fiery Indian maid," as illustrated in the opening verse, whose protest whites could share. Another was the "savage fury" that marked an irreconcilable difference from her audience. The fact that each of these forms of anger is itself a stereotype challenges the equation that is often made between anger and resistance: the idea that the expression of emotion is "the means by which women can become conscious of their oppression and mobilize for change" (Pinch 54). How could Johnson's protest be subversive if it was, as I will suggest, often figured as a subject of white men's desire—an anger that they demanded of her? My ultimate intent is not to argue that Pauline Johnson was either subversive or not—clearly her self-presentation was more complicated than any such binary would suggest—but to examine the relationship between her genres, her audience, and the anger she articulated. As with Alice Callahan, Johnson's anger was at times posited in service of Anglo nationhood. Yet Johnson's writing departs from Callahan's, I argue, in its ability to sustain an indigenous anger in certain genres. Johnson finds this voice most successfully in works that are not dependent on a hetero, cross-racial romance. In the two poems I consider, her anger can be imagined as the reader's own despite its service to indigenous nationhood; in the maternal essays, it is a distinct form legitimated in First Nations terms. Before analyzing these genres, however, we should examine the context in which she learned to perform anger—and Indianness.

Emily Pauline Johnson was born on March 10, 1861 on the Six Nations Reserve in Southern Ontario. Her father, George Martin Johnson (Onwanonsyshon), was a prominent Mohawk chief, an Anglican, and a government interpreter for the reserve; her mother, Emily Howells, was an Englishwoman from a Quaker background. Emily's cousin was the American writer William Dean Howells, although neither Emily nor Pauline was close to him.[3] In "My Mother," a thinly veiled biography of Emily Howells Johnson, Pauline describes the harmonious relationship between her mother (known here as "Lydia Bestman") and father (George "Mansion"):

> Their loves were identical. They loved nature—the trees, best of all, and the river, and the birds. They loved the Anglican Church, they loved

> the British flag, they loved Queen Victoria, they loved beautiful, dead Elizabeth Evans, they loved strange, reticent Mr. Evans. They loved music, pictures and dainty china, with which George Mansion filled his beautiful home. They loved books and animals, but, most of all, these two loved the Indian people, loved their legends, their habits, their customs—loved the people themselves. Small wonder, then, that their children should be born with pride of race and heritage, and should face the world with that peculiar, unconquerable courage that only a fighting ancestry can give. (*Moccasin* 70–71)

As this passage suggests, Pauline and her siblings grew up with pride in their Mohawk heritage—and a sense of its compatibility with an English-Canadian empire. Her father was a staunch imperialist who idolized Napoleon (Pauline was named after the French leader's sister) and who disapproved of the Métis rebellions of 1869–70. Much of this pride originated in the Loyalist narrative that her grandfather John Smoke Johnson (Sakayengwaraton) told her of the American Revolution. Pauline grew up listening to her grandfather's personal accounts of the Revolutionary War: stories in which the heroes were the Mohawks who were awarded Canadian land after fighting on the British side.[4] Accounts of Johnson's childhood suggest that her parents were eager to share their marriage of Mohawk and English customs with the public; once, when Pauline invited some school friends to her home, her parents held what Mrs. Garland W. Foster refers to as a "war dance" after tea (28). This domestic harmony was severely disrupted, however, on the three occasions that George Johnson suffered life-threatening beatings as a result of his campaign against illegal alcohol and timber sales on the reserve. These assaults contributed to his early death in 1884.

Johnson was educated at home and for a brief period at the Brantford Collegiate, an institution that offered young women all of the elements of a proper "moral training" (C. M. Johnston 85). Taking advantage of her parents' extensive book collection, she read Longfellow, Byron, Shakespeare, and Tennyson at a young age. She is reported to have first published in 1883, when her poem "My Little Jean" may have appeared in the New York magazine *Gems of Poetry* (Gerson and Strong-Boag 290). The publication of numerous poems and prose pieces followed. In addition to her later articles in *Mother's Magazine*, *Boys' World*, and other newspapers and magazines, several books were eventually published: *The White Wampum* (1895); *Canadian Born* (1903); *"When George Was King" and Other Poems* (1908); *Legends of Vancouver* (1911); *Flint and Feather* (1912); *The Moccasin*

Maker (1913); and *The Shagganappi* (1913). The latter two books were published shortly after she died of breast cancer in March 1913.

According to Paula Bennett, Johnson's biography and writing betray a significant disconnect between her and the Mohawk community. Bennett suggests that in her use of European conventions, her address to a dominant audience, and her tenuous connection to her Mohawk nation, Johnson occupies a questionable position as a Native writer. Bennett describes Johnson's father (and presumably, Pauline herself) as having two options: either traditionalism or assimilation. Like Callahan, then, Johnson is suspected of not being adequately tied to her nation. But is it fair to measure indigenous writers in such terms? Doing so, I would argue, neglects both their complicated approach to writing, representation, and resistance, as well as the complexity of their identities themselves. In other words, instead of trying to fix her into a rather narrow assimilated/nonassimilated divide, we should concentrate on her tactics of survivance, to borrow Gerald Vizenor's term. For Bennett, the irony of Johnson's literature comes in her critique of an audience that she herself was included in. In contrast, I contend that like Winnemucca, Johnson is most successful in performance and text when she is able to convince her predominantly Anglo audience that it is included and then, at that very moment, draw a sharp line between her nation and theirs.

Johnson's position as an exalted member of the Canadian nation is evident in her inclusion in a number of Canadian anthologies, most notably William Douw Lighthall's *Songs of the Great Dominion* (1889). It was this collection, coupled with Theodore Watts-Dunton's enthusiastic review of her poetry in London's *The Athenaeum*, which secured her literary fame. Even during the mid-twentieth century, when some scholars criticized Johnson's "sentimental" poetry, she had the honor of being one of only two women included in most of the Canadian anthologies published before 1980.[5] Johnson has remained a popular figure in Canadian culture, as newspaper articles throughout the twentieth century attest.[6] On the hundredth anniversary of her birth, commemorative celebrations were held at her grave in Stanley Park, Vancouver, and at Chiefswood. At the same time, a postal stamp—the first to honor a Canadian woman or a First Nations writer—was issued. It was so successful that it sold 40,000 copies instantly.[7] Such ongoing acclaim testifies to Johnson's position—much more than Alice Callahan or even Sarah Winnemucca—as an icon of the Anglo community. This popularity is due at least in part, I argue, to her articulation of an anger with which her Anglo audience could align itself. I turn now to one key audience: those who watched her on stage, a platform for her famous incarnations of anger, Indianness, and femininity. Here Johnson demonstrated her ability both to conform to and challenge Anglo expectations.

FEMALE INDIANNESS

Pauline Johnson learned to perform Indianness—and whiteness—at an early age. As a child she played roles like Pocahontas for elite individuals such as Horatio Hale and Thomas Edison who frequented her parents' estate. Her professional stage career began at age 30 when she debuted at a prestigious Canadian Literature Evening in Toronto. The audience's enthusiastic response to her recitation of the poems "A Cry from an Indian Wife" and "As Red Men Die" inaugurated her stage career throughout Canada, the United States, and England. She and her fellow performers took advantage of the bourgeoning theater scene; the railroad made one-person shows and platform tours increasingly feasible even in remote areas.

Despite the growing respectability of the theater in the late nineteenth century, women who appeared on stage were still considered morally suspect. As Chad Evans claims in his book *Frontier Theatre*, there was a relatively fine line between the somewhat disreputable performers who appeared in vaudeville, magic, and phrenology shows, and the more respectable "elocutionists" who read literary selections. Elocution itself was not thought suitable for school curricula until at least the early twentieth century (Saddlemyer 14). Ever vigilant about her family's reputation, even when their financial situation made such concerns less realistic, Pauline's mother initially disapproved of her daughter's stage career.

Johnson's stage presence was shaped not only by her gender but by her indigenous heritage. Native women were particularly stigmatized: the Indian Act of 1869 required that First Nations women prove their "good moral status" before they could vote or inherit property. Anglo-Canadian women were regarded the moral superiors of indigenous women (Strong-Boag "Ever" 1). Despite (or perhaps because of) the public fascination with the "Mohawk Princess," an indigenous woman on stage was doubly stained. Chad Evans notes that the success of many Canadian soloists depended on their enactment of the racial and ethnic stereotypes that their audiences expected: "No one did this better than Miss E. Pauline Johnson, a woman who actually became her role and as such became perhaps the quintessential Canadian speaker, as important to Canada as Mark Twain was to the United States" (184). Given that her contemporaries were the indigenous actors of Buffalo Bill's Wild West Shows—the first Native Americans to appear as "themselves" on stage—Johnson confronted a particularly demanding set of expectations from her audience.[8] Her writing indicates that she was aware of how an Indian was supposed to look and was occasionally pained by her failure to live up to that image. As she lamented in a letter to her friend Arthur Henry (Harry) O'Brien during an August 1894 speaking tour, "We are getting into Indian country now. Every town is full of splendid complexioned Ojibawas [sic], whose copper colouring makes me ashamed of my washed out Mohawk skin, thinned with European blood, I look yellow and 'Chinesey' beside these Indians" (quoted in S. Johnston 125). As she recognized, the public preferred a "pure-blood" Indian to a biracial one.

In performing the "fiery Indian maid"—a key player in this female Indianness—Johnson borrowed from prominent constructions of the Haudenosaunee (Iroquois) and of anger itself. As she claims in her essay "The Six Nations," this fierceness makes the Haudenosaunee superior to other indigenous peoples: "the Iroquois roused with a just ire, impassioned by a taunt, marched northward, and in one fell battle exterminated Jesuit and Huron, leaving the little christian hamlet a desolation, and dancing a triumphant war dance on the hills that overlook Penetanguishene." They were "savage," she continues, "with a righteous patriotism" (souvenir number). The word "righteous" introduces a moral element to this image, suggesting that they are entirely justified in making this "savage" assault. Likewise, Pauline's father was remembered for his destruction of a Delaware idol. Infuriated by the Delawares' idolatry, he had allegedly crushed the figure before the people who worshiped it and, in the process, converted many of them to Christianity. Anger that is motivated by "proper" religious beliefs—and that motivates others to convert—is thus accepted and even admirable. In his discussion of this event, Horatio Hale emphasizes that Johnson's indignation originates in his reason, as if to distinguish it from an erratic, prohibited anger: "In the ordinary intercourse of society the chief was always gentle, courteous and unassuming; but in dealing with the corrupters and despoilers of his people his manner totally changed. . . . To them he was stern and imperious, as if the spirit and temper of twenty generations of the great chiefs, his ancestors, had been concentrated in his tone and manner" (139). This image of George Johnson as the firm disciplinarian of a wayward people accords with popular conceptions of the "civilized" (that is, the Christianized) Mohawk versus the more "primitive" Indian. The male counterpart to the "fiery Indian maiden," this Mohawk man is characterized, again from the perspective of whites, with the "good" anger that affirms his aristocratic, noble status.[9] We are left with an "Indian" anger that is sanctioned and even shared by Anglo-Canadians who, after all, are not its target.[10]

In accounts of her childhood, Johnson mobilizes another kind of anger that serves to affirm her femininity and respectable class status: virtuous indignation. Her biographical essay "From the Child's Viewpoint" recalls her mother's emphasis on anger management: "I can never recollect having seen her more than 'irritated' or 'annoyed,'" she writes. "She had conquered her temper very early in life—completely subdued it. Early, too, in our infancy she looked for those traits in us, expected them, recognized them and grappled with them" (30). Johnson describes her mother's relationship to anger as rather imperialistic, as if her "conquest" of anger secured her noble status like her father's temper had secured his. The energy that Mrs. Johnson devoted to curbing her own and her daughters' temper ironically suggests anger's potency: it requires one's constant vigilance. Mrs. Johnson's attempts to control her daughters' anger are consistent with Carol Zisowitz Stearns and Peter N. Stearns's description of the emphasis on temper management in nineteenth-century middle-class households. Notably, the description of the "stern and imperious" George M. Johnson doesn't contain the same anxiety about anger's potential excesses; it is as if this is a particularly female—and female Indian—concern. Indeed, in the second installment of "From the Child's Viewpoint," Johnson emphasizes that one form of anger was required of her: an indignant response to courtship. Her mother often told her that it was "not aristocratic" to allow boys to touch her; only "ill-bred girls" permitted such behavior (60). As a result of these somber lessons, Johnson recalls, she was appalled when a schoolboy once threatened to kiss her. In her account of this incident, she proves a daunting adversary: "I never stirred, only stood and glowered at him, and, with all the indignation my eight years could muster, I shouted at him, 'Don't you dare insult me, sir!' The 'sir' was added to chill him, and it did" (60). Her moralistic anger is intricately linked to her class status: a "good girl" would not tolerate a boy's advances.

This image of the indignant lady drew in part from the extremely influential organizations of white, middle-class, women reformers in the nineteenth century. As both Carroll Smith-Rosenberg and Lori D. Ginzberg have demonstrated, the extremely popular moral reform societies of the 1830s and 1840s were driven by an indignation at men who were free to seduce and prostitute innocent young women. In Ginzberg's words, "One cannot exaggerate the hostility toward men in their journals, auxiliary constitutions, and, most important, discussions of poverty and prostitution" (20). A letter to the editor of the New York Moral Reform Association's publication, the *Advocate,* asserts, "Men who seek to destroy [women's] virtue and happiness, are more dangerous than the wild animals that roam their native forests" (quoted in Ginzberg 20). The moral indignation of these publications characterizes white women's political efforts throughout the nineteenth century, from abolition to antebellum Indian reform. Johnson and her sister were involved in associations that espoused a similar ideology: Evelyn was a member of Ohsweken's Indian Moral Association, and Pauline performed at least once for a Massachusetts Indian Association (Strong-Boag and Gerson *Paddling* 54; 69). Such affiliations remind us that the "fiery Indian maid" cannot be seen apart from what was, for Johnson, a feminine and class-based virtue.

Regardless of how Johnson defined the "fiery Indian maid," once on stage she faced whites who saw her anger as evidence of an Indianness they narrowly defined. Much was made of the fact that Johnson had no formal theatrical training (although she later received lessons in elocution from her stage partner, Owen Smily). Reviewers noted approvingly of her natural aptitude for public performance. Charles Mair comments on how her "intense feeling" about the oppression of people of the First Nations "poured red-hot from her inmost heart" (14–15). One might attribute this emphasis on Johnson's emotionality to contemporaneous conceptions of acting talent; the famous Sarah Bernhardt, for instance, was said to exert "a strange and thrilling power" over her audience (Hewitt 241). Fans of Bernhardt, however, considered her emotionality a sign of her acting ability rather than her racial status. As Mrs. W. Garland Foster confidently notes of Johnson, "But with her, passion was racial rather than individual as in the case of Mrs. Browning," a white actress (97). Browning's performance meant that she was a real actor; Johnson's assured that she was a real *Indian*.

The "fiery Indian maid" who protests racial mistreatment appears in reviews like the following from the *Des Moines Leader:* "['The Cattle Thief'] was probably the best number of the evening. It was an Indian's appeal to the white man, an Indian's wail at the injustice which the evolution of civilization has made necessary. It was read with the intensity which is not a product of art but of nature" (n.p./n.d.).[11] This association between Indianness and emotionality extended to Johnson's patrons. Gilbert Parker's popular novel, *The Translation of a Savage* (1893), notes that since "primitive people are quicker in the play of their passions," one of the primary lessons in "civility" is emotional restraint (142). Her indignation was read, then, not necessarily as a confirmation of a respectable woman's virtue or acting talent, but as a confirmation of her fervent "Indian" emotions.

The popularity of Johnson's performances stemmed in part from the image of the "eloquent Indian" that Sandra Gustafson has described. Beginning with the delegations of Haudenosaunee leaders who visited England in the eighteenth century, the figure of the articulate Indian had particular cultural currency. This image was solidified during the Great Awakening, when men like Samson Occom (Mohegan) served as influential orators. Similarly, as C. M. Johnston notes in his study of Brantford, Methodists were deeply impressed by the Iroquois' "highly emotional behaviour" at campfire meetings (89).[12] This emotionality complemented the personal, intense religiosity encouraged at such gatherings. In voicing her own version of eloquent (and appropriately Christian) anger, Johnson tapped into this legitimation of indigenous voices. Accounts such as Lewis Henry Morgan's *League of the Iroquois* describe the orator as the hallmark of indigenous eloquence, which stems in part from "passions untaught of restraint" (107). Hailing from a long line of Mohawk leaders, Johnson makes frequent reference to her predecessors' speeches. The figure of the eloquent Indian is often invoked in her work: as she explains in her essay "The Lodge of the Law-Makers" (1906), the chief matron is always free to "publicly make an address to the chiefs, braves, and warriors assembled, and she is listened to not only with attention, but respect" (4). While she herself was not a clan matron, Johnson draws from the power of this position in order to validate her own public voice.

Although a woman's indignation was typically regarded as a protection against potential male suitors, reviews of Johnson's performances indicate that her anger was sexualized. Here, the disconnection between her high-minded anger and the anger her audience responded to is most obvious. Reviews of Johnson's performances suggest that her white male audience members found her emotional display—and her anger in particular—sexy. As one white male commentator noted, "Such is the train of thought that the poems arouse in the minds of the audience, and when the anger of an Indian maiden, feeling from experience the sufferings of her race, is depicted in every line; dull indeed is the man that cannot be aroused by Miss Johnson's recitations" (quoted in Strong-Boag and Gerson *Paddling* 107). Although we should not necessarily read the word "arouse" in terms of its present-day sexual connotations, a sense of the erotic quality of Johnson's performances characterizes this and other reviews. As Jack Scott writes in his 1952 article, "The Passionate Princess," Johnson possessed a "disturbing exotic look" such that "brave men went weak when she smiled"

(12). Scott and other white men seem to imagine and even fantasize about an Indian woman who overpowers them with her charms—who, in other words, crosses the line from prudent indignation to provocative rage. She was, Scott recalls, "a tempestuous and often flamboyant person who liked to rock her audiences on their heels by sheer passion" (12). O. J. Stevenson remarks that he cannot remember one of her recitals "without an indescribable thrill" (145). This response of white men, who had certain financial and cultural resources that Johnson lacked, was in some cases advantageous: admirer Frank Yeigh secured her first performance in Toronto, and the eminent Sir Gilbert Parker made sure that some of the city's most important editors and publishers were in the audience of her Steinway Hall recital. The attractiveness of Johnson's indignation undermines its potency as a reproof of men's attentions; in this scenario, the schoolboy is not corrected but aroused by her reprimand. Ironically, the indignation that her mother believed would affirm her virtue was often perceived as one of her most alluring qualities.

In turn, the supposed sexiness of Johnson's anger often sparked the fears of white women who believed she would overwhelm their husbands or sons with desire. What appears in *Wynema* as a relatively benign, coquettish indignation on the part of the title character here generates tremendous anxiety. After one recitation, the mother of a young man who was to escort Johnson to her next show was so convinced by Johnson's act that she forbade him from accompanying her farther. During another recital, Johnson "was delighted to overhear a small mild man whisper aside to his wife, 'Wasn't she Savage? I wouldn't like her for a wife'" (J. Scott 12).[13] As Michael Pickering points out, this delight in the exoticized woman is another version of the derogatory "us/them" division: "The Other represents an attempt to make the unfamiliar familiar, to make what is disturbing safe, but the stereotypical Other is thereby set up as a source of contradictory responses: providing pleasure in the exotic, say, and reawakening fear or disgust in relation to what is foreign" (157). As with any stereotype, this image of the exotic woman tells us much more about the people who create such representations than those who are represented by them. In this case, it indicates white men's desire for (and white women's fear of) what both imagined as an alternative, disruptive sexuality. The fact that Johnson often repeated this story suggests her intervention in and appropriation of her image: she was not simply clay in their hands. Part of the allure of this position was perhaps its sense of empowerment; this was not the conventional, submissive wife.

The degree to which Johnson's enacted anger was raced is evident in

Chapter 2

FIGURE 1. Pauline Johnson, BHS Image #635 ("First English Dinner Dress"). Courtesy of the Brant Museum & Archives.

her audience's accounts of her "fiery" spirit in half of her performances, when she appeared as an Indian woman, versus her "gentle" demeanor as an Englishwoman. A piece from the magazine *Saturday Night* (1892) declares that "Miss Johnson on the platform is very different from the accomplished lady so well known in social circles; when reciting one of her own fiery compositions on the wrongs suffered or heroism displayed by her Indian race, she becomes the high-spirited daughter of her warrior sires and thrills the reader through and through" (quoted in Strong-Boag and Gerson *Paddling* 70). This quotation suggests that it is the recitation

"A Woman to Let Alone"

FIGURE 2. Pauline Johnson ("London, 1895"); reprinted in Walter McRaye, *Pauline Johnson and Her Friends* (Toronto: Ryerson, 1947), frontispiece. Courtesy of the Newberry Library, Chicago.

of these "fiery" words that is believed to effect her transformation from a well-known and "accomplished lady" into an Indian daughter of a warrior: the fiery Indian maid. Another review describes Johnson as moving expertly between identities "ranging from gentle to ferocious" (MacEwan 67). A reviewer for the *Carberry News* similarly comments, "At times she is terrible in her ferocity and in a few moments will be as winsome as a girl" (quoted in Strong-Boag and Gerson *Paddling* 106–7). Both identities are defined by affect: the fury of the Indian woman contrasts with the composure of the English "lady."

This chameleonlike quality was understood not only in terms of Johnson's affect but her clothing as well: she moved from the elegant and "modest" dress to the "bare-armed" Indian attire, a transformation that likely called to mind Anglo fantasies about the scantily clad Native woman. Strong-Boag and Gerson have noted that her stage photos emphasize this distinction; as an Indian she appears with visible ankles and long, loose hair, often in assertive poses, while she wears a more demure expression in the corseted evening gown (*Paddling* 113). As a December 1897 article from the *Winnipeg Free Press* illustrates, Johnson's transformation into an "English lady" made a profound impression on her audience: "When Miss Johnson, in the second half of the programme, appeared in a rich and beautiful dress made in fashionable, civilized style, the impression upon the audience was entirely changed. People then thought she must surely be at least almost white, in her features and her complexion they could see nothing of the Indian" (quoted in S. Johnston 145). Given their desire for a "real" Indian, the onlookers' delight in Johnson's transformation might seem surprising. On the other hand, it makes perfect sense as a version of the fantasy that a white woman—even an upper-class English lady—is just a costume away from the "savagery" that she ostensibly counters. Likewise, the "winsome" girl might suddenly become the seductress. This fine line between the two recalls the image from the *American Phrenological Journal* in which the "lady" is made "Indian" by her anger.

Johnson was not, however, the helpless dupe of these stereotypes; like Winnemucca, she demonstrated a marked ability to manipulate them. Once, a white woman asked her with surprise if her father were indeed an Indian. When Johnson assented, she replied, "I would not have known it." Not missing a beat, Pauline quickly asked the woman if her father was "of pure white blood." When the other woman managed a startled yes, Johnson replied, "I would never have known it!" (quoted in McClung 34). In a letter to William Douw Lighthall she writes, "For my Indian poems I am trying to get an Indian dress to recite in, and it is the most difficult thing in the world. Now I know *you know* what is feminine, so you can tell me if the 'Indian stores' in Montreal are *real* Indian stores, or is their stuff manufactured? ... My season begins Oct 20th, so I must have my costume by that date, but I want one that is made up of *feminine* work" (quoted in Strong-Boag and Gerson *Paddling* 110). To be convincingly Indian, Johnson realized, not just any clothing would do; she needed something feminine—something, it seems, that was made by hand. Like Sarah Winnemucca, Johnson borrowed from popular images of Native Americans: in her case, Longfellow's Minnehaha rather than Pocahontas.

"A Woman to Let Alone"

In her effort to secure a wardrobe of convincingly Indian garments, few of which had any relationship to Mohawk traditions, Johnson demonstrates her awareness that this was indeed a role—a performance—that she could command. She appears to have made the desired effect: a reporter for the *Chicago Tribune* of January 28, 1897 notes, "Dangling at her girdle there is an American Sioux scalp, taken at Fort McCloud by a Canadian Blood Indian, while the necklace of bear's claws which encircles her brown throat has a history almost as thrilling" (8). Again, to be "Indian" was to evoke particular emotions.

For interpretations of the significance of Johnson's racial maneuvers on stage, we might turn to scholarship on a key phenomenon of nineteenth-century theatre: blackface minstrelsy. David Roediger has argued that minstrel shows affirmed both the whiteness of the actors and the importance of whiteness itself, while Eric Lott sees them as a complex display of the identification and desire embedded in whites' constructions of blacks. What happens, however, when the performer underneath the clothing is a member of the racial group she's enacting? As a Mohawk and Anglo woman who knew both wealth and financial difficulty, Johnson inhabited each of these positions on and off the stage. The power of Johnson's transformation was her ability to make the audience forget that it was a transformation at all: when she was an Indian, she became "the high spirited daughter of her warrior sires" while in her evening dress, "They could see nothing Indian at all." Race was, at these moments, what she made it: a production based in part on whites' desires for (and fears of) such seamless transformation.

A PLEASANT KIND OF ANGER: TWO POEMS

I begin my analysis of Johnson's writing with two of her most famous poems, "The Cattle Thief" and "Ojistoh," both of which illustrate her construction of an indigenous anger that her predominantly white audiences believed they could share. These poems appeared during what Strong-Boag and Gerson refer to as Johnson's "prolific years" of 1889–98. "The Cattle Thief," first published in *The Week* in 1894, tells the story of a Cree chief killed by English "settlers" after he takes their livestock.[14] The historical backdrop for the poem is the depletion of buffalo and the government's efforts to restrict indigenous groups to reserves with insufficient resources (Gerson and Strong-Boag *Collected* 306). The poem begins with the Englishmen's stereotypical description of the chief: "That monstrous, fearless Indian, who lorded it over the plain, / Who thieved and raided, and scouted, who rode like a hurricane!" (7–8). In these opening lines, only one word challenges the image of the "monstrous" Indian: the chief is, we learn, "desperate." The initial representations of the Indians and the settlers are called into question in the second stanza. As the settlers, "Bent on bullets and bloodshed," close in on "their game," the chief emerges as the more human and dignified of the two (12). With "all their British blood aflame"—a phrase that suggests the settlers' own excessive anger and plays on racial concepts of blood—they corner the chief and proclaim him a coward for not showing his face (11). The description of the Cree man recalls popular sentimental images not only of the elderly but, more specifically, of the noble, and doomed, chief; declaring his resolve through "shrunken lips" (24), "the gaunt old Indian Cattle Thief dropped dead on the open plain" (28). When he then appears in response to the British taunts, vowing to fight each of them, they drill him with bullets. As he falls to the ground dead it is the settlers who are described as "savage": one tells the others to dismember the body and leave it for the wolves to devour. So although Johnson challenges the binary of the "civilized" whites and "savage" Indians, she does so within a conventional sentimental frame that tells of an indigenous figure's death.[15]

At this point the poem makes a dramatic shift to the perspective of the chief's daughter:

> But the first stroke was arrested by a woman's strange, wild cry.
> And out into the open, with a courage past belief,
> She dashed, and spread her blanket o'er the corpse of the Cattle Thief;
> And the words outleapt from her shrunken lips in the language of the Cree,
> "If you mean to touch that body, you must cut your way through *me*."
> And that band of cursing settlers dropped backward one by one,
> For they knew than an Indian woman roused, was a woman to let alone.
>   And then she raved in a frenzy that they scarcely understood,
>   Raved of the wrongs she had suffered since her early babyhood. (34–42)

In the whites' eyes the woman remains "strange" and "wild," raving in unintelligible Cree words. Yet the speech that follows is delivered in English and in first person, so that the reader hears what is in fact an eloquent, forceful speech.

"A Woman to Let Alone"

"Stand back, stand back, you white-skins, touch that dead man to your shame;
You have stolen my father's spirit, but his body I only claim.
You have killed him, but you shall not dare to touch him now he's dead.
You have cursed, and called him a Cattle Thief, though you robbed him first of bread—
Robbed him and robbed my people—look there, at that shrunken face,
Starved with a hollow hunger, we owe to you and your race.
What have you left to us of land, what have you left of game,
What have you brought but evil, and curses since you came?
How have you paid us for our game? how paid us for our land?
By a *book*, to save our souls from the sins *you* brought back in your other hand.
Go back with your new religion, we never have understood
Your robbing an Indian's *body*, and mocking his *soul* with food.
Go back with your new religion, and find—if find you can—
The *honest* man you have ever made from out a *starving* man.
You say your cattle are not ours, your meat is not our meat;
When *you* pay for the land you live in, *we'll* pay for the meat we eat.
Give back our land and our country, give back our herds of game;
Give back the furs and the forests that were ours before you came;
Give back the peace and the plenty. Then come with your new belief,
And blame, if you dare, the hunger that *drove* him to be a thief." (43–62)

The desperation mentioned early in the poem returns in vivid form as the Cree woman proclaims that the cattle theft was not a crazed, selfish act but a leader's valiant attempt to secure food for his starving people. In the midst of the dispossession that pervades the poem, both of the cattle and, more centrally, of the Crees' land and game, the daughter asserts her right to her father. The poem is thus a poignant illustration of anger as a claim of possession: for land, for food, and for her father's body. Through the use of italics for emphasis, the rhetorical questions, and the repeated declarations "You have," "Go back," and "Give back," she mounts a furious and effective prosecution. In these final lines, which literally and figuratively silence the settlers, the indigenous woman reclaims what has been stolen from her community, making the title a more appropriate reference to the whites than to her father. The poem's form lends her speech even greater force: instead of being broken up into various stanzas it is delivered in one uninterrupted block.

This speech recalls mourning conventions of both Anglo and indigenous cultures. As critics of Greek, Russian, French, and Irish literature have shown, in many cases the lament is an oration expected of women after the death of a loved one. In some cases, their grief is combined with what Colette H. Winn calls a "public denunciation of oppression" (148).[16] An instance of personal mourning becomes an opportunity for the speaker to protest not only the loved one's death but also the larger social structures that brought it about. It may even be, Winn notes, a call for revenge. Although the lament is associated with a grief that is beyond words—in some sense sublime—the actual literary work is forceful and articulate. The mourning ritual is also, as Mary Jemison describes of the Senecas, an opportunity for the bereaved to make certain claims (22).[17] Similarly, in "The Cattle Thief" the "frenzy that they scarcely understood" is in fact an eloquent protest of the whites' wrongdoing.

While this protest would seem to create a divide between the white readership and the narrator, the audience is positioned to identify with an Indian daughter who has the last word. As opposed to the English settlers who cannot understand her Cree speech, the English-speaking reader has access to her oration. In effect, the reader is aligned with the speaker against the others. That is, Johnson reverses the binary to which her predominantly white audience was accustomed, describing white Englishmen as "savage." The fact that the heroine speaks to the settlers in Cree but to the reader in English is an important difference; it is as if what happens in the poem is secondary to the narrator's communication and affiliation with the reader, a central characteristic of sentimentality. Thus the reader, despite her whiteness, is allowed a part of the anger of the "Indian maid" who asserts both her dispossession and her rights. In turn, the success of a poem like "A Cry From an Indian Wife," which also articulates indigenous claims to the land ("They but forget we Indians owned the land"; "By right, by birth we Indians own these lands") makes more sense if we see it as a righteous indignation the Anglo audience could somehow share (21; 58). As Frank Lawson notes in *The London News* of 19 May 1900:

> In her literary work when E. Pauline Johnson pours forth lamentations for her injured kinsmen, when she portrays the life of the red-men of the forest, extols the virtue of the Indian women, the valor of the Indian men, her verse-making is perfect; while, when she tries to write a little sentimental poem on ordinary topics, she weakens often into the common methods of the amateur rhymester. (9)

As with the stanza that opens this chapter, the white reader calls on Johnson to "pour forth" a lament for her people.

"Ojistoh," the opening poem of *The White Wampum* (1895), also presents through sentimentality an anger that the white audience can share. The narrator introduces herself in the first line as a woman and as the spouse of a Mohawk leader: "I am Ojistoh, I am she, the wife." Her relation to him is repeated throughout the poem: in lines ten and eleven, she claims, "me, Ojistoh, chosen wife / Of my great Mohawk, white star of his life." At the end of the third stanza these lines are echoed: "—then they thought of me, his wife" (23). This emphasis on her position as a leader's wife might seem to diminish her individual worth, suggesting that she is important only because of her relation to him. The remainder of the poem, however, affirms her authority. During a battle with the Hurons, Ojistoh is captured by a man who claims her as his wife. As he gallops away with her tied behind him, she delivers a surprising response:

> I smiled, and laid my cheek against his back:
> "Loose thou my hands," I said. "This pace let slack.
> Forget we now that thou and I are foes.
> I like thee well, and wish to clasp thee close;
> I like the courage of thine eye and brow;
> *I like thee better than my Mohawk now.*"
>
> He cut the cords; we ceased our maddened haste.
> I wound my arms about his tawny waist;
> My hand crept up the buckskin of his belt;
> His knife hilt in my burning palm I felt;
> One hand caressed his cheek, the other drew
> The weapon softly—"I love you, love you,"
> I whispered, "love you as my life."
> And—buried in his back his scalping knife. (46–59)

Here a feminine gentleness is intertwined with a masculine penetration of the male captor. In murdering him and thus freeing herself from captivity, Ojistoh demonstrates a self-determination that the reader might initially doubt given the earlier line, "Ojistoh, chosen wife / Of my great Mohawk." Ojistoh may be chosen by her husband, but here she chooses him in a dramatic fashion. Ironically, her seduction of the Huron brave as a tool for vengeance ultimately affirms her purity: "My hands all wet, stained with a life's red dye, / But pure my soul, pure as those stars on high—. /

'My Mohawk's pure white star, Ojistoh, still am I'" (68–70). Ojistoh takes advantage of her captor's (and perhaps the reader's) assumption that she could fall for the enemy so easily in order to affirm her undying devotion to her husband. In this instant the conventional romance narrative, in which people fall in and out of love with relative ease, is disrupted even within the standard iambic pentameter line. Her anger is aligned with her liberty; "Mad with sudden freedom, mad with haste," she makes her escape (61). This version of female desire—and anger—is possible, I would argue, because it is directed at an indigenous rather than a white man. These poems disrupt stereotypes of femininity and savagery, but maintain an alliance with the white reader, who can still imagine the Indian woman speaking for a shared nation. Its status as a "national" poem is evident in that it is one of the two poems by Johnson that are included in Margaret Atwood's anthology of Canadian literature. While Strong-Boag and Gerson maintain that "Ojistoh" is less political than "The Cattle Thief," I would argue that both poems engage in the political act of asserting indigenous dignity in terms that the reader can believe are her own.

In contrast, in two of Johnson's most popular short stories, the heroine's fury emphatically marks her separation from her white lover—and reader. These stories, I contend, indicate the necessary (and necessarily fraught) female/Indian anger produced by a cross-racial, heterosexual relationship. Unlike the poems, where the indigenous woman speaks a lament that her Anglo readers can share, these stories require her to assert a separate indigenous nationhood. The same virtuous indignation that secures Ojistoh's reunion with her husband ultimately precludes the marriage of the Indian woman and white man in "A Red Girl's Reasoning." A cross-racial, heterosexual relationship, that is, marks the beginning—and end—of a shared nation.

FACING FURY: CROSS-RACIAL RELATIONS IN JOHNSON'S SHORT STORIES

"A Red Girl's Reasoning," which won first-place in a contest held by *Dominion Illustrated* in the fall of 1892, enjoyed tremendous popular success; actor George Alexander wanted to turn it into a "full-length emotional drama" (Charlesworth 102). The story centers on a mixed-blood woman named Christie who has just married Charlie McDonald, a white man. When the couple attends a local dance, Christie acknowledges to the gossipy townspeople that her white father and Native mother were married by indigenous rather than Anglo rites.[18] McDonald, who discovers that she has shared this information with the townspeople, is furious with her for "staining" their reputation. When McDonald chastises her once again for this admission, she responds with righteous indignation. As if to emphasize the degree to which he has wounded Christie—and to affirm her own alliance with the Indian heroine—Johnson includes the footnote "Fact" after Christie's claim that for the two of them to remarry according to whites' customs would be to admit the illegitimacy of their first marriage (*Moccasin* 115). Christie then declares that for her to continue living with him when he doubts the validity of their marriage would be to assume the name of "squaw," a word she equates with sexual indiscretion (118). Here Johnson inserts a word that epitomizes derogatory representations of indigenous women in order to critique it. The Indian heroine voices an eloquent anger that affirms her dignity: "The girl turned upon him with the face of a fury. 'Do you suppose,' she almost hissed, 'that my mother would be married according to your *white* rites after she had been five years a wife, and I had been born in the meantime? *No*, a thousand times I say, *no*'" (115). To accept a white man's definition of marriage above her own would be to sacrifice her respectability as an indigenous woman.

Indeed, the story suggests, the heroine's dignity as an indigenous woman requires her termination of the cross-racial relationship. When Charlie begs her to return, she refuses to do so. "'You cannot *make* me come,' said the icy voice, 'neither church, nor law, nor even'—and the voice softened—'nor even love can make a slave of a red girl'" (124). Words like "the icy voice" and "the voice" suggest the heroine's distance not only from Charlie but from the reader as well. Ultimately, it is Charlie who is sentimentalized, taken to kissing dogs "as women sometimes do" with "tones that had tears" and "burning moisture" in his eyes (122). Christie, in contrast, shows no tears, demonstrating a blankness normally filled by sentimental signifiers. In contrast to the diminutive descriptors of *Wynema*, in this narrative, phrases like "little girl wife" don't win her over (124); she refuses his claims to her. The narrator implies that this anger comes at a cost: as she watches him leave, dejectedly, "She was conscious of but two things, the vengeful lie in her soul, and a little space on her arm that his wet lashes had brushed" (125). Yet she rejects even the sight of his "wet lashes," an endearing image of conventional sentimentality.[19] This hint of her lingering love for Charlie is not followed by a romantic conclusion in which all is forgiven; such a resolution is incompatible with her narrative. Even a "vengeful lie," a phrase that suggests a particular kind of anger, is preferable to their reunion. Johnson's heroine occupies a thorny position: her self-dignity requires her anger at her white husband, but that anger severs her from the man she still loves. This can be no traditional happy ending, although for the heroine it seems favorable to one that would require her betrayal of her indigenous identity. The final line of the story seems unsatisfying; we are left with an image of Charlie sobbing, alone, with his dog. It is as if the sentimental language here realizes its own inadequacy. Yet to return to it, the story suggests, would be to sacrifice the national pride that Christie will not relinquish.

The story "As It Was in the Beginning," which was first published in the Christmas 1899 edition of *Saturday Night*, enacts a similarly fraught anger that challenges a conventional sentimental resolution. The first-person narration positions the reader in intimate relationship to the protagonist, a young Cree girl; we see firsthand her longing look into the horizon, wondering what lies beyond her view. As in Zitkala-Ša's *American Indian Stories*, the heroine is initially curious about the outside world, a curiosity quickly satisfied by the white minister who removes her from her parents' home in order to "civilize" her. Despite the minister's efforts, however, she maintains a strong attachment to her Cree culture, dreaming of those days when she might again wear moccasins and buckskin: "as my girlhood passed away, as womanhood came upon me, I got strangely wearied of them all; I longed, oh, God, how I longed for that old wild life! It came with my womanhood, with my years" (*Moccasin* 147). More tribally specific than Callahan's novel, "As It Was in the Beginning" twins Esther's racial consciousness with her development as a woman. She wants "my own people, my own old life, my blood called out for it" (147). This longing to return home registers the short-sightedness of her earlier desire for independence from her family and the failure of the colonizing project itself.

This explicitly indigenous female desire is soon redirected rather inexplicably to the minister's nephew, Laurence. The awkward switch from Esther's erotic longing for her Cree culture to this white man is marked by the juxtaposition of lines like "Oh, the wild wonder of that wood-smoked tan, the subtilty [sic] of it, the untamed smell of it!" (148) and "I felt the blood from my heart swoop to my very finger-tips. I loved him. O God, how I loved him!" (149). As in *Wynema*, a romance script seems to derail, or subsume, any other. When she and Laurence become engaged, the minister, horrified by the thought of his nephew marrying a Native woman, convinces him to marry a white woman instead. The Cree woman is, he claims, as dangerous as a snake: a simile that makes the story's underlying biblical connotations explicit. Like Eve, she is associated with the perilous temptation that the snake represents. Upon overhearing these words, the previously demure girl adopts this very image: "What had that terrible old man said I was like? *A strange snake.* A snake? The idea wound itself about me like the very coils of a serpent" (155–56). In her fury, she becomes the person he has described: "then, with bowed head and his pale face wrapped in thought, he left the room—left it with the mad venom of my hate pursuing him like the very Evil One he taught me of" (154). This poignant image of indigenous anger takes physical form when she uses actual snake venom to exact revenge on the minister; it is with "a small flint arrow-head dipped in the venom of some *strange snake*" that she kills her beloved (156). These words recall both "A Red Girl's Reasoning," in which the protagonist's anger is likened to a "flint-tipped arrow" (120) as well as Johnson's foreword to *Flint and Feather,* a collection so named because "Flint suggests the Red Man's weapons of war; it is the arrow tip, the heart-quality of mine own people" (xvii). In a striking example of anger as a statement of entitlement, the narrator kills her lover rather than his uncle in order to take from him something as valuable as that which he has taken from her. As she thinks to herself, "He has killed the best of you, of your womanhood; kill *his* best, his pride, his hope—his sister's son, his nephew Laurence" (155). The narrator's anger is directed not only at Laurence and his uncle, however, but at the white woman whom Laurence is now to marry. As she declares, "I hated her. I hated her baby face, her yellow hair, her whitish skin. 'She shall not marry him,' my soul said. 'I will kill him first'" (155). Her fury is thus directed at a female whiteness that carries with it an undue entitlement to Laurence's affection. In place of virtuous indignation or "savagery" comes a new form of anger: an entitlement that separates the indigenous heroine from the white woman, an alliance that sentimentality would conventionally depend upon.

The phrase "blood stained her face" from "A Red Girl's Reasoning" is an intriguing example of this convergence of race, anger, and virtue (118). Her "blood," a common synonym of "race," marks her rage in a visual form of female indignation. In both stories, the husbands' appearance is of equal import: Johnson is careful to point out that they (and the woman Laurence is to marry) have blond hair. As in particular sections of *Wynema* and "A Red Girl's Reasoning," italics or quotation marks indicate the narrator's distance from and critique of certain stereotypes: a line like "*it is a different thing to marry with one of them*" has special force when italicized (152).

As in "Ojistoh," anger affirms her virtue and her connection to her nation: at the end of "As It Was in the Beginning" the heroine is restored to her Cree home. It is as if a Native woman, once dignified by her anger towards a white man, can no longer be his wife: her righteous anger precludes a cross-racial and heterosexual romance.

In the classroom I have used "As It Was in the Beginning" to illustrate a rather complicated phenomenon of racial formation. It exemplifies, I argue, not an essentialist take on race—that she kills Laurence with snake venom because she is, in his uncle's words, a "savage" or a "snake"—but because he has described her as such. So what may be read as a stereotypical account is in fact a brilliant enactment of labeling theory or, in broader terms, the social construction of race. As a chilling last line reads, "Was it not merely a snake bite?" (156). But as some of my students have asked, is this really what the story's original readers would have taken from it? Wasn't the reader more likely to see it as an affirmation of the dangers of indigenous anger, and as such a reiteration of existing stereotypes? Indeed, I respond, Johnson's story demonstrates the very difficulty and determination of early indigenous women writers in asserting an anger that would be taken seriously.

This anger of entitlement draws in part from stereotypical images of the vengeful Indian. Although this figure is usually male, there is a strand of fictional Indian women who delight in an enemy's persecution. This was a figure Johnson was familiar with; as she once told stage partner Walter McRaye, "'I love everything Indian, and I am fond of reciting my poem, "The Avenger," which that picture illustrates. You know the iron Indian law of blood for blood?'" (quoted in McRaye 40).[20] The figure of the vengeful Indian woman is a readily available narrative that on one hand asserts an attractive power and on the other suggests the stereotypical savagery that Johnson seeks to distance herself from. These stories demonstrate, then, Johnson's attempt to articulate the anger of a First Nations woman who refuses dispossession. The difficulty of this articulation is due in part to the incompatibility of femininity and violence. While the male writers of color whom Ronald T. Takaki studies find a certain self-assertion in violent acts against their oppressors largely because violence (and anger) is consistent with the masculinity they have been denied, women of color often find femininity at odds with anger.

Indigenous women's anger is most potent in both stories in the figure of the protagonist's mother. "A Red Girl's Reasoning" opens with Christie's white father warning Charlie not to mistreat her, for "'there's a good bit of her mother in her, and,' closing his left eye significantly, 'you don't understand these Indians as I do'" (102). His self-proclaimed expertise is based not only on his experience in the multiracial community but, more importantly, his marriage to a First Nations woman. Thus the story begins with another, ostensibly successful cross-racial relationship; yet it is one in which racial (and gender) difference requires some caution. The indigenous mother becomes the epitome of Indianness: "Christine's disposition is as native as her mother's," a disposition that is kind but also capable of violence when scorned (102). Similarly, in "As It Was in the Beginning," Esther's mother laughs scornfully at the minister's initial approach: "even then my mother must have known" (145). She, it seems, can see past the minister's seductive words. "No" is the first word she speaks to him, her eyes "snapping," when he asks to take Esther with him (146). Although she is overruled by Esther's father, it is she who remains Esther's role model: "[I] only thought of the time when I should be grown, and do as my mother did, and wear the buckskins and the blanket" (146).

Johnson presents mixed-raced relationships in ambivalent terms. As in *Wynema*, Natives are at times positioned as objects. As a boy, Christie's father "had the Indian relic-hunting craze, as a youth he had studied Indian archaeology and folk-lore, as a man he consummated his predilections for Indianology by loving, winning and marrying the quiet little daughter of the English trader, who himself had married a native woman some twenty years ago" (103). On one hand Christie's parents have a loving match, but on the other, such unions seem to lead inevitably to "'the white man's disease,' consumption" as if they might consume one another (104). Johnson's take on these relationships seems as mixed as the relationships themselves, which in this case has produced an ambiguous child: "She belonged to neither and still to both types of the cultured Indian. The solemn, silent, almost heavy manner of the one so commingled with the gesticulating Frenchiness and vivacity of the other, that one unfamiliar with native Canadian life would find it difficult to determine her nationality" (104). Christie and Charlie's marriage ceremony incorporates both white and indigenous traditions, but in a way that appears to accommodate or at least complement Anglo desires: Charlie is only too glad in their wedding to "escape the flower-pelting, white gloves, rice-throwing, and ponderous stupidity of a breakfast, and indeed all the regulation gimcracks of the usual marriage celebrations" (105). From the first words that follow their idyllic ceremony, however, Charlie is subtly critiqued, a censure that Callahan's Robin escapes. Such critique is accomplished through sarcasm; Johnson places quotation marks around the following to suggest a distance between Charlie's assessment of Christie's position in her new community and her own: "he was proud that she had 'taken' so well among his friends" (105). There is also a skepticism about idolatry that is absent from Callahan's novel. Johnson suggests Christie's "almost abject devotion" of her husband (106), a phrase that both invokes the idolatry typically associated with Indians and checks it with the word "almost." Further critique of her position is evident in the quoting of her "newness," a word that likens her to a fashion to which the superficial townspeople are drawn (106). In other words, the description becomes more of a commentary on their construction of this supposed "relic" or new fashion than on Christie herself. Similarly, Esther acknowledges that she is the whites' "pet" (147), a word complicated by the retrospective bitterness in which it is uttered and the fact that it is delivered from her viewpoint.

Christie refuses the tears that are the hallmark of sentimentality; when Charlie's brother declares that "the little woman will cry her eyes out" if they were to move, she responds that she would not and never does cry (107–8). She goes even further in joking that Charlie might be exchanged as a duplicate relic, placing him in the position of the usual sentimentalized object. Such lightheartedness quickly disappears when the townspeople inquire about the legality of her parents' marriage. While the narrator sides with Christie's anger as righteous indignation, Charlie's anger—his humiliation about being disgraced before the town—is represented as selfish and destructive. Christie's anger, in turn, moves her to negate in stunning terms white superiority over indigenous peoples: "Do you mean to tell me, Charlie—you who have studied my race and their laws for years—do you mean to tell me that, because there was no priest and no magistrate, my mother was not married? Do you mean to say that all my forefathers, for hundreds of years back, have been illegally born? If so, you blacken my ancestry beyond—beyond—beyond all reason" (115). Their marriage becomes, then, a metaphor for a nation-to-nation relationship that she negates: if he won't honor her nation's legitimacy, she won't honor his.

The anger of Johnson's heroines is better understood if we consider it in light of an essay she wrote denouncing the traditional representation of indigenous women. "A Strong Race Opinion: On the Indian Girl in Modern Fiction," which appeared in Toronto's *Sunday Globe* in May of 1892, criticizes white writers who present Indian women as self-effacing, pathetic figures who bear no relation to actual indigenous women. She charges that these authors inevitably end the story with the heroine's suicide, a radical form of dispossession: "[The author] knows what she did and how she died in other romances by other romancers and she will do and die likewise in his (she always does die, and one feels relieved that this is so, for she is too unhealthy and too unnatural to live)" (1). This dismal end occurs, she notes, despite the fact that suicide is exceedingly rare among indigenous peoples. What's more, this character calmly accepts that the white man is meant for a white woman, and so sacrifices her own life for his happiness. The character does not, in other words, get angry: she does not lay claim to her lover. In Jessie M. Freeland's story "Winona's Tryst," Johnson points out, the Indian woman "manages by self-abnegation, danger, and many heartaches to restore him to the arms of Rose McTavish who of course he has loved and longed for all through the story. Then 'Winona' secures the time honored canoe, paddles out into the lake and drowns herself" (1). The Indian girl of such fiction lacks, Johnson argues in her first sentence, the self and in turn the national possession of actual Native women: "Every race in the world enjoys its own peculiar characteristics, but it scarcely follows that every individual of a nation must possess these prescribed singularities, or otherwise forfeit in the eyes of the world their nationality" (1). Forfeiting indigenous nationality is not something Johnson is willing to do. As she expresses in a letter from 1890, "I have a double motive in all my work and all my strivings—one is to upset the Indian Extermination and noneducation theory—in fact to stand by my blood and my race" (quoted in Gerson and Strong-Boag *Collected* xvi).

In contrast to sentimental poems like "The Cattle Thief," which make space for the reader to join in (or at least evade) the heroine's anger, this essay establishes an impermeable boundary between the English and the indigenous peoples. This anger is communicated through a biting sarcasm: "one cannot love or admire a heroine that grubs in the mud like a turtle, climbs trees like a raccoon, and tears and soils her gowns like a mad woman" (1). The reference to the Indian girl who "climbs trees" recalls the scene in which Wynema is perched from a branch, reading Tennyson. The character must "develop from 'the dog-like,' 'fawn-like,' 'deer-footed,' 'fire-eyed,' 'crouching,' 'submissive' book heroine into something of the quiet, sweet womanly woman she is, if wild, or the everyday, natural, laughing girl she is, if cultivated and educated" (1). Johnson goes on to observe that for all that the Indian woman devotes herself to a white man, she never kisses him, which to her indicates the clear limits placed on the character's sexuality. This stereotypical Indian woman is somewhat reminiscent of Callahan's Wynema, who also lacks both dignified anger and sexual desire. In these stories, Johnson finds little more than caricatures of innocence and submission: figures that have no ability to assert their rights.

Despite Johnson's frustrations with a Wynema-like character, however, her short stories indicate that she too found it difficult to portray a fictional cross-racial relationship that allowed for a Native woman's anger. Strong-Boag and Gerson note that "A Strong Race Opinion" appeared early in Johnson's career, before she faced the challenge of appealing to a mass audience (*Paddling* 187). The fact that this essay went relatively unnoticed compared to her stories and poems suggests that like Callahan, Johnson was limited to conventional sentimental scripts that were not necessarily conducive to indigenous anger. The challenge of depicting such anger is evident in critical responses to "As It Was in the Beginning." A reviewer of her Steinway Hall performance in July 1906 notes that compared to "Ojistoh," the story's "mixture of bitterness and savagery makes it less pleasant."[21] Faced with either the dismal drowning of Winona or the Indian woman's angry self-assertion, Johnson opted for the latter, crafting a story in which the First Nations heroine acknowledges and in some sense avenges her lover's betrayal. So although it is no neat happy ending, at the closure of "As It Was in the Beginning" we find the heroine restored to her indigenous community, her anger rewarded with the nationality that the "popular Indian girl of modern fiction" is denied.

Johnson's essay seems a fitting dialogue with Womack's *Red on Red*. Womack would likely agree with her desire for indigenous characters that are "distinct, unique and natural," terms that seem compatible with the tribal nationalism that Womack and other critics espouse (1). She places the word "Indian" in quotes as a marker of the generic, and inaccurate, figure who lacks tribal distinction. Johnson insists that writers demonstrate a realistic knowledge of indigenous cultures, criticizing those who presume knowledge even if they have "never met or mixed with them" (1). If they are not "competent to give tribal characteristics," they should at least render believable characters (1). Johnson applauds Charles Mair, who shows "upon every page evidence of long study and life with the people whom he has written of so carefully, so truthfully" (1). In turn, she would likely find fault with Wynema; the "popular Indian girl" she describes always has a "Winona sound about it" and doesn't have a surname (1). One of the most disturbing aspects of the stereotypical Indian girl, Johnson claims, is that she sells out, getting herself "despised by her own nation" (1). Accordingly, neither Christie nor Esther betrays her indigenous community; Christie refuses to negate her culture's legitimacy, and Esther returns to her Cree home. Terms that usually mark sentimentality here convey a biting sarcasm: "Poor little Wanda!" (1). In contrast to writers like Jessie M. Freeland, Johnson doesn't "restore" the white man to the white woman; indeed, Esther violently refuses this restoration.

"A Woman to Let Alone"

JOHNSON'S INDIAN MOTHER

It was in the form of the Mohawk mother that Johnson found an alternative, successful form of female Indianness—in part because the sentimental advice essay in which she appeared did not involve the inevitably charged relationships between indigenous women and white men that characterize these short stories. Between 1907 and 1912, she published twenty-nine pieces in the popular *Mother's Magazine,* which boasted a circulation of 600,000 in 1909 (Strong-Boag and Gerson *Paddling* 209). In circulation from 1905 to 1920, the magazine offered short stories, poetry, and advice pieces in the tradition of an earlier periodical of the same name. The editors' introduction to the essay "Mothers of a Great Red Race" suggests that the Mohawk mother of Johnson's pieces was popular because she complemented many white women's images of ideal motherhood in the early twentieth century. In her article, Johnson describes the Indian mother as occupying a kind of domestic Eden, "exempt from unceasing war which the white mother wages—the war against unnatural foods, unseasonable apparel and unhealthy hours and environment which are a menace to the frail little bodies of the majority of white children. No worry enters into the wigwam to fret the placid red mother, to upset her nerves, to irritate her temper and thereby to warp her baby's upbringing" (5). The editors make clear that Johnson's submission should be for mothers in particular, "not women in general."[22]

In a move consistent with conventional sentimentality, the mother Johnson describes is figured as the cornerstone of morality. Like other women of color such as Harriet Jacobs, motherhood becomes a means for the writer to establish a connection with her white reader. Many of Johnson's pieces that draw explicitly from family history describe the Mohawk mother as one whom all women should emulate. In "Mothers of a Great Red Race," the supposed backwardness of Indian women is refigured as the source of their maternal skills: the "grace of motherhood," she claims, "is to her a primitive glory" (5). The magazines in which Johnson published encourage parents to quell their own and their children's tempers. In an interview with H. I. Cleveland, for example, one woman tells how she once held her screaming son down until his tantrum subsided. It never occurred again.[23] In a tone that fit nicely with contemporary concerns about how modern life threatened children's lives, Johnson describes the Mohawk mother as one who protects her children from such malignant influences within the seclusion of the forest:

> [T]here are two terrors the Indian mother is happily free from: one is the haunting fear that her children may fall into evil company, temptation or crime—she knows nothing of this anxiety. The other is that thieves, marauders, or alarmists may enter her little home. These threatening evils do not exist in the wilderness, and for weeks together, unprotected and unguarded, she and her little ones may lay themselves down to sleep without fear or misgiving, for no harm will ever approach from God's primal world about them. ("Outdoor Occupations of the Indian Mother" 23)

Like Sarah Winnemucca, albeit in more subtle terms, Johnson challenges the traditional binary of the "savage" wilderness and the "civilized" city; here the outdoors is the safest place of all. Cognizant of the precise function of the Indian mother in these magazines, Johnson tacks back and forth between comparing Indian and white mothers and suggesting the former's superiority. Many of her "Indian mother" essays mark her indigenous status with the name "Tekahionwake" in parentheses after "E. Pauline Johnson." In "Heroic Indian Mothers," the familiar "calling card" is replaced with the "little red kernel," so that a marker of social privilege and decorum is neatly translated into indigenous terms, reminding us that we should not read these pieces as erasing Mohawk tradition (23). As the essay "Outdoor Occupations of the Indian Mother and Her Children" notes, the Indian mother is free from the hazards of city life.[24] Unlike other women, she enjoys a domestic seclusion free of "discontent" ("Winter Indoor Life" 5). The "circle of warmth," a perfect synonym for the ideal home, is a place of "healthy children," "fortunate" wives, and "manly" husbands (22). Such rhetoric was particularly appealing in a time when mothers were encouraged to avoid such "impurities" as caffeine, spices, and excessive indoor activity, which were thought to harm children. Like Sarah Winnemucca, at times Johnson posits indigenous traditions as more domestic and moral than whites'. Two articles that share pages with Johnson's essays, "The Child's Life and Character Begins in the Youth of the Mother and Father" and Sceva Stephen's "Housekeeping Responsibilities Outside of Home," give advice that complements hers: the former extols the virtues of fresh air and proper nutrition, while Stephen rails against unsanitary conditions and unwholesome food.[25] Editor Elizabeth Ansley's invitation to Johnson echoes these sentiments: "you might have something very good to offer the mothers in the way of Outdoor Sports, Mother and Child out-of-doors, Health Exercises, Picnics, Camping, etc., all written especially for the mother, and her family" (quoted in Strong-Boag and Gerson *Paddling* 170). Johnson fills this order with essays such as "Winter Indoor Life of

"A Woman to Let Alone"

the Indian Mother and Children," in which she claims that

> the Indian mother never loses sight of the fact that, although her children must first learn the indispensable arts of practical living, mental and physical recreations must not be overlooked. No matter how deep the snow, the sturdy youngsters are bundled outdoors for an hour's pastime daily, during which time they accomplish the useful function of water-carriers, drawing on their little toboggans all the water needed for household purposes. (5)

Such examples illustrate Johnson's balance between incorporating the required components of Anglo-Canadian culture and modeling an alternative and even superior maternalism. The same thread appears in her later Chinook story "The Legend of Lillooet Falls": "there is a strange tie between them and their children. The men of magic say they can *see* that tie, though you and I cannot. It is thin, fine, silvery as a cobweb, but strong as the ropes of wild vine that swing down the great canons. . . . *Nothing* breaks it" (19). The Indian mother thus becomes the very epitome of maternal love.

Anger is not absent from Johnson's maternal essays; "Mothers of a Great Red Race," for example, portrays a mother's anger that is deemed crucial to the Mohawk nation. The essay describes her paternal grandmother's indignation when her Mohawk clan tried to deny her son a position as a head chief because the leaders felt his position as an interpreter for the Canadian government would conflict with his duties as a leader of the Mohawks: "after a bitter, scathing, ironical speech, in which she reprimanded the entire council for about forty minutes, she capped her argument with the threat that, unless they accepted her nominee she would annul the title forever, thus weakening by one the Mohawk portion of the council and shattering a constitution that had existed for centuries" (5). In an instance that demonstrates women's power in the Mohawk political system as well as the potential weight of their anger, the clan matron threatens to block anyone else from filling the position created by her brother's death. The Mohawk mother articulates an anger that is not trivialized or condemned as it would be within Anglo-European or American political structures. Her anger is legitimated in part because it is thought to be in service of the family and the nation rather than an individual whim. As Johnson notes, her grandmother ultimately won out, although George was not allowed to vote in the council as long as he was a salaried interpreter.[26] Thus a valid female—and Mohawk—anger emerges in the form of the powerful clan matron.

Chapter 2

The mother's relationship to the nation is mapped onto a classic Anglo-Canadian narrative of nationhood in Johnson's story "Her Dominion—A Story of 1867, and Canada's Confederation," which was published in the *Mother's Magazine* in July of 1907. The story begins with a white mother's delight that she finally has a son, who she longs will be "good and manly and useful" (10). When Malcolm Farleigh later shares his hopes for the union of Canada, his mother is heartbroken by his aspirations since they will require him to leave home and devote himself to the political arena. Attempting to steel her feelings for him, as does the Mohawk mother of Johnson's essays, Mrs. Farleigh manages:

> "It would be great, Malcolm—a great thing for you to mother such an idea, to mother the scheme of confederation of those scattered provinces into one vast family—"
>
> "To 'father' such an idea, don't you mean, mother?" He laughed, his excitement deepening as he saw her ready grasping of his ambitions. "Yes, it would be great to 'father' the confederation of those provinces. Mother, you've invented the right word—'Confederation.' I'll make that word of yours go down in history." (11)

Notably, Mrs. Farleigh describes political union in distinctly familial—and maternal—terms. In contrast, Malcolm replaces the word "mother" with "father," symbolically usurping her role in producing "his wonderful child, the Dominion of Canada, awaiting the moment of its birth" (40). Malcolm refers to confederation in paternal terms until his first speech after it is achieved. In this closing scene, he acknowledges her linguistic contribution to the nation's formation: "Gentlemen, my mother—the first one I ever heard make use of that glorious word—'Confederation.' And, gentlemen, she used it in speaking of Canada. Whatever I have done that is creditable I owe to her and her dominion—a dominion of love and understanding" (40). While he credits her vision, it is up to him to do so. Recognizing that a white mother would lack the political voice that Johnson's Mohawk grandmother enjoyed, Johnson grants Mrs. Farleigh a compromised voice through her son by acknowledging "her ready grasping of his ambitions." Positioned alongside Johnson's maternal essays, the comparatively limited power of the white mother becomes apparent. And while the story seems a rather celebratory vision of the nation's founding, it is worth noting that "Canada" is figured as a primarily male and Anglo creation.

"A Woman to Let Alone"

THE FEMALE RACIAL COMPLAINT

I conclude my analysis of Pauline Johnson's strategies onstage and in writing with a reformulation of "The Female Complaint," Lauren Berlant's term for women's collective, and insufficient, public lament, which often takes the form of (conventional) sentimental literature. As Berlant writes, "Situated precisely in the space between a sexual politics that threatens structures of patriarchal authority and a sentimentality that confirms the inevitability of the speaker's powerlessness, the female complaint registers the speaker's frustration, rage, abjection, and heroic self-sacrifice, in an oppositional utterance that declares its limits in its very saying" (243–44). In *Uncle Tom's Cabin,* Berlant claims, the female complaint is perhaps most poignant when the senator's wife, moved by the presence of a runaway slave mother, asks him to aid Eliza in a way that does not challenge his superiority. Although this "aesthetic 'witnessing' of injury" is a form of resistance to patriarchal systems, it is also perceived as evidence of the speaker's feminine—and benign—discontent (243). Given that women are in an odd position, expected to desire their oppressors in a patriarchal society that resists direct attacks on its authority, they are left to mount a rather ineffectual complaint against men. This framework is somewhat reminiscent of the stereotypical coquette whose "no" doesn't really mean no, whose protest is in fact attractive to the man who knows he doesn't have to take it seriously. For performance artist Karen Finley, a man's response that a woman's anger "turns him on" is his attempt to tame or control her (Juno 49). Sentimentality, Berlant contends, is one of the forms that the female complaint assumes: a complaint that invariably ends in heterosexual marriage. A central problem with the female complaint, she notes, is its construction of a community of supposed "sameness," where there is no acknowledgment of the differences that exist between women.

As a performer, Johnson needed the regard of both men and women—but as an indigenous woman, she found that her relations with white men were potentially threatening to white women. In "A Strong Race Opinion," she notes that in earlier stories by white men, the relationship between the Indian woman and the white man ends tragically:

> But the hardest fortune that the Indian girl of fiction meets with is the inevitable doom that shadows her love affairs. She is always desperately in love with the young white hero, who in turn is grateful to her for services rendered the garrison in general and himself in particular during red days

of war. In short, she is so much wrapped up in him that she is treacherous to her own people, tells falsehoods to her father and the other chiefs of her tribe, and otherwise makes herself detestable and dishonorable. Of course, this white hero never marries her! Will some critic who understands human nature and particularly the nature of authors, please tell the reading public why marriage with the Indian girl is so despised in books and so general in real life? (1)

As I consider at greater length in my reading of Sarah Winnemucca's *Life Among the Piutes,* the phrase "of course" marks the author's sarcastic response: in this case, to narratives in which a woman's Indianness and her "feminine" desire cannot coexist. Johnson was painfully aware of the "constraints and contradictions" of desire: her own engagement to a white man was broken off in part because his family resisted his marriage to a mixed-blood woman.[27]

The ostensible solidarity that is key to the female complaint is invoked in the final, powerful sentence of Johnson's story "As It Was in the Beginning." The narrator imagines a community of women linked by their shared anger at men—an anger that, like "the female complaint," seems to transcend racial distinctions. As the narrator remarks, "They account for it by the fact that I am a Redskin. They seem to have forgotten I am a woman" (156). Here the narrator contends that it is her sex rather than her race that makes her capable of this rage. Anger and womanhood are presented here not as opposites, but as mutually constitutive. What Johnson attempts, then, is a portrait of anger that is not "Indianized," but womanized. Yet this gesture of solidarity with white women is made impossible not only by their resentment of her but by her own anger at them. This anger is communicated through the sarcasm and irony that marks her departure from conventional sentimentality—and from white women readers.

While the audience Johnson most often imagined and indeed faced on stage was a white one, she leaves us to ask how her performances would have been altered for an indigenous community. Sarah Winnemucca, the final writer I consider, is the most successful at affirming her nationhood through sentimental anger. Her toughest audience, however, would prove to be her own people. Anger was for her, as for Johnson and Callahan, a valuable and yet potentially dangerous resource.

3

Lost (and Gained) in Translation

LANGUAGE, ANGER, AND AGENCY
IN SARAH WINNEMUCCA HOPKINS'S
LIFE AMONG THE PIUTES

In her editorial preface to the first edition of Sarah Winnemucca Hopkins's *Life Among the Piutes*,[1] reformer Mary Elizabeth Mann claims that Winnemucca's authority stems from her position between Native American and white cultures:

> It is the first outbreak of the American Indian in human literature, and has a single aim—*to tell the truth* as it lies in the heart and mind of a true patriot, and one whose knowledge of the two races gives her an opportunity of comparing them justly. At this moment, when the United States seem waking up to their duty to the original possessors of our immense territory, it is of the first importance to hear what only an Indian and an Indian woman can tell. (2)

This truth claim, which resembles those of slave narratives in its assertion of authority, positions Winnemucca as a unique—and uniquely credible—speaker. As a translator for the whites, Winnemucca is said to speak the "truth" of both the whites and the Northern Paiute community. But for whom does she speak this truth? If she is indeed a "true patriot," exactly to what (or to whom) is she patriotic? Further, how is our reading of this early self-narrative by a Native American woman altered when we consider her a mediator between whites and Paiute Indians? Is there any space for her critique—her anger—when she is paid to speak whites' words?

All three of the writers I consider encounter obstacles to the articulation of an anger that affirms their indigenous nationhood: Alice Callahan was largely limited to the Indian reform scripts that could only imagine an anger of a white woman on behalf of Native Americans; Johnson's virtuous indignation was read by her white audiences as sex appeal; Winnemucca was a translator, a kind of spokesperson, for whites. But each writer manages to use some form of sentimentality to disrupt, if only briefly, conventions that deny Native women's anger. Winnemucca is most successful in this endeavor, offering a narrative that combines sentimentality and sarcasm both to criticize whites and to affirm her Northern Paiute nation.

Growing up during the critical period when the Northern Paiutes first encountered white settlers in large numbers, Sarah Winnemucca (Thocmetony) was confronted at an early age with complex questions of identity. Born around 1844, she spent her childhood living with the Northern Paiutes—the Numa, as they call themselves—in the arid stretch of the Great Basin now known as Nevada. As a member of the band known as the Kuyuidika-a (Eaters of the Cui-ui, an ancient fish in Pyramid Lake), Winnemucca spent her first years in a nomadic community that depended on hunting, gathering pine nuts, and fishing. Her mother, Tuboitony, was the daughter of a distinguished Paiute leader, and Sarah's father came to be known as Chief Winnemucca. Sarah was only a young girl when white settlers, seeking land and promised gold, began to enter Paiute territory. When she was about thirteen, her grandfather sent her and her sister to live with Major William Ormsby and his family in Genoa. It was during this period, when she worked as a housekeeper and companion for various white families, that she became fluent in both Spanish and English. Returning to Pyramid Lake in 1866, she discovered that because she could speak and write English, she was expected to serve as a go-between for the white and Paiute communities that were increasingly at odds. Upon her arrival, military officials asked her to urge her father to bring his people to the reservation. Serving as an interpreter for the military and the white agents who ran the reservations, Sarah Winnemucca was one of the few

Paiutes who could support herself in a time when the tribes were increasingly exploited by whites. Her work as a translator illustrates the kind of transformation the Northern Paiute and other Native communities were enduring as they moved from communal subsistence to a capitalist economy. Her position as an individual and a member of the community is, in turn, an important tension in her narrative.

Winnemucca's English proficiency allowed her a control over her literary self-representation that few Native Americans had known.[2] In her self-narrative she attests that she is in a unique position to expose the government's exploitation of her people: "Oh, it is a fearful thing to tell, but it must be told. Yes, it must be told by me" (77). Her sense that the narrative is a powerful means of publicizing government corruption is also evident at the end of the narrative, where a petition for the reader to sign and send on was enclosed. The reformer Mary Elizabeth Mann, who met Winnemucca through her sister, Elizabeth Peabody, suggests that *Life Among the Piutes* is powerful also because it is written in English by Winnemucca herself. Although she acknowledges correcting Winnemucca's spelling and grammatical errors, Mann insists in her preface that she has not interfered with the style or content of Winnemucca's prose: "I am confident that no one would desire that *her own original words* should be altered" (2, my emphasis). Using words like "command" and "fervid," Mann emphasizes Winnemucca's individual speaking authority and, accordingly, the text's authenticity.[3] While this authenticity is said to stem in part from Winnemucca's capacity as an individual, I will argue that she ultimately returns to a more collective model of agency to defend herself against accusations of betrayal.

By the time Winnemucca wrote *Life Among the Piutes*, she—like Pauline Johnson—was adept at representing herself before white audiences. She began her stage career in the mining town of Virginia City, Nevada, in 1864. In between performances, she, her father, and her sister Elma rode through the streets in elaborate attire that the white residences understood as "Indian": leather and feather headdresses. Well-versed in English, Sarah interpreted her father's speeches for the audience. Soon after, the three performed at the Metropolitan Theatre in San Francisco. Their show, which was advertised as an illustration of "Indian Life," had little relationship to actual Northern Paiute culture (Canfield 39). It was intended to cater to Anglo expectations of Indianness: the troupe again sported headdresses and buckskin. Like Johnson, Winnemucca was aware of the importance of dress in her public performances; at one point in her narrative she describes her family's "mourning dress," which she plans to wear during her lectures (75). In one performance the family reenacted the Pocahontas legend, a tale that had nothing to do with Northern Paiute history but that was a sure crowd-pleaser. One newspaper review describes Sarah's use of language to charm the audience:

> [Old Winnemucca's] part of the speech being loudly applauded by the appreciative audience, the old fellow became inspired and rattled off at such a telegraphic rate that we couldn't come up with him at all. Not so with Shell Flower: she had been there and knew just what to say, and it came to us in her sweet English voice to this effect, "My father says he is glad to see so many of you here, and he hopes there will be a great many more tonight when he hopes to accommodate you—I mean please you better." (quoted in Canfield 41)

Although the three did not earn enough money to assist the financially strapped Paiutes, Winnemucca became adept at entertaining white audiences. She did so in part by marshaling sentimental conventions. A spectator of one of her lectures in 1870 noted Winnemucca's sentimental effect on the white audience: she spoke with "such persuasion and conviction . . . that many people were moved to tears" (quoted in James 629). Tears have a prominent place in the narrative, as my students invariably notice; references to weeping occur on no fewer than 18 of the first 50 pages. Recounting an early incident in which one of her uncles was shot by whites, Winnemucca notes that as Truckee urges restraint, "he wept, and men, women, and children, were all weeping. One could hardly hear him talking" (21). Paiute elders later comment on the whites who have committed the ultimate sentimental outrage of laughing at them when they weep (102). Whether or not it actually occurred, this weeping recalls Karen Sanchez-Eppler's assessment of the importance of tears in sentimental literature:

> Sentiment and feeling refer at once to emotion and to physical sensation, and in sentimental fiction these two versions of sentire blend as the eyes of readers take in the printed word and blur it with tears. Reading sentimental fiction is thus a bodily act, and the success of the story is gauged, in part, by its ability to translate words into pulse beats and sobs. This physicality of the reading experience radically contracts the distance between narrated events and the moment of their reading, as the feelings in the story are made tangibly present in the flesh of the reader. (*Touching* 26–27)

Lost (and Gained) in Translation

In Winnemucca's narrative, weeping serves not only to forge this alliance between character and reader but to assert Paiute dignity. It also becomes a form of resistance: early on, Winnemucca's tears mark her refusal to trust the whites. Washoe women cry in protest when their innocent husbands are accused of killing two white men: "Such weeping was enough to make the very mountains weep to see them" (63). Weeping registers that this violence is not simply against the Washoe or Paiute Indians but the very earth itself.

In the 1880s, Winnemucca incorporated such sentimental conventions into her lectures across the Northeast about white Americans' mistreatment of indigenous peoples. These lectures indicate her astute sense of what should be included in—and perhaps more importantly, excluded from— her speeches. Mary Elizabeth Mann's sister, Elizabeth Peabody, another spirited advocate of Indian reform, affectionately recalls Winnemucca's first lecture. It was directed exclusively to women: "she unfolded the domestic education given by the grandmothers of the Piute [sic] tribe to the youth of both sexes, with respect to their relations with each other both before and after marriage,—a lecture which never failed to excite the moral enthusiasm of every woman that heard it, and seal their confidence in her own purity of character and purpose" (*Practical Solution* 28). Winnemucca's framing of Paiute culture in these terms suggests that, like Johnson, she found that such sentimental, moralistic language made her message more attractive to white, middle-class women. In turn, Winnemucca omits the details of her marriages and her alleged bar fights. According to biographer Gae Whitney Canfield, Winnemucca married military officer Edward Bartlett in 1871 and filed for divorce in 1876 after falling in love with a man named Joseph Satewaller (109).[4] Her last husband was Lewis H. Hopkins, whom she married on December 5, 1881. Hopkins was an alcoholic and an inveterate gambler who ultimately squandered much of Winnemucca's money before his death in 1887. Although multiple marriages were common and divorce was easily attained in Paiute culture, Winnemucca realized that her white, middle-class women readers would not likely approve of her marital history. And while at least one scholar has noted that Sarah's father had several wives, Winnemucca refers only to her mother as if to satisfy her white readers' investment in monogamy—an investment very much linked to the sentimental conception of a "stable" nuclear family.[5] Such sentimentalism may continue in our current treatments of her: Carolyn Sorisio has suggested that critics' choice to drop "Hopkins" when referring to Winnemucca may be an effort to "protect" her from a bad husband, or to authenticate her as a Native American.

Nor does Winnemucca mention her various brushes with the law, which were covered with tabloid enthusiasm in local newspapers and would not complement the sentimental image of femininity that her readers expected. According to the *Silver State*, she fought with another Indian woman in 1875 and later attacked a man with a knife after he threatened to assault her (Canfield 92). Colorful newspaper accounts emphasize her temper: in one she is described as "using language more forcible than polite," while another notes that in response to defamations of her character, "her royal blood boiled in her veins."[6] A woman who carried a knife, rode bareback, and physically defended herself had to tailor herself carefully in a sentimental narrative. Winnemucca's campaign to portray herself in an acceptable light became even more critical when Agent William Rinehart, in retaliation for her critiques of his mismanagement, filed several affidavits against her in 1880. Written by men who had various investments in her demotion, these and other documents described Winnemucca as a "notorious liar and malicious schemer" who "had been several times married, but that by reason of her adulterous and drunken habits, neither squawmen nor Indians would long live with her" (quoted in Canfield 173). To challenge her cultural authority, these white men accused her of violating sentimental norms of domesticity and chastity. Given these allegations, it is no wonder that Winnemucca omitted details of her life, whether true or alleged, that could only be used against her. Her inclusion of several letters of recommendation by white men in the appendix of *Life Among the Piutes* further indicates her attempts to intervene in these representations.

Historical accounts have tended to position Winnemucca as either an influential mediator who accomplished significant reforms in Indian policy or "a tool for the military" who had little control over the words she used (C. S. Fowler "Foreword" 4). For her white supporters, she fit into a storyline of famous American Indian women who made personal sacrifices on behalf of Anglos. One of Winnemucca's allies, General Oliver Howard, likens her to the Indian figure who is perhaps most prominent in the Anglo imagination: "She did our government great service, and if I could tell you but a tenth part of all she willingly did to help the white settlers and her own people to live peaceably together I am sure you would think, as I do, that the name of Toc-me-to-ne should have a place beside the name of Pocahontas in the history of our country" (237). What Howard saw as noble mediation, however, others considered treason. The latter point to Sarah's family's commitment to reconciliation with the whites and her own support of assimilation as evidence that the Winnemuccas were "what would be labeled today 'White-men's Indians'" who betrayed the Paiutes (quoted in C. S. Fowler "Sarah Winnemucca" 40). Some of this criticism originated in Winnemucca's alleged support of the General Allotment (Dawes) Act.[7] Today, Winnemucca's fiercest critics are certain Paiutes who maintain that she and her family do not deserve such prominence in the historical records. According to them, the Winnemuccas were considered the leaders of the Paiutes simply because they were the ones, beginning with the amenable "Captain Truckee," who had the closest ties with whites. One such critic is Nellie Shaw Harnar, who claims that while Sarah's father was an influential man among the Paiutes, "he was not considered the chief of the tribe as stated by [Frederick] Dodge in 1859" (104).[8] Lalla Scott's biographical account of the author's mother also alleges that the Winnemuccas had a traitorous alliance with the whites. Contemporary literary critics Gretchen M. Bataille and Kathleen Mullen Sands have faulted *Life Among the Piutes* for its "acculturated and Christianized" bias, suggesting Sarah Winnemucca was more faithful to the Anglos than the Paiutes (21). These accusations that Winnemucca sold out might recall the story of an indigenous woman who was Cortés' advisor, translator, and mistress: a figure known in Chicano culture as a "sellout to the white race" (Moraga 39). Alternative accounts of the life of this woman indicate that she was raped by Cortés, or that she believed he was the only hope for her peoples' survival. It is as an interpreter for the colonists' language that the indigenous woman allegedly betrays her people: in speaking the others' words, she becomes them.[9]

Defending the author against the accusation that she betrayed the Paiutes, Fowler's foreword urges the reader to acknowledge the tremendous obstacles that Winnemucca faced:

> But in evaluating Sarah, one must also place oneself as much as possible within the times and in the conditions under which she lived and worked—not such an easy task. For example, what was the role prescribed for a woman, let alone a Native American woman, in the mid- to late 1800s? What could she hope to accomplish given that role and what means were available to her? Could speaking out ever go unchallenged? (4)

Chapter 3

In order to consider Winnemucca's ability to "speak out"—specifically, to articulate her anger about whites' treatment of Native Americans—I turn to theories of agency and translation. As a translator, Winnemucca was not strictly an agent of others' words (and thus wordless herself) or an entirely free agent; rather, as an ostensibly passive conduit of others' words, she intervened in their meaning.

THE AGENT AS VENTRILOQUIST

The relationship between agency and language immediately arises when one studies nineteenth-century women writers of color, many of whom confronted illiteracy and other forms of exclusion from the literary marketplace. At the same time, in assuming that nineteenth-century autobiographers such as Harriet Jacobs could not have written their own self-narratives, some scholars have underestimated writers' ability to express and represent themselves. David Murray's analysis of American Indian autobiographies illustrates this tension between acknowledging these writers' limitations and their interventions. Early autobiographies ostensibly written by Native Americans, he argues, are more appropriately described as *bio*graphies, since the white editor often turned the Native American into an object of a white reading audience rather than a subject of his or her life story. Because of their assumed (or actual) unfamiliarity with the English language and their existence as "others" in the national imaginary, he contends, Native Americans autobiographers were less agents in their own right than agents *for* white discourse. The autoethnographic act necessarily makes authors objects to themselves:

> This sense of the "othering" of the "I," as it is uttered and "outered" in a text, and the consequent problematic relation between this notion of text and the claims for certain sorts of authenticity contained within autobiography, become particularly relevant with Indian autobiography, where the production of the text often operates to turn the speaking subject into an object, whether for study, entertainment or even the *frisson* of the exotic. (*Forked* 65–66)

In this sense, Native autobiographers of the nineteenth century were doubly objectified. Noreen Groover Lape, somewhat similarly, claims that because Winnemucca writes the narrative in English, she "already loses much of the cultural context that her own words, her native language, would embody" (*West* 42).

But can we ever say that our words are entirely our own? If we agree that agency demands or operates through representation, we can identify opportunities for the Native American writer to narrate her life in spite of her objectification. Even in cases where the author's narrative is altered by a white editor, aren't there spaces where the writer can intervene in the editorial process, or otherwise participate in his or her own representation? I do not mean to downplay the respective power of white editors like Mary Elizabeth Mann, who obviously had access to resources that Winnemucca lacked.[10] But I would question whether our emphasis on the censorship of such authors denies the complexity of their self-presentation.

Our reading of Native American autobiographies, Arnold Krupat contends, must also account for the ways in which indigenous conceptions of self and community differ from those of whites: "Whereas the modern West has tended to define personal identity as involving the successful mediation of an opposition between the individual and society, Native Americans have instead tended to define themselves as persons by successfully integrating themselves into the relevant social groupings—kin, clan, band, etc.—of their respective societies" (*Native American* 4). Although such emphasis on the collective—an emphasis that Jace Weaver terms "communitism"—is indeed a frequent element of Native American literature, Winnemucca's narrative communicates a certain egotism that appears to challenge this characteristic. After saving a group of Paiutes from the Bannock Indians, she proudly declares, "Yes, I went for the government when the officers could not get an Indian man or a white man to go for love or money. I, only an Indian woman, went and saved my father and his people" (164).

We might reconcile these apparently conflicting models of selfhood by considering how Winnemucca once described herself as the Spirit Father's "special messenger" (quoted in Peabody *Practical Solution* 25). Although Winnemucca imagined herself as a vehicle for this god-like figure, she maintained a sense of herself as unique: she, after all, was the one chosen to be this messenger. Winnemucca understood her dynamic position in between discursive systems: even as a conduit for others' words she maintained a voice (albeit an always complicated, even contradictory, voice) of her own. In her words, "Many Indian wars would be avoided if interpreters were only true instead of being the tool of the Agents.... I attribute the success of my school not to my being a scholar and a good teacher but because I am my own Interpreter, and my heart is in my work."[11] As Siobhan Senier writes, "This does not mean she is never individualistic, for we have seen that she most emphatically can be; nor is it to romanticize her, as an Indian, as somehow essentially more communal than her white contemporary. It is, however, to observe that she characteristically allows other viewpoints to speak through her writing, including those of radically conservative Paiutes" (*Voices* 103). Agency is not neatly equated, then, with either the individual or the collective.

My analysis of language and agency in *Life Among the Piutes* borrows in part from feminist theories, where words like "agency" and "the subject" are as pervasive as they are contested. Challenging the humanist concept of the self-determining subject in *Feminists Theorize the Political*, Judith Butler contends that both agency and the subject who is thought to assert that agency are products of discursive systems:

> My position is mine to the extent that "I"—and I do not shirk from the pronoun—replay and resignify the theoretical positions that have constituted me, working the possibilities of their convergence, and trying to take account of the possibilities that they systematically exclude. But it is clearly not the case that "I" preside over the positions that have constituted me, shuffling through them instrumentally, casting some aside, incorporating others, although some of my activity may take that form. The "I" who would select between them is always already constituted by them. (9)

For Butler, agency is neither a quality that preexists the subject nor a prerequisite to action. The idea that we must retain a concept of woman, the subject of feminist discourse, *forecloses* the potential for agency: to speak of "the subject" as if it is a single, stable position is to normalize one particular position while precluding others.

Butler's assessment of agency has been criticized by Seyla Benhabib, who claims it is incompatible with feminist goals of empowerment and social change because of its insistence on agency as a product of social systems rather than a characteristic that the subject possess *a priori*. Benhabib notes Butler's inability or refusal to imagine the individual as anything more than the agent of the discourses that she or he inhabits. As she argues, "Not only feminist politics, but also coherent theorizing becomes impossible if the speaking and thinking self is replaced by 'authorial positions,' and if the self becomes a ventriloquist for discourses operating through her or 'mobilizing' her" (216). Benhabib's use of the word "ventriloquist" is worth noting, for it captures the disagreement between the two theorists: for Benhabib, the ventriloquist epitomizes the dangers of being spoken for, while for Butler it is *through* a kind of ventriloquism that agency is produced. Malea Powell's more indigenous-centered interpretation, which argues that Winnemucca draws from both Euro-American and Paiute tactics, can be imagined as a bridge between the two: one that considers how the colonized might find opportunities for resistance in existing discourse (404).[12]

The translator, another sort of ventriloquist, is a productive figure through which to consider the relationship between language and agency since he or she is located squarely in the midst of discursive systems and yet has some ability to manipulate them. Theorist Lawrence Venuti has claimed that the translator is considered successful when his or her presence is forgotten: "The translator remains subordinate to the author of the original work.... [T]he originality of translation lies in self-effacement, a vanishing act, and it is on this basis that translators prefer to be praised" (*Rethinking* 4). In other words, the ideal translator disappears in the process of translation. Venuti's descriptions of translation are eerily, though not intentionally, reminiscent of colonization. He associates contemporary English-language translation with terms such as "intervention"; "faithful"; "uniformity"; "identification"; "self-annihilation"; "marginal status"; "ambiguous legal definition"; "imbalance"; "aggressively monolingual"; "exploitation"; "insidious domestication"; and "ethnocentric violence" (*Translator's* 2–21). My juxtaposition of the colonizing project and the "inevitable" violence of translation makes me uneasy because of the prominent myth of the colonization of the Americas as "inevitable" and thus somehow justified (*Translator's* 19). But Venuti's project, which is "to combat the translator's invisibility," is one that anti-racist and anti-imperialist forces can surely embrace (*Translator's* 39). Indeed, if the "vanishing Indian" has particular resonance with the "vanishing translator," the American Indian who refuses to disappear must be equally compelling.

At various moments in *Life Among the Piutes,* Winnemucca manages to refuse the disappearance expected of the translator/American Indian. In one intriguing scene, she reads a letter that she is asked to transmit from a corrupt agent to another white man. Although she acknowledges that reading the letter is a "wicked thing," she delights in it, for it validates her suspicion of the agent's corruption (135). By keeping the letter, she intervenes in this transaction, insisting on her presence. In this role, Sarah Winnemucca has a rare ability to produce meaning for white and Paiute audiences—and for the readers of her self-narrative, all of whom are dependent upon her translation. Instead of disappearing in the process of linguistic exchange, Winnemucca asserts herself as an interpreter and as an American Indian; to borrow Venuti's terms, she refuses linguistic "self-annihilation" (*Translator's* 8). But it is not merely her self that is at stake; it is also her nation.

TRANSLATING AGENCY INTO NARRATIVE

Aware that her own position as an interpreter places her in danger of either being betrayed or being seen as a betrayer, Winnemucca distinguishes herself from interpreters like the "half breeds" who are willing to say anything for the right price and thus are purchased like objects (91). Some of these "half-breed" traitors are her own relatives, and so enact a very personal, familial betrayal: "I am sorry to say these Indian interpreters, who are often half-breeds, easily get corrupted, and can be hired by the agents to do or say anything" (91). Here Winnemucca fuses racial and linguistic positions, declaring that in transmitting commands from whites to the Paiutes, the "half-breeds" are the conduit of colonial control. Conscious of her own intermediary position, Winnemucca tries to imagine a space in which she is not simply a voice box for her Anglo-American employers, a space where she can evaluate and manipulate the language that she speaks. Winnemucca experiences an increasing tension between being loyal to her white employers and speaking her "own" voice. When working for the corrupt agent Rinehart, she informs him that she will do her "duty as far as it goes," suggesting that it is not without limit (128). She is careful to account for and condemn the one occasion when she accepted money for a deceptive purpose: to help the government move her people to the Malheur Reservation. Recounting her motivation, she remembers thinking, "'[White people] make money any way and every way they can. Why not I? I have not any. I will take it.' So I did, for which I have been sorry ever since,—many times" (217). Whiteness is defined not only in terms of individual greed but the betrayal of one's community.

The Paiutes' complicated relationship to the English language is further embodied in Truckee's "white rag friend," a letter written by General Frémont, an early white explorer of the area. The letter commends Sarah's grandfather's performance in the Mexican-American War. His amiable relations with whites—his sentimental alliance with them—are evident in the name Frémont gives him: "Captain Truckee," which according to Winnemucca means "all right" or "very well" in her "Indian" language (9). Truckee believes that the power of the letter rests in its ability to speak: "This is my friend.... Does it look as if it could talk and ask for anything? Yet it does. It can ask for something to eat for me and my people" (43). For

Sarah's grandfather, the note is not simply a symbol of their friendship; it is an object so valuable that he insists on being buried with it. As he tells the Paiutes, "Just as long as I live and have that paper which my white brothers' great chieftain has given me, I shall stand by them, come what will.... Oh, if I should lose this ... we shall all be lost" (22). His sense that he and the other Paiutes will be "lost" without this English message suggests their dependence on it. Indeed, the English words are so powerful that he fears they speak "too much": that they have a voice of their own. When a group of Mexicans who are enemies of the whites visit his camp, he remarks, "I am not going to show them my rag friend, for fear my rag friend will tell of me" (28). Although the paper allows him to travel through contested territory and acquire food, it also has the potential to betray him by speaking in his place. The paper, which Truckee kisses "as if it was really a person," thus becomes another figure of white betrayal (22).

One could argue that in the act of presenting the letter, Truckee becomes the "successful" and thus the annihilated translator, for he has transmitted this message from one white man to another without intervening in it. But it would be too simplistic to argue that Truckee is entirely effaced by the white rag friend, since it carries with it a history of his relations with whites and a record of his service in the war. Indeed, the letter is powerless without Truckee's wise management of its distribution. He also intervenes in this transmission of meaning by insisting that it be interred with him. In other words, he takes it out of circulation, claiming it as his own. On the role of objects in sentimental texts, Gillian Brown notes, "As this extension of the proprietor into his or her valued articles, property reflects and represents the individual; as emblems of their owner, cherished things ratify the individual sovereignty of their proprietors" (42).[13] In relation to the paper, Truckee is both owner and object; at the same time that it marks his individuality, he relies on it as proof of his loyalty to whites.

In turn, it is as a spokesperson for whites that Sarah Winnemucca both endangers and ultimately secures her national loyalty. When an agent declares he will pay her only if she does not communicate the contents of a letter from the U.S. government to the Northern Paiutes, she responds, "I did not promise, and went away. I did not say anything for five or six days" (235). Silence, perhaps the most effective form of resistance a translator can exert, has the potential to mark her complicity with the corrupt agent or, on the other hand, to excuse her from participating in this exchange. Her salary as an interpreter for whites helped finance her lectures on the government's exploitation of the Paiutes. Her visit to the East culminated in a meeting with President Hayes in 1880. During Winnemucca's stay, her right to deliver speeches is challenged by several government officials; one tells her, "[Y]ou must not lecture here" (219). He refuses to allow her to speak with the reporters—to "talk on" some of the most powerful papers in existence. Knowing that her every word is scrutinized, Winnemucca makes sure an official is in hearing distance when she informs her father and brother of her plans to lecture—just to make the government representatives angry. Anger is thus not only something she works to articulate; it is also a response from whites that signals her success.

SENTIMENTAL NATIONHOOD

Having sketched some of the difficulties of Winnemucca's position as an interpreter, I turn now to her use of conventional and unconventional sentimentality to affirm Paiute nationhood. The narrative's vision of nationhood is evident from its early pages in the form of a Paiute creation story. According to this story, or at least to Truckee's reconstruction of it, the Paiutes were originally comprised of two dark and two white children.[14] When a quarrel ensued between them, their parents insisted that they separate. As Truckee claims, the white settlers are the descendants of these white brothers, and so their arrival is cause for celebration. Awed by his words, the community accepts his version and agrees not to harm the whites. Sarah goes on to describe how a medicine man later gathered his people in order to share with them one of his dreams. His words are tremendously effective; as she recalls, "We all wept, for we believed this word came from heaven" (16). In the midst of these references to such speeches, she refers to herself as the "chieftain's weary daughter," as if to legitimate her own speaking authority in sentimental terms (12). Truckee himself is sentimentalized in such language; voicing mixed feelings about her grandfather's relationship to the whites, Sarah seems to share his surprised disappointment in them at the same time that she suggests his optimism is naïve. As she notes, "But he was disappointed, poor dear old soul!" (6). Winnemucca portrays her grandfather, and his version of this origin story, as well-meaning but ultimately misguided. Yet in the following paragraph she claims that she can "imagine his feelings, for I have drank deeply from the same cup" (6). In this sense she both identifies with her grandfather's worldview and distinguishes it from her own. In pronouncing, "How good of him to try and heal the wound, and how vain were his efforts!,"

Lost (and Gained) in Translation

Winnemucca notes both his optimistic faith in including the whites in the Northern Paiute family/nation as well as whites' disregard of their familial obligations to American Indians (7). This is, in other words, a moment of distinction between Truckee's conventional sentimentality and her more critical one. A blatant example of this distinction comes a few pages later when she refers to "the people that my grandfather called our white brothers" (12). By inserting the reference to her grandfather, Winnemucca indicates that despite his feelings about the whites, she herself is not willing to include them in the Paiute family. According to Winnemucca, on his death bed Truckee drew an ultimate distinction between "his people" and the whites, suggesting that even for him there were limits to the inclusiveness of the Paiute family/nation.

Readers are often troubled by Sarah Winnemucca's use of the term "Great Father" in reference to the U.S. President, viewing it as a disturbing reminder of the paternalism with which whites treated American Indians in the nineteenth century. Yet if we examine this and other familial terms through the lens of Winnemucca's revision of her grandfather's origin story, it becomes possible to see them as her means of critiquing whites' misconduct and, accordingly, their violation of this familial/national narrative. As Winnemucca states, "we call all good people father or mother; no matter who it is,—negro, white man, or Indian, and the same with the women" (39). By honoring familial obligations, one earns authority and respect. Her words echo Truckee's origin story: "Have I not been kind to you all, and given you everything your hearts wished for? You do not have to hunt and kill your own game to live upon. You see, my dear children, I have the power to call whatsoever kind of game we want to eat; and I also have the power to separate my dear children, if they are not good to each other" (7). Someone like Samuel Parrish, the agent of Malheur Reservation whom the Paiutes come to trust and admire for his fair dealings with them, is described as "our Father." The term "my children," which Parrish uses to refer to Paiutes on the reservation, may in fact be Sarah Winnemucca's version of his words rather than those he actually said; she might have inserted them into her retelling of his speech in order to honor his membership in their community (106). On the other hand, Parrish could have used this phrase to indicate his understanding of, and respect for, the Paiutes' conception of nationhood. Likewise, Winnemucca's description of herself as "mother" may be read as her assertion of authority: as she declares at one point, "Tell [the Northern Paiutes] I, their mother, say come back to their homes again" (182). To regard such terms as titles of honor bestowed upon those whites who live up to their obligations (and so are recognized as members of a familial community) requires acknowledging Native Americans' agency and self-definition rather than focusing on how they were *viewed by* whites.

Winnemucca finds familial language a powerful vehicle for her sentimental anger. As one petition to Congress states:

> And especially do we petition for the return of that portion of the tribe arbitrarily removed from the Malheur Reservation, after the Bannock war, to the Yakima Reservation on Columbia River, in which removal families were ruthlessly separated, and have never ceased to pine for husbands, wives, and children, which restoration was pledged to them by the Secretary of the Interior in 1880, but has not been fulfilled. (247)

The U.S. government's policies are thus described as a violation of American Indian families. It is in similar terms that Winnemucca ultimately appeals to President Hayes, calling on him as a "husband and father" to consider the horror of being forcibly separated from his wife and children (246). Reframing the U.S. president in terms of his familial status rather than his political position, Winnemucca suggests that he and the American Indians are equals: both would be devastated if they were separated from their family members. The image of familial separation that she presents in the petition also contrasts her grandfather's origin story, in which separation is a justified punishment for wrongdoing. In the case of the Malheur Reservation, the U.S. government, acting unlawfully as the "father," divides families for no good reason. Winnemucca, as "their faithful 'Mother,'" testifies to this crime (Peabody *Practical* 35).

Winnemucca rewrites racial language so that a word like "white" refers not to skin color but to one's betrayal of family or, by extension, one's nation. In this sense, Winnemucca distinguishes the soldiers, whom she generally finds more trustworthy than other colonists, from "whites": "Brother and my people always say 'the white people,' just as if the soldiers were not white, too" (86). This distinction allows her to maintain a sense of family that is not based exclusively on blood but on an individual's fulfillment of certain moral obligations. In being "good," a white person thus loses his whiteness in some sense and is honored as a member of the Paiute family/nation. At least initially, the Paiutes—or at least Truckee—regard the whites as potential family members: in his telling of the origin story Truckee declares he would like "to love them as I love all of you" (7). In a following scene, Sarah uses the conventional sentimental language usually reserved for Native Americans to sympathize with a group of whites: "So, poor things, they must have suffered fearfully, for they all starved there" (13). Here the stranded whites assume the "othered" position as objects of pity. In turn, Winnemucca describes a cruel Anglo woman as "white": "Dear reader, this is the kind of white women that are in the West. They are always ready to condemn me" (168). Directing her words to a white woman reader, Winnemucca presents her with the opportunity (and the challenge) to prove her own goodness and, accordingly, her departure from these "white women." The powerful position of "whiteness" is framed as what the reader (if she is indeed "dear" and "good") is *not:* a striking rhetorical move that challenges and denaturalizes Anglo-American racial hierarchies. American Indians themselves aren't necessarily admirable in Winnemucca's account: she distinguishes between those who are "good," the "hostiles" (167), and, sarcastically, "the civilized." Particularly shameful are Egan and Oytes, who betray their Native communities and in so doing enact a certain whiteness. Similarly, the so-called "bad" agent Parrish is kind and fair, while the "good" agent Rinehart tries to cheat them. Winnemucca thus shows how professed Christianity does not necessarily guarantee one's morality; indeed, as in many slave narratives, religion is used by some as a license for cruelty. In another scene, a white woman's "Bible" is revealed to be a deck of cards, an image that functions to show whites' religious hypocrisy.

While I am uncomfortable with any neat distinction between Anglo and Indian conceptions of family—those, for example, that would see the former as strictly exclusionary and the latter as entirely tolerant of difference—it is important to acknowledge a difference between how Winnemucca invokes family and how she believes it is envisioned by her opponents. Consider the following passage:

> Alas, how truly our women prophesied when they told my dear old grandfather that his white brothers, whom he loved so much, had brought sorrow to his people. Their hearts told them the truth. My people are ignorant of worldly knowledge, but they know what love means and what truth means. They have seen their dear ones perish around them because their white brothers have given them neither love nor truth. Are not love and truth better than learning? My people have no learning. They do not know anything about the history of the world, but they can see the Spirit-Father in everything. The beautiful world talks to them of their Spirit-Father. They are innocent and simple, but they are brave and will not be imposed upon. They are patient, but they know black is not white. (258–59)

Winnemucca strategically portrays her people in terms of a firm distinction with which the nineteenth-century white reader would be familiar: the "unlearned" Indian versus the educated white person. The last two sentences, however, complicate this distinction: the Northern Paiutes "are brave and will not be imposed upon.... [T]hey know black is not white." Recast in familial terms, relations between whites and Paiutes are marked by Anglo neglect of their kinship responsibilities. Winnemucca thus severs goodness, whiteness, and learning—concepts intricately linked in conventional sentimentality—to assert the Paiutes' dignity. Without (familial) love, she claims, there is no truth. And so the all-knowing Anglos are reduced to ignorance.

This centering on the Northern Paiute family is particularly poignant in Winnemucca's chapter "Domestic and Social Moralities," which, like Pauline Johnson's maternal essays, can be read as a kind of conduct manual. While the initial switch of pronouns from "our children" to "their parents" resembles the shifts of *Wynema*'s first pages, Winnemucca speaks with a distinct cultural authority, making it clear that the whites have much to learn from a Northern Paiute lifestyle. The chapter begins with the assertion, "Our children are very carefully taught to be good" (45). They learn immoral habits like swearing not from each other but from whites. It is difficult not to hear the sarcasm in the following comparison between whites and Northern Paiutes: "We don't need to be taught to love our fathers and mothers," she declares, implying that whites, on the other hand, do (45). Unlike *Wynema,* where the medicine man is described as "weird," here his role is admirable and even divine: "We do not call him a medicine man because he gives medicine to the sick, as your doctors do. Our medicine man cures the sick by the laying on of hands, and we have doctresses as well as doctors. We believe that our doctors can communicate with holy spirits from heaven" (15). As in Johnson's "A Red Girl's Reasoning," Winnemucca asserts the legitimacy of indigenous and courting rites, correcting the reader's assumption that marriage might be forced on Native women: "She is never forced by her parents to marry against her wishes" (49). Later, when she receives a marriage offer, she is careful to point out that she cannot marry someone she does not love. When she asserts, "It is always the whites that begin the wars," Winnemucca holds whites responsible for violating the peaceful reunion (51). Marshaling such evidence of the Paiutes' morality, Winnemucca uses it to bolster their nation: "We have a republic as well as you. The council-tent is our Congress, and anybody can speak who has anything to say, women and all" (53). Here the conventional use of sentimental language as a means for the "civilized" whites to educate the "savage" Indian is reversed; the Paiute family—and nation—is equal to that of the white reader. Just as the family she envisions is strengthened, so too is her "republic," a word that to an Anglo-American reader would have connoted a virtuous, egalitarian political unit. Winnemucca goes so far as to suggest that the Northern Paiute republic is even more democratic than the United States, for "anybody can speak ... women and all." Instead of "civilizing" the Paiutes, the whites have made them "savage": as she claims, when the whites first arrived, "my people were less barbarous than they are nowadays" (10). She later reflects on a time when "my people had not learned to steal" (59). In both instances Winnemucca directly challenges the expected "progression" from savagery to civility. As with Pauline Johnson's poem "The Cattle Thief" and the late chapters of *Wynema*, it is the whites who are most savage.

Winnemucca's exposition of Northern Paiute culture becomes a platform for a sustained sentimental critique of colonialism. Even as she describes Northern Paiute culture in her second chapter, she shifts to past tense, making clear how certain traditions have been threatened by colonization: "Many years ago, when my people were happier than they are now, they used to celebrate the Festival of Flowers in the spring. I have been to three of them only in the course of my life" (46). While past tense is often a means of suggesting the "extinction" of Native peoples, here it becomes a powerful indictment of whites' cultural violence. In a scene that is strikingly similar to one from Callahan's novel, Winnemucca tells of an elderly blind man who is murdered before his blind wife: "[T]he poor woman could only hear her husband's groans as the man was cutting him to pieces. At last his groans died away. She felt so thankful she could not see!" (183). Winnemucca also utilizes the conventional sentimental images of dying or assaulted children to demonstrate whites' outrages: "After the soldiers had killed all but some little children and babies still tied up in their baskets, the soldiers took them also, and set the camp on fire and threw them into the flames to see them burn alive. I had one baby brother killed there" (78). She adds the last sentence to underscore the event's truth. Such statements indicate that Winnemucca sees her narrative as a legalistic document chock-full of evidence, such as the exact salary (spelled out) of the whites who benefit from the agency system. Hers is a record of atrocities; she follows the words of a corrupt doctor with the declaration, "I heard all this" (130). This evidence, she asserts, is lacking in many of the whites' accounts, which "had no proof" (79). In these instances conventional sentimentality becomes another tool for a condemnation of whiteness.

The power of Winnemucca's voice rests in part on her astute manipulation of gender. As a young girl, she accompanies her mother and grandfather on their journey to California. Terrified of the whites they encounter, Winnemucca asks her mother if they can return home instead of continuing with her grandfather. Her mother tells her that they cannot possibly return by themselves: "We can't go alone; we would all be killed if we go, for we have no rag friend as father has" (26). The rag friend becomes a kind of Phallus: the elusive power that the women lack. But as an interpreter, Winnemucca is admired by both men and women. As her father tells the community, her oratory skills have made her more "manly" than the Paiute men: "Now hereafter we will look on her as our chieftain, for none of us are worthy of being chief but her, and all I can say to you is to send her to the wars and you stay and do women's work, and talk as women do" (193). So while speech is aligned with masculinity, it is not limited to the Paiute men. Winnemucca does not simply assume the Phallus; she proves she does not need it. Her "manliness" depends not on her biology or physical courage but on her language skills (both at the time of the speech and, of course, in her retelling of it). As David H. Brumble has argued, Winnemucca's description of her impressive ride to save her band of Paiutes from the Bannocks resembles a coup tale in that it affirms, through words, her valiant reputation. With her prominence as an interpreter growing, Winnemucca locates herself in the position she once reserved for her father and grandfather. When she receives a letter from an army captain regarding an Indian attack, she recalls, "My people all gathered round me waiting for me to tell them something" (82). Lacking a pen, she improvises with a stick dipped in fish's blood, a moment that illustrates indigenous ingenuity in using one's own materials to produce a written text. She recounts several instances when the Paiutes ask her to "talk for them" (139). Her description of her meeting with an army captain illustrates her command of language:

> I told him everything from the first beginning of the trouble. I told him that the agent sold some powder to an Indian, and that his own men had killed the Indian. I told him how brother and I went to him and asked him and his men to go away, as we had heard that our people were going to kill him. I told him that he talked bad to brother and me, because we went to tell him of it. (83)

Winnemucca's repetition of the phrase "I told him" emphasizes her position as a powerful speaking subject. Her indignation also differs markedly from the childish anger of the white agent, Rinehart. When the Paiutes show skepticism about his orders, he gets angry, trembling "as if he was afraid" (124). Following his angry retort, some of the Paiutes respond, "Let us go; why do we fool with such a man?" (125). Ironically, while he refers to them as boys, they refuse this language and assert their masculinity and his weakness: "I am not a boy, I am a man. I am afraid he will die if I talk to him" (124). Here the agent's anger comes off as a mark of insecurity that deserves no respect.

Shaming, itself an exercise of authority, is a particularly effective form of sentimental critique in *Life Among the Piutes*. In a blistering account of the United States, Winnemucca speaks directly to the white reader, both drawing from and revising her grandfather's origin story:

> Oh, for shame! You who are educated by a Christian government in the art of war; the practice of whose profession makes you natural enemies of the savages, so called by you. Yes, you, who call yourselves the great civilization; you who have knelt upon Plymouth Rock, covenanting with God to make this land the home of the free and the brave. Ah, then you rise from your bended knees and seizing the welcoming hands of those who are the owners of this land, which you are not, your carbines rise upon the bleak shore, and your so-called civilization sweeps inland from the ocean wave; but, oh, my God! leaving its pathway marked by crimson lines of blood, and strewed by the bones of two races, the inheritor and the invader; and I am crying out to you for justice,—yes, pleading for the far-off plains of the West, for the dusky mourner, whose tears of love are pleading for her husband, or for their children, who are sent far away from them. Your Christian minister will hold my people against their will; not because he loves them,—no, far from it,—but because it puts money in his pockets. (207)

Here Winnemucca incorporates the very words Anglo-Americans use to articulate their Americanness in order to expose the hypocrisy of this vision: she includes "Plymouth Rock" and "home of the free and the brave" to show how far removed these "citizens" are from such lofty ideals. The familial language of her grandfather's narrative remains, but this time it is used to mark the difference between the "civilized" invader who is motivated not by kinship but by monetary reward and the rightful "inheritor" who grieves for her spouse and children. The inheritor—the lawful owner—is Northern Paiute; the invader is the returning, disobedient (and perhaps disowned) sibling.

Winnemucca's use of shame is reminiscent of Truckee's origin story, in which the father asks his children before separating them, "Why are you so cruel to each other?" The children then hang their heads: "They were ashamed" (7). Similarly, when the U.S. president's failure to live up to his promise becomes clear, Winnemucca uses language to shame him: "Every night I imagined I could see the thing called President. He had long ears, he had big eyes and long legs, and a head like a bull-frog or something like that" (205). Here shaming and sentimentalism work hand in hand to enforce certain morals, challenging the idea that the latter is useful only to whites. In another passage she describes the generosity with which the Paiutes provide the white settlers food: "They did not hold out their hands and say:—'You can't have anything unless you pay me.' No,—no such word was used by us savages at that time" (10). "Savage" is associated with one who, unlike the "civilized" whites, graciously offers food to those in need. In turn, "civilized" becomes a synonym for "greedy": "They did not come because they loved us, or because they were Christians. No; they were just like all civilized people; they came to take us up there because they were to be paid for it" (209). This sarcastic tone suggests Winnemucca's conscious repetition of the word, a repetition that serves to trouble that very distinction between civilized and savage. It is through the rearticulation of the original—the dominant discourse—that she exposes it as a fabrication.

In presenting this angry sarcasm in the intimate terms of sentimentality, Winnemucca is able to critique the very readers with whom she has aligned herself. In a particularly cynical moment, Winnemucca declares, "Now, dear readers, this is the way all the Indian agents get rich" (86). Often the "dear reader" is positioned as a sympathetic individual who stands apart from, and presumably condemns, the actions of the corrupt whites. But there are moments when even this dear reader is challenged to take action, suggesting that simply lending a sympathetic ear is not sufficient. "Oh, my dear good Christian people, how long are you going to stand by and see us suffer at your hands? Oh, dear friends, you are wrong when you say it will take two or three generations to civilize my people. No! I say it will not take that long if you will only take interest in teaching us" (89). This moment resembles the passage in *Wynema* when Callahan refuses to differentiate between her white readers and those who participated in the Wounded Knee massacre: even the "dear reader" is implicated in the violence Winnemucca describes.

In a more sustained example of the sarcasm that appears toward the end of *Wynema*, Winnemucca repeats the words "of course" in an illustration of her ironic tone and the anger that underlies it. By beginning numerous statements about the whites' mistreatment of the Paiutes with "of course," she indicates her full awareness of the extent of this mistreatment. These two words also suggest that the following statement is so matter-of-fact that it hardly merits mention. Consider these examples:

> That same summer another of my men was killed on the reservation. His name was Truckee John. He was an uncle of mine, and was killed by a man named Flamens, who claimed to have had a brother killed in the war of 1860, but *of course* that had nothing to do with my uncle. About two weeks after this, two white men were killed over at Walker Lake by some of my people, and *of course* soldiers were sent for from California, and a great many companies came. (78, my emphasis)
>
> *Of course,* they did not know any better; they put their names to the paper, and signed their chief away! So the soldiers came and took brother to San Francisco, Cal. Brother was only there a little while when two white men whose lives he had saved went and took him out and sent him home, and wrote to our minister agent. *Of course* I knew not what was in the letter. (89, my emphasis)

In perhaps her most striking use of the term, she declares, "*Of course,* that is the kind of men that are called good,—men who talk to the Spirit Father three times a day, but who will kill us off as they would kill wild beasts" (132, my emphasis). By referring to the whites as if they were already convicted and sentenced, Winnemucca moves beyond the position of having to persuade her readers of these crimes: *of course* the whites are guilty.

One of the central elements of irony, Linda Hutcheon has argued, is its effective deployment of and engagement with anger. Ross Chambers has described irony as a "possible model for oppositionality whenever one is implicated in a system that one finds oppressive" (quoted in Hutcheon 16). As an interpreter for the colonizers, Winnemucca finds irony a subtle means of distinguishing herself from and even criticizing the whites whose words she is paid to speak. So while she presents the whites as guilty, she exonerates herself. Similarly, the word "outrage" communicates Winnemucca's disgust with white men's treatment of Paiute women. On several occasions she refers to sexual harassments and assaults as "outrages." By using a synonym of rape or sexual assault that was familiar to white women, Winnemucca asserts not only that such violations occurred but that they were, indeed, violations. Like Harriet Jacobs, who exposes the sexual abuse of black women in her slave narrative, *Incidents in the Life of a Slave Girl,* Winnemucca uses white women's language of respectability and domesticity to gain the reader's empathy. That is, she counters stereotypes of the hypersexualized or subhuman woman of color in asserting that these sexual assaults are violations of Paiute women's dignity. Winnemucca's use of the word "outrage" is particularly notable since her enemies, many of whom were affiliated with the Bureau of Indian Affairs, used it in their accusations of her sexual misconduct; as an issue of *The Council Fire and Arbitrator* declares, "It is a great outrage on the respectable people of Boston for General Howard or any other officer of the army to foist such a woman of any race upon them" (quoted in Canfield 204). In appropriating "outrage," Winnemucca aligns white and Paiute women against the depraved, dangerous white man and at the same time shores up her own reputation. Unlike Callahan, who for the most part relies on a representation of the white man as protector, Winnemucca demonstrates the danger he presents to Native American women. Newspaper accounts illustrate Winnemucca's angry response to such dangerous white men. In 1872, an edition of the *Humboldt Register* noted that "Sally" (as she was sometimes known in the popular press) "rushed across the street to procure a warrant for the arrest of her adversary, but before the papers could be made out, she went into spasms, and soon after was taken in charge by the Indians and carried off to camp."[15] The article goes on to mention that while some claim Winnemucca was drunk at the time, others "say it was nothing but an overdose of 'mad' that caused the stupor." In this statement, different conceptions of anger, femininity, and Indianness converge: like Pauline Johnson, the "outraged" lady who faints is also the "furious" Indian who will not tolerate such abuses. Winnemucca seems to have understood that her anger—whether represented as "hysteria" or a mode of self-defense—was central to her public image.

In *Life Among the Piutes*, "outrage" signifies not only a violent act against an innocent victim but an angry response to this attempted violence as well. While describing white men's behavior, Winnemucca declares that she will not permit such assaults: "I thought within myself, 'If such an outrageous thing is to happen to me, it will be not be done by one man or two, while there are two women with knives, for I know what an Indian woman can do. She can never be outraged by one man; but she may by two'" (228). Her words are couched in sentimental terms: as she continues, "My dear reader, I have not lived in this world for over thirty or forty years for nothing, and I know what I am talking about" (228). The intimacy of "my dear reader" is complicated by an authoritative edge that suggests the "dear reader" may not know what *she's* talking about. Winnemucca challenges the stereotype of the debased woman of color who deserves or even enjoys a sexual assault, declaring that an *Indian woman will never allow herself to be raped*. She further takes issue with the assumption that women are too weak to defend themselves; indeed she suggests it is unwomanly (and un-Paiute) *not* to do so. As in Pauline Johnson's "As It Was in the Beginning," the mother is particularly wary of white men, while the father seems rather naïve: Winnemucca's mother frequently expresses her fear of the whites to Truckee, whether through tears or verbal protests. Accordingly, it is elder Paiute women who at times afford the best protection of the younger girls; after Winnemucca's sister expresses her fear of being left with a group of white men, Sarah announces, "From that day my grandma took my sister under her care, and we got along nicely" (41).

Winnemucca repeatedly notes Paiute women's determination to defend themselves. When describing a Native woman who was threatened with sexual assault, she remarks, "every minute she cried out to her Spirit Father that he might kill her right away, and not let her person be outraged, for she would rather die a hundred deaths than be outraged by a white man" (183). Winnemucca implies that Native American women are more moral than white women, for they are willing to go to extreme lengths to preserve their virtue—especially from abuse at the hands of a *white* man. So while at times Winnemucca appeals, as Malea Powell notes, to the "moral authority" of white women (411), here she uses sentimentality to assert that Paiute morality is greater than theirs.[16] She later contrasts the barbarity of white and African American men with the civility of the Paiutes: "I am so proud to say that my people have never outraged your women, or have even insulted them by looks or words. Can you say the same of the negroes or the whites? They do commit some most horrible outrages on your women, but you do not drive them round like dogs" (244).[17] Finally, she quotes another Paiute who uses "outrage" as an adjective: "[White men] do not care for anything. They do most terrible outrageous things to our women" (228). In this and other instances, the word "outrage" functions as an ironic contrast between the uncivilized white men, who regularly violate Paiute women, and Paiute women, who have never committed such crimes and yet are considered savage.[18] It also voices an anger that is legitimated within the sentimental discourse of her predominantly white, female audience. This anger is distinguished from the stereotypical vengeance the white reader might have imagined. She makes clear that any violence Paiutes engage in is justified self-defense: "when people are too bad they rise up and resist them. This seems to me all right. It is different from being revengeful. There is nothing cruel about our people. They never scalped a human being" (54). At one point, Winnemucca quotes a newspaper account of the "'bloodthirsty savages,'" using quotation marks to critique this representation (71). On other occasions, the lack of quotation marks only strengthens her critique: "It is the way we savages do when we meet each other; we cry with joy and gladness" (101). So while Pauline Johnson deems the action of her heroine as vengeance only because she has been driven to it by racist stereotypes, Winnemucca refuses this stereotype altogether.

Winnemucca's use of the word "outrage" is but one example of her adoption of sentimental discourse. In the *Second Report of the Model School of Sarah Winnemucca* (1887), Elizabeth Peabody argues that such instruction should "be given to Indians . . . by Indians themselves who have spoken both languages from childhood, and are able to ground their methods, as [Sarah] does, upon their own inherited natural religion and family moralities" (3). Winnemucca makes clear that this "natural religion" bears a comfortable similarity to Christianity: she describes the link between medicine men and the heavens, she likens her people's cries to those of Methodist revivals, and she criticizes the whites for not waiting "to find out how good the Indians were, and what ideas they had of God, just like those of Jesus" (51). Fluent in both languages, Winnemucca was uniquely positioned to teach other Paiutes English and, accordingly, domesticity as it was defined by white women. For Peabody, the school was the site where Winnemucca worked her magic: "The school is thus an enlarged home, of which [Winnemucca] is the recognized mother" (*Second* 13). Accordingly, the whites' mistreatment of the Paiutes is portrayed as an assault on domesticity. Peabody recalls Winnemucca's disappointment when she returned to Nevada in August 1884 to discover that the students were living in poverty and had lost confidence in her:

> It was one of Sarah's acutest trials to find . . . how the last seven years of homelessness depriving her people of all opportunity for family councils and the hereditary domestic discipline, had told on their morals. She found them divided into small squads scratching for mere bread under captains elected for their smartness in getting along, instead of their goodness, as when the fatherly chief appointed them; and that they had partially lost their old confidence in her as their faithful 'Mother,' though she could not blame them for it, as she said she had been made the mouthpiece of so many lying promises. (*Practical Solution* 35)

Peabody's earlier updates are full of glowing testimonials. The Paiute

Lost (and Gained) in Translation

children, she reports, love English words so much that they write them all over the fences in Lovelocks, literally encoding the land with the colonizers' language. English words become in Peabody's terms "acquisitions" which, like the land they are written on, affirm their personhood (*Second* 13). Such acquisitions are framed not in opposition to domesticity but as affirmations of it. These statements indicate the complicated links between domesticity, language, and agency that Winnemucca encountered as a teacher of English, a spokesperson for Indian reform, and an interpreter. As Gillian Brown has demonstrated, although scholars have tended to regard the domestic sphere (imagined as female/private) as the antithesis of the capitalistic economy (imagined as male/public), the two were in fact intricately linked: domesticity instilled individualism with qualities of interiority and privacy. Lori Merish, who also links sentimentality with possession in the nineteenth century, describes "sentimental ownership" as the imagined move from enslavement/savagery to agency/civility. Put simply, to own things is closely linked to owning oneself. This ownership supposedly distinguished whites from Native Americans and blacks, who were imagined as having a lack of "work discipline as well as an insufficient sense of private property, figured as an inadequate psychological and affectional 'attachment' to things" (Merish 36). Winnemucca learns early on the degree to which property is invested with individuality and sentiment for whites: her grandfather warns her to "never take anything unless they give it to you; then they will love you" (27). She then assumes the whites have no concept of shared property; she has to be assured by her mother that the daughter of a white man will not be whipped for sitting in his chair. Winnemucca takes this concept of individual ownership to its logical extreme, demonstrating how much it contrasts with the Paiute model of familial/national property. Thus, her narrative serves as a subtle critique of this individualist economy even as she inserts herself within it.

As the "mother" of these Paiute children, Winnemucca would—within the confines of the "home"—teach them to be productive citizens (and owners), a task not unlike that of white, middle-class women. In a *Silver State* article of 1886, Winnemucca emphasizes that education is key to Paiute assimilation: "It seems strange to me that the Government has not found out years ago that education is the key to the Indian problem. Much money and many precious lives would have been saved if the American people had fought my people with Books instead of Powder and lead. Education civilized your race and there is no reason why it cannot civilize mine."[19] It is American Indian women, she argues, who are the best teachers and agents.[20] Winnemucca's use of sentimental conventions, from the phrases "poor Indian" and "dear reader" to her maternal self-descriptions, affords her agency in Peabody's domestic terms. In the letter that opens *Sarah Winnemucca's Practical Solution of the Indian Problem*, Peabody asserts, "instead of being, as usual, a passive reception of civilizing influences proffered by white men who look down upon the Indian as a spiritual, moral, and intellectual inferior, it is a spontaneous movement, made by the Indian himself, *from himself*, in full consciousness of free agency, for the education that is to civilize him" (3). Contrary to popular belief, Peabody maintains, American Indians are anxious to learn English and, accordingly, to become self-sufficient citizens: a sentiment that was the cornerstone of the General Allotment Act. The "free agency" that Winnemucca imagines for Native Americans thus accords with the white women's concepts of the relationship between English language, domesticity, and possessive individualism: the concept that each person "is free inasmuch as he is proprietor of his person and capacities. The human essence is freedom from dependence on the wills of others, and freedom is a function of possession" (Macpherson 3). Yet *Life Among the Piutes* complicates the reduction of agency to a pure individualism; Winnemucca's voice is dependent on her relationship to others. A statement in the book's appendix by a white defender describes her as one firmly linked to whites: "you have displayed an unusual intelligence and fearlessness, and loyalty to the whites in your capacities of scout, interpreter, and influential member of the Piute [*sic*] tribe of Indians" (261). It was this very linkage between the author and white women reformers that would threaten Winnemucca's influence among the Paiutes.

AGENCY, REASSERTED

When the Paiutes ultimately accuse Winnemucca of betraying them for failing to read the letter she received from the president, her response poignantly illustrates the tension between being an agent and the agent "of" someone else. Standing before the group, she holds the paper over her head in a defiant gesture, declaring,

> "I have suffered everything but death to come here with this paper. I don't know whether it speaks truth or not. You can say what you like about me. You have a right to say I have sold you. It looks so. I have told you many things which are not my own words, but the words of the agents and the

soldiers. I know I have told you more lies than I have hair on my head. I tell you, my dear children, I have never told you my own words; they were the words of the white people, not mine." (236)

Winnemucca acknowledges that as an interpreter hired by the whites, she is a carrier—an agent—of their lies, and so has been contaminated by the meanings she passes on. In Peabody's words, she understands herself as one who has "been made the mouthpiece of so many lying promises" (*Practical Solution* 35). One of the critical questions this scene raises is to what degree Winnemucca's admission compromises the credibility of her own speaking voice. Does her entire narrative then become a medium for white discourse? Is there no space outside of white discourse—white subjectivity—from which she can articulate her anger?

The "successful" translator eradicates his or her own existence by ostensibly reproducing the original, enacting what Venuti calls "ethnocentric violence" (21). In his words, "By producing the illusion of transparency, a fluent translation masquerades as true semantic equivalence when it in fact inscribes the foreign text with a partial interpretation, partial to English-language values, reducing if not simply excluding the very difference that translation is called on to convey" (*Translator's* 21). Winnemucca accomplishes the kind of resistance Venuti calls for by reminding the Northern Paiutes of her role in the translation. Having created this cross-racial sentimental community, she at this point steps out of it to affirm Northern Paiute nationhood. As she contends, "It is not my own making up; it came right from him, and I will read it just as it is, so that you can all judge for yourselves" (236). She thus inserts a distinction between her "own words" and "the words of the white people"—between the Northern Paiute nation and the United States. In the final sentence, she returns authority to the Paiutes, declaring that now that they are aware of the duplicity of the whites' language, they can judge it for themselves. This appeal to audience has a long history in Native cultures; as Kimberly M. Blaeser writes, "Traditional native literature has always entailed both performance and commentary with, in Dennis Tedlock's language, the 'conveyer' functioning as the 'interpreter' as well. We get, says Tedlock, 'the criticism at the same time and from the same person'" (59). Winnemucca's speech has a powerful effect on her people, who beg her forgiveness for having accused her—that is, for believing her to be white. By translating whites' words but at the same time pointing out the distinction between their words and her own, she demonstrates the failed repetition: the (literal) white lie. While she translates the message as it is written, she shows that the whites' words do not mean what they say—and thus exposes the falsity of the original text.

Winnemucca's transmission of the colonizers' message recalls what Homi Bhabha has termed "colonial mimicry": the not quite perfect duplication of colonial power that both affirms that power and, in exposing its ambivalence, calls it into question. Although Noreen Lape maintains that Winnemucca "cannot disengage herself from the false language forced upon her by the White government," I contend that she in fact intervenes in the translation, refusing to be effaced by it ("'I Would'" 266). Winnemucca further reminds the reader that her speech is prompted not only by her white employers but also by Paiutes' requests that she speak for them. As she recalls, "Very late in the fall my people came again . . . and once more they asked me to talk for them. I then told them I would do what I could" (139). This sentiment is echoed a few pages later: "Then they all asked me if I would go if they would give me the money to go with. I told them I would only be too happy to do all I could in their behalf, if they wanted me to" (146). Her authority within the Paiute community is jeopardized the moment she is suspected of not speaking for her people. She regains this authority by declaring, "I have said everything I could in your behalf, so did father and brother" (236). Although agency is typically defined in terms of individual will, Winnemucca complicates this concept, claiming her words are not entirely her own. She follows this scene by comparing herself to those interpreters who are motivated by their individual profit or who have no ability to decipher the truth of what is said. Not incidentally, it is in the form of the autobiography—a genre that ostensibly epitomizes self-command and yet for nineteenth-century Native Americans is so fraught—that Winnemucca is able to assert this ventriloquism. Within this form she can both assert and downplay her individual voice. As the returning family member, Sarah Winnemucca pledges her fidelity to this family, this nation, and the origin story itself. Imperfect translation thus becomes a means for her to write her own loyalty—and accordingly, her (and their) survival.

EPILOGUE

I end with a story about the present-day Pyramid Lake Reservation that illustrates the ongoing relationship between anger and nationhood in one indigenous community. This story, which centers on the teaching of Sarah Winnemucca's *Life Among the Piutes,* indicates that while for many Northern Paiutes Winnemucca is an impressive representative of this indigenous nation, for others she remains an object of suspicion. The late scene in her narrative when she tries to convince the Paiutes that she has not betrayed them is thus reenacted on a twenty-first-century stage.

A teacher at the Pyramid Lake Junior and Senior High School, Harriet Brady has a reputation in the community for speaking her mind. Nowhere has her voice been more tested than in the classroom. During her first year of teaching there, she was surprised by the degree of animosity that the mere mention of Sarah Winnemucca's name provoked. "She's a traitor," several of her students claimed, voicing a sentiment that had been repeated over many a dinner table.[21] Like the Paiutes who in the late nineteenth century charged Winnemucca with selling out to the whites, some residents of the reservation still believe that she was a tool of white society—or perhaps even a willful traitor. The fact that these accusations, like those of the *Council Fire*, are tied to Winnemucca's alleged promiscuity indicates the presumed link between her tribal loyalty and her sexuality. Some of the same accusations made by white men are now voiced by Paiutes. Although Sally Zanjani's biography opens with a note that "Victorian morality" no longer has a stranglehold on Winnemucca's reputation, Brady describes some students' attitude that Sarah married too often or was promiscuous (1). One young woman said simply, "She was a slut." Brady recalls one boy who was very much against Winnemucca until he learned more about her. Yet when she saw him after the school year had ended, she found that he had returned to calling Winnemucca a traitor. Winnemucca's own words seem fitting here: "Every one knows what a woman must suffer who undertakes to act against bad men. My reputation has been assailed, and it is done so cunningly that I cannot prove it to be unjust. I can only protest that it is unjust, and say that wherever I have been known, I have been believed and trusted" (258).

When Brady first started teaching Winnemucca's book, the most vocal resistance came from two men, one of whom had a child enrolled in her class during her first year as a full-time teacher at Pyramid Lake. Their distaste for Winnemucca and their influence in the community was such that initially Brady did not attempt to purchase copies of *Life Among the Piutes* for her classes, knowing that the school board (of which one of the men was a member) would never approve it. With the 2000–2001 school year, the first for the spotless, completely wired facility, a diverse student body and a new school board made the book's purchase more feasible. Brady promptly ordered an entire stack of plastic-wrapped copies. With the addition of Washoe and Shoshone students (members of the other two indigenous groups in Nevada) she has found that while some of the criticisms prevail, many of her students have never heard of Sarah Winnemucca: a fact that presents its own set of challenges. As in Winnemucca's time, the school is a nexus for tensions about community allegiance and sedition—perhaps because it is perceived as a powerful site for language and the production of meaning. As with many reservations, the schools witnessed some of the most brutal colonialism; many Paiute students ran away from a boarding school that was opened in 1883 (Inter-Tribal 67). Now, as then, questions of what it means to be Paiute are of paramount importance. To address the collective and individual memories of Winnemucca at Pyramid Lake today is to realize that some residents' anger stems from disagreements about how Northern Paiutes should be represented and remembered, and in turn, how their nation is defined. As in Audra Simpson's account of the attempts of the Kahnawake Mohawk nation to define its membership, anger about what constitutes Native identity often draws sharp lines between individuals.

Brady proudly tells her students that Winnemucca was the first American Indian woman to write a book, and that "she comes from *our* reservation."[22] Students also read Lalla Scott's *Karnee*, a biography that is critical of Sarah and her family, sections from Dee Brown's *Bury My Heart at Wounded Knee*, and contemporary newspaper articles about American Indians. One of the highlights of Brady's second year at the school was the visit of Alex Voorhees, a Walker River Paiute who performs a quite convincing Sarah Winnemucca. Her presentation ended with a question-and-answer period when she appeared first as "Sarah" and then as herself. Some students asked "Sarah" point blank whether or not she was a traitor. Voorhees's answer, Brady remarks, was strikingly true to the author of *Life Among the Piutes:* "I'm human," she said, admitting that she had made mistakes, but adding that she had always done what she thought was best for her people: a sentiment that Brady finds her students understand. "I ask them to place themselves in her moccasins. When it's done that way, given the circumstances, they said they would find it hard to be in her place and probably do the same."[23] Brady compares current representations of Winnemucca to the game of telephone, in which one statement inevitably changes as it is transmitted from person to person. Brady's goal, she explains, is simply to get her students to read *Life Among the Piutes* and other materials and then decide for themselves how to remember Sarah Winnemucca. "It's okay to listen to your relatives, but open your mind.... You might just learn something from someone else."[24] In a culture that places a high premium on the respect of one's elders (and their stories), such advice can be controversial.

Lost (and Gained) in Translation

Pyramid Lake High School is not the only location where Sarah Winnemucca's place in the community is contested. Some ambivalence toward this historic figure is also evident at the Pyramid Lake Visitor Center, which I visited in April of 2001. A sign refers to Winnemucca in a lukewarm tone:

> Sarah has been notoriously known to the Neh-muh as a traitor and is blamed for many lives lost on a forced march to the Fort Malheur Indian Reservation in Oregon (this was a direct result of the Pyramid Lake War of 1860).
>
> Despite the controversy, Sarah Winnemucca-Hopkins remains one of the most well-known members from the Pyramid Lake Paiute Reservation.

The second part of this sign suggests the organizers' frustration with Winnemucca's fame: "despite" their knowledge of her treachery, she "remains" (to the rest of the world) one of the most recognized Paiutes. Another display shows Pancho, Truckee's brother, receiving a medal for his service in the Mexican-American War, while he is typically overshadowed by Truckee in historical accounts. The organizers seek to tell what they say is the Paiute side of the story—a side they claim has too often been obscured or omitted altogether. Given the differences between these displays and much of the scholarship on Northern Paiutes, they have a point. Ben Aleck, director of the Pyramid Lake Visitor Center, suggests that Sarah is controversial in part because she was "raised by" Major Ormsby, who would lead U.S. military troops against the Paiutes in the Pyramid Lake War of 1860.[25] Although Ormsby is for many Paiutes an undisputed enemy, Sarah Winnemucca paints him in a rather positive light, noting that her brother Natches attempted to save his life in the battle. Yet Zanjani's biography indicates that Sarah lived at Ormsby's house for only a year at most. The Visitor Center staff also attempts to correct what it sees as a common misrepresentation of the Pyramid Lake War. A document on the Pyramid Lake Battles, which the staff hoped to post on their website, emphasizes the heroism of the Paiute women, elders, and children who fought the whites in hand-to-hand combat. Given their frustration with historical accounts that diminish the significance of the Paiute victory, it is no wonder that Winnemucca's favorable presentation of Ormsby only works against her. Trying to find a middle ground, Aleck notes that while "tribal people got killed" because of certain decisions that Winnemucca made, "she did some good." As a testament to that good work, the center now displays photographs of the Sarah Winnemucca statue that was installed in the U.S. Capitol in the spring of 2005.[26] Although some might find it surprising that Northern Paiutes at Pyramid Lake would try to distance themselves from their most famous ancestor—even resenting others' efforts to honor her—these competing narratives make their frustration more understandable.

The presentations at the Visitor Center also suggest an attempt on the part of the organizers to find a space for Northern Paiute women that is not eclipsed by memorials to Sarah Winnemucca. As one sign reads, "Prior to John C. Fremont's 'discovery' of Pyramid Lake (Jan. 13, 1844), women played an immeasurable contribution for the Ku-yui survival." It goes on to explain that women harvested seeds and berries, cooked, cared for children, made baskets, and assumed "spiritual responsibility that included 'curing' or 'doctoring' sick people." Today, it notes, many women are elected to the Tribal Council, maintaining "high status jobs within the Tribal structure" while also serving as traditional caretakers. "It is with this respect, we the people of Pyramid Lake, acknowledge the contributions of the grandmothers of before and the present women of Pyramid Lake so that future generations of the Ku-yui Dicutta may continue our survival and Ki Na Sumoowakwatu (Never to be Forgotten)." This note of women's participation in the Tribal Council was affirmed in the 2001 Tribal Council elections, when (as Harriet Brady enthusiastically reported) seven women were elected.[27] The gender role of Paiute women is thus inseparable from their contributions to the nation, so that accusations about their nonallegiance have important implications for their femininity.

As in the late nineteenth century, a group of white women have organized themselves in defense of Sarah Winnemucca. One of these is Georgia Hedrick, a writer and former teacher from Reno. Hedrick first stumbled upon *Life Among the Piutes* at a public library over a decade ago and was immediately drawn to the author.[28] As a member of the Nevada Women's History Project, Hedrick took her fascination with Winnemucca beyond the classroom, calling for a day and an elementary school named in the Paiute woman's honor. After mobilizing legislators, Hedrick was rewarded with a statewide Sarah Winnemucca Day in 1991. An elementary school was christened with the Paiute woman's name in 1994. Most ambitiously, Hedrick spent several years campaigning for a statue of Winnemucca in the rotunda of the U.S. Capitol. In March of 2001, the Nevada legislature passed a bill in support of the Sarah Winnemucca statue, and the Nevada Women's History Project raised the necessary funds for its creation. That spring, Harriet Brady planned to ask her students if they would be interested in participating in a fund-raiser; she was not sure how the community would respond.[29] When I asked Ben Aleck in April 2001 about the tribe's positions on the statue, he said that most tribal leaders had "reserved judgment" on it.

The statue was installed in the U.S. Capitol in March of 2005; two replicas were dedicated in Nevada. In Reno a year later, Harriet Brady led the discussion of the film "Sarah Winnemucca: The Dream Fulfilled," which documents the statue campaign. Given the long history of whites laying claim to Indians for their own benefit, it is not surprising that some Paiutes would hold Hedrick and other whites in suspicion. Placed in the Capitol, the statue becomes a vivid symbol for the U.S. nation, once again raising questions about Sarah Winnemucca's Paiute loyalty. For Brady, however, the statue is a testimony to her Paiute nation: "she is where she belongs—both at DC and in Carson City. It is very fitting that she is acknowledged. It is just so cool for our little desert nation to have that connection."[30] The students she takes to DC as part of a special program gain new appreciation for Winnemucca when they see her image in bronze. In turn, Brady notes, more people from the community support the statue now that Winnemucca has been officially endorsed. For others, that official endorsement may make her all the more galling.

During the statue campaign, Hedrick and the other members of the Nevada Women's History Project marshaled support from one of Sarah Winnemucca's descendants, an elderly woman by the name of Louise Tannheimer. With pride, Tannheimer speaks of her great-great aunt as another Frank Sinatra—someone "who did it her way."[31] Now living in Portola, California, Tannheimer periodically returns to Nevada to meet with members of the Women's History Project and with Paiutes. Her mission, as she sees it, is to increase awareness of and support for Sarah Winnemucca—something she claims has been a long time in coming. "These young people need something to be proud of. She belongs to everyone of the Paiute nation—especially Northern Paiutes." Although she understands why some Paiutes harbor bad feelings toward her famous relative, she believes most of their discontent springs from jealousy and a lack of familiarity with Sarah Winnemucca. "They haven't read the books," she says, simply, of Winnemucca's critics. As a two-time member of the Fort Yuma Tribal Council, Tannheimer witnessed first-hand the consequences of a woman speaking out. She laughs, recalling her outspokenness as an appointee of a governmental commission on women: "I think I have a little bit of Sarah in me!" Like her great-great aunt, Tannheimer was regarded with some suspicion by other Paiutes for living among whites.

When she returned to the community after growing up in Phoenix, others questioned her allegiance—even though, she notes, she had attended the Phoenix Indian School. Again, school is a place where one's tribal identity is affirmed or called into question.

Hedrick repeats Tannheimer's words, which seem to fuel her campaign: "The spirit of Sarah is in you and she won't let you go until [the statue] is done." In a spirited, colorful voice, Hedrick—who even changed her e-mail unique name to a version of Winnemucca's name—declares, "She is a phenomenon. If the world would recognize what they had . . . ." Although Hedrick is mindful of those who call Winnemucca a traitor, they certainly have not dissuaded her; she spoke forcefully at the 1994 meeting on the naming of the elementary school (Zanjani 300). With a "contained fury," Hedrick noted indignantly that this early Native American woman author had no official memorial (Zanjani 300). As Zanjani reports, some Paiutes at the meeting "rejected Sarah as a turncoat who married white men and favored assimilation" (299). Like the English words that Winnemucca encouraged her students to write on the fences, the renaming of this elementary school was a symbolic act of possession.

These women's relationships to Sarah Winnemucca raise a series of questions about the intersection of anger, femininity, and race today. If the school were to be named after Winnemucca, whom would it honor? Winnemucca and all Paiutes? Hedrick and the other members of the Nevada Women's History Project? Who has the right to tell Winnemucca's story? Questions of voice—of who may speak for this Northern Paiute community—inevitably arise when Sarah Winnemucca's name is mentioned. Harriet Brady remembers being irritated during the school board meeting that some members of the community would speak as if they represented all Pyramid Lake Paiutes—as if they, in other words, could lay claim to Winnemucca. Given the competing narratives that exist, anyone who speaks publicly about her is likely to raise someone else's ire.

Once again, Sarah Winnemucca is championed by white women reformers, placing her—as well as American Indian women like Harriet Brady and Louise Tannheimer—in a complicated relationship with the Paiute community. Questions of who can represent Sarah Winnemucca abound; Brady expresses her frustration that some of the individuals, including Tannheimer, have been at the center of the spotlight while other relatives, like Dorothy Ely, are overlooked.[32] Like Sarah Winnemucca, Harriet Brady is in the tricky position of translating what are often perceived as "white words" in her representation of the past and present. In teaching her students about Sarah Winnemucca, she has discovered the degree to which gender figures into attitudes about this famous Northern Paiute woman—and herself as well. While attending the University of Nevada at Reno, Brady began to think more about the position of women in her community, and realized that while her people might "pat [her] on the back," they don't necessarily listen to women as much as men or believe that they should speak out. When I ask Harriet whether she believes that women are more likely than men to be labeled traitors, she assents. She adds that although her students are often able to recognize and discuss racial discrimination, they have more difficulty acknowledging sexism. Consequently, one of Brady's goals is to encourage young people to think about how Winnemucca's position as a woman affected and continues to affect her reputation and her ability to be heard. As Brady declares, "We can forgive whites, but when it comes down to Sarah Winnemucca we haven't forgiven her."

Both Hedrick and Brady may be indignant about those who, in their eyes, fail to appreciate Sarah Winnemucca, but the implications of that anger differs; while Brady is a member of the community, Hedrick is always located outside of it. An alliance between the two seems difficult for some of the same reasons it was for Johnson and white women. Like Sarah Winnemucca, Brady occupies a delicate position as a mediator between whites and American Indians: as a white woman like Georgia Hedrick aligns herself with Winnemucca, some Paiutes may regard Brady as a potential traitor. In turn, Brady is constrained; since women of color must contend with both sexism and racism, anger at the men of their community is necessarily fraught. As Mary Crow Dog notes in her account of the Wounded Knee occupation of 1973:

> At one time a white volunteer nurse berated us for doing the slave work while the men got all the glory. We were betraying the cause of womankind, was the way she put it. We told her that kind of women's lib was a white, middle-class thing, and that at this critical stage we had other priorities. Once our men had gotten their rights and their balls back, we might start arguing with them about who should do the dishes. But not before. (131)

According to Crow Dog, American Indian women's anger directed at Indian men was in some cases a betrayal of their nation.

The fact that an undercurrent of anger at Winnemucca persists suggests that while attempts to distinguish herself from whites' words are successful within the pages of her book, for certain Paiutes she has remained tainted by the association. So for some, when Harriet Brady teaches *Life Among the Piutes* or supports the Winnemucca statue, she participates in that betrayal. In turn, white women may choose to see Brady or Winnemucca as Pauline Johnson's fans viewed her: an indignant Indian woman who articulated a protest they could share. Again, the anger Winnemucca (and Brady, by extension) raises is about possession. Winnemucca's and Brady's power (and danger) is their ability to communicate with a wider audience, whether the audience is the reading public or the high school classroom, whites or Paiutes. Like Winnemucca, Brady has found some success in positioning herself as the conduit rather than an absolute advocate of Sarah Winnemucca's voice, leaving her audience to determine the truth of Winnemucca's words. The difficulty is that, as Winnemucca found, the "untainted" translator may be a tricky role to pull off. Sarah Winnemucca's name continues to raise such emotion, I would argue, because she represents "the" story about the Northern Paiute nation that is most commonly heard.

The "contained fury" with which Georgia Hedrick spoke at the school board meeting is not unlike the moral indignation expressed by the fictional Genevieve and the historic white women Indian reformers of the nineteenth century. In each instance, a white woman finds a measure of self-worth on behalf of American Indians. Genevieve separates herself from a man who would devalue her, and Hedrick finds purpose in aligning herself with Winnemucca (via her e-mail address) and dedicating her time to restoring Winnemucca's honor. The dedication of women like Georgia Hedrick and other members of the Nevada Women's History Project indicates that the complex relationship between white and American women so central to *Life Among the Piutes* persists. I too am implicated in these relations; I wonder, for example, how my representation—my translation—of Brady's words might affect her relationship with her community, and what motivates my own affiliation with her. For me, Winnemucca is proof of the vitality of early American Indian women's writing; in studying her I simply am not faced with the knotted questions of tribal commitment and betrayal that Brady regularly confronts.

The story of Pyramid Lake today, then, like the early American Indian literature I have examined, leaves us to ask under what conditions an alliance between Native and non-Native women might be possible. Is the non-Native anger that motivates someone like Hedrick inevitably self-sustaining, misguided, or provocative? Non-Natives, it appears, must first acknowledge anger's history as a divisive force before we can hope to use it as an instrument of alliance. Audre Lorde offers us hope in translation: "But anger expressed and translated into action in the service of our vision and our future is a liberating and strengthening act of clarification, for it is in the painful process of this translation that we identify who are our allies with whom we have grave differences, and who are our genuine enemies" (127). It is only through such clarification, when we examine our own motivations and our community's past and present understanding of anger, that American Indian and non-Native women may become allies.

Conclusion

An Anger of Their Own

> As I understand ten years later after the slow changing
> of the seasons
> that we have just begun to touch
> the dazzling whirlwind of our anger,
> we have just begun to perceive the amazed world the ghost dancers
> entered
> crazily, beautifully.
>
> —Joy Harjo, "For Anna Mae Pictou Aquash . . ." (34–40)

In Harjo's poem, "the dazzling whirlwind of our anger" is associated with the Ghost Dance, the phenomenon of the late 1800s that was interpreted by whites as a call for war and yet was at once a more drastic and a more peaceful protest than they could have ever imagined. The Ghost Dance is an apt illustration of the ways that American Indians' anger has been misinterpreted, forced into a narrative other than their own. The adoption of the Ghost Dance among the Lakotas was followed by the deaths of nearly 300 men, women, and children from Big Foot's band of Miniconjou Sioux at Wounded Knee Creek in December 1893.[1] Charles Alexander Eastman (Ohiyesa), a Santee Dakota doctor who treated some of the survivors, speaks of the "so-called hostile" camp (63) and the "friendlies" (55), two words that epitomize the racialization of anger in the nineteenth century. As the words indicate, Native Americans were defined (and in some cases, defined themselves) by certain emotional responses, which in turn were thought to determine their relationship to whites. With these quotation marks, Eastman attempts to distance himself from these terms. His simultaneous use of and separation from these words indicate his complicated relationship to Native American communities and non-Native discourses about them. In an attempt to lay claim to an Indianness that exists outside of the simplistic terms "hostile" or "friendly," Eastman emphasizes an "Indian etiquette" that is measured and peaceful and yet acknowledges the travesty of the massacre (57). As a Santee Dakota man who had been educated among whites, he searched for the words to interpret a ceremony and the Wounded Knee massacre that in many ways defied expression. A century later, Joy Harjo invokes a literary Ghost Dance in which Native Americans once again articulate an anger of their own. Drawing from a shared memory of—and outrage for—Native Americans, Harjo presents a collective, "an amazed world," a nation of their own.

To this point, I have concentrated on anger and sentimentality in early American Indian women's texts, arguing that while Alice Callahan, Pauline Johnson, and Sarah Winnemucca each employ a sentimentality in which sarcasm and irony mark anger, Winnemucca is most successful at using it to affirm her indigenous nationhood. Their success is related to the genres they employ: Callahan is hindered by the script of the Indian reformer, for example, while Johnson's short stories are marked by a tension between a cross-racial romance and a Native woman's loyalty to her nation. Winnemucca, in the form of a self-narrative, is most able to command language for her (and her nation's) own ends, ultimately showing the distinction between her own words and those of whites. When we juxtapose these authors and their works, other things become clear: for one, the phenomenon of playing angry, which in *Wynema* is limited to the white reformer, is more available to Johnson and Winnemucca. For them, however, it is not without its costs: Johnson is sexualized on stage and Winnemucca's response to attacks on her virtue are described as "an overdose of 'mad,'" a phrase that indicates how anger was used to stereotype American Indian women.[2]

All three women, whether during their lives or after, have been charged with disloyalty to their indigenous nations. Such charges are perhaps inevitable for the first published writers of any group, especially those who wrote in English and worked closely with whites. As I have shown, Winnemucca is most able—at least within the pages of her narrative—to confront this criticism head on. Conversations with Northern Paiutes at Pyramid Lake today indicate that anger about her disloyalty remains, a likely response to the enduring power of *Life Among the Piutes*. It is the book, after all, that prompts white women like Georgia Hedrick to embark on a campaign to memorialize Sarah Winnemucca.

Conclusion

As I have demonstrated, sentimentality has its costs: each author, at various times, positions Native Americans as objects in need of white protection. For all of its cultural authority, even Winnemucca's narrative defers at times to the white "expert," as Mann's footnotes illustrate. Johnson is perhaps least willing to cede this authority, presenting her own footnotes—for example, the declarative "Fact" in "A Red Girl's Reasoning"—to underscore her heroine's statements. Her essay "A Strong Race Opinion" is one of the most emphatic statements of cultural authority that I examine. Here Johnson critiques those authors who write "Indian literature" with no real experience with indigenous peoples. In this sense, her essay seems a prescient forerunner to contemporary calls for acknowledging American Indian literary nationalism.

Given that anger is inevitably raced and gendered, these texts are explorations of not only Native nationalism but masculinity and femininity as well. Gender roles are particularly differentiated in Callahan's novel, presenting an interesting contrast to Gail Bederman's claim that in the late nineteenth century people of color were represented as lacking the rigid gender distinctions of whites. Perhaps in response to such stereotypes, Callahan imagines male and female Creeks who embody conventional (white) masculinity and femininity. Yet this ultra-femininity, marked by deference and selflessness, offers Wynema none of the anger that drives Genevieve's self-development. It is only the white woman who can access, at least briefly, a healthy assertion. One of the tragedies of the story Callahan tells, then, is that there was little room, at least in her imagination, for a three-dimensional indigenous woman. Chikena, the one Native woman who raises a forceful protest, is described in both masculine and feminine terms. To imagine an angry Native woman, it seems, Callahan must look outside the Creek community to the Lakotas. While the heroines of Pauline Johnson's "As It Was in the Beginning" and "A Red Girl's Reasoning" witness the demise of their cross-racial, heterosexual relationships by the end of each story, Wynema's survives and indeed culminates in the requisite bliss of marriage and motherhood. The difference is that while the Native woman of Johnson's stories makes certain claims—first to Laurence and second to her indigenous wedding rites—Wynema is claimed *by* her white lover. Her emotional expression is limited to a passive response to his desire rather than an insistence of her own. In this sense, she does not lay claim to her rights, a central aspect of empowering anger as I have described it.

It is this deferent, selfless Indian woman that Johnson blasts in her essay "A Strong Race Opinion," indicating her desire to create indigenous heroines who would refuse mistreatment. Throughout her poetry and fiction are women who raise voices of protest: the chief's daughter slams the English for their oppressive tactics, Christie leaves her white husband when he refuses to acknowledge the legitimacy of her parents' indigenous marriage, and Esther kills the white man who chooses a white woman in her place. Notably, in this last instance, Esther locates the anger that rouses her to murder in her gender rather than her race. This effort epitomizes the attempts of all three writers to articulate a justified anger that would be taken seriously. It is this struggle that Harjo describes in the lines "we have just begun to touch / the dazzling whirlwind of our anger" (36–37).

The writer's ability to articulate an indigenous anger, these texts suggest, is correlated with her tribalism. As Craig Womack has demonstrated, the Indians Callahan describes bear little relation to actual Creeks; they live in "tepees," they do not engage in historic resistance efforts, and no Creek language appears in the novel. In contrast, Johnson's essays specify Haudenosaunee (Iroquois) traditions such as the hanging of the Maternity Mask ("Heroic Indian Mothers" 23) and the clan matron's nomination of tribal leaders. Winnemucca devotes an entire chapter to the ethnography of the Paiutes, in which she makes statements such as "we have a republic as well as you" (53). In moments like this Winnemucca writes herself into a tribalist position—an "explication of specific Native values, readings, and knowledges" (Weaver, Womack, and Warrior 6)—from which she can critique non-Paiutes. That is, her tribalism offers her a speaking authority: a place from which she can judge others. As Jace Weaver, Craig Womack, and Robert Warrior note in *American Indian Literary Nationalism*, "At its most profound, literary nationalism is not a confrontation, not a tearing down, but an upbuilding" (6) While these critics suggest writers like Sarah Winnemucca and Zitkala-Ša too easily satisfy a non-Native desire for a Pocahontas or Squanto-like surrender to colonialism, I would argue that these authors make important contributions to tribalist discourse (2). Certainly, they are not the only writers who do so—the field of Native American literary studies benefits from attention to a broad range of voices—but it seems dismissive to cast these writers off as products of colonialism.

I end my analysis in the twentieth century, where discussions of Native American resistance usually begin. One bridge between these early texts

Conclusion

and Harjo's poem is the Native-centered organizations like the Society of American Indians (SAI) and the National Council of American Indians (NCAI) that were established early in the 1900s. While the overall success of organizations like the SAI is debatable, they offered people like Zitkala-Ša and Arthur Parker opportunities for resistance and critique (8).[3] One such opportunity came in the form of the *American Indian Magazine* (originally known as the *Quarterly Journal*), the main organ of the SAI.

The contributions of Zitkala-Ša, secretary of the SAI and later founder of the NCAI, are an especially useful link between the anger of the nineteenth and the twentieth centuries. As her essay "What It Means to be an Indian Today" concludes, "To be an Indian today means to be an inarticulate subject under the plenary power of Congress, presumed by the United States Supreme Court to be governed by Christian motives in its dealings with this ignorant and dependent race. It means to be hungry, sick, and dying while still used for a national political football" (46–47). Combining a sentimental image of Native persecution with a sarcastic edge, Zitkala-Ša's words resemble Callahan's biting account of the public's reaction to the slaughter of American Indians, the daughter's response to her father's murder in Johnson's poem "The Cattle Thief," and Winnemucca's clever critique of words like "civilization" and "savagery." Similarly, Zitkala-Ša's poem "The Indian's Awakening" creates a stark image of the boarding school that contrasts Colonel Pratt's ominous call for the Indian to "save his life only by losing it by quitting all race distinctions and climbing into the great big all containing band wagon of real American citizenship through industrial usefulness."[4] Zitkala-Ša details precisely why American Indians should hesitate before jumping onto Pratt's bandwagon:

> I snatch at my eagle plumes and long hair.
> A hand cut my hair; my robes did deplete.
> Left heart all unchanged; the work incomplete.
> These favors unsought, I've paid since with care. (1–4)

In Zitkala-Ša's hands, Pratt's school is unsuccessful in two terms. It deprives students of their cultural heritage and fails even according to his standards: the work is not complete. The rest of the poem is stocked with the imagery of failure: "My light has grown dim, and black the abyss / That yawns at my feet. No bordering shore; / No bottom e'er found by hopes sunk before" (9–11). As she continues, "I've lost my long hair; my eagle plumes too. / From you my own people, I've gone astray. / A wanderer now, with no where to stay" (17–19). The individuality that Pratt would herald as a sign of progress is here a mark of decline: "I stand isolated, life gone amiss" (24). This failure has two facets: it is both the individual isolation that sentimentality decries and the divide from the community that scholars like Jace Weaver and Arnold Krupat have shown is so undesirable in Native American literature. Zitkala-Ša's line recalls Winnemucca's effort in *Life Among the Piutes* to restore her position within her tribal community; as she realizes, to "stand isolated" is to lack authority.

In a scene of *American Indian Stories*, her semi-autobiographical account of boarding school education, Zitkala-Ša forges this critique in domestic terms. Reprimanded for some trivial "misconduct," the young narrator is forced to mash turnips for the evening dinner. The turnips instantly become the target of her anger. "I hated turnips, and their odor which came from the brown jar was offensive to me" (60). In a vivid description of the relationship between her body and the turnip jar, she describes taking the wooden tool, climbing up on the stool, and grasping the handle firmly with both hands.

> I bent in hot rage over the turnips. I worked my vengeance upon them . . . I saw that the turnips were in a pulp, and that further beating could not improve them; but the order was, "Mash these turnips," and mash them I would! I renewed my energy, and as I sent the masher into the bottom of the jar, I felt a satisfying sensation that the weight of my body had gone into it. (60)

Standing "fearless and angry," she recalls, "I whooped in my heart for having once asserted the rebellion within me" (61). Her unjustified punishment ironically becomes the vehicle for her revenge. Not insignificantly, it is in the kitchen—the ultimate domestic space—that this is carried out. Quite unlike the docile, obedient girl who is supposed to quietly mash the turnips, she takes this order to the extreme, challenging the stereotypes to which she is expected to conform. She has devoted her whole body to the task, but for a very different end. From a conventional domestic stage, she uses irony to enact her anger. According to Laura Wexler, this scene, as well as the moment when she cries to no avail, illustrates the narrative's anti-sentimentality: the tears that would otherwise be effective here go unheard. But I would argue that through this invocation of the reader's sympathy and outrage about her treatment—in this case her inability to be heard through tears—the genre's emphasis on the power of tears remains intact. To say that her "self-conception had been so effectively ensnared within the codes of sentiment that there was no Indian in them that was left untouched by Western codes" (Wexler 32–33) is to neglect the ability of this indigenous author to represent her experience in powerful, and sentimental, terms.

Zitkala-Ša was not the only early-twentieth-century Native American activist to employ sentimentality in the *American Indian Magazine;* Seneca writer Arthur Parker (Gawasa Wanneh) uses the familiar image of persecuted innocence to articulate anger about the representations of Native Americans in school textbooks:

> Our school books do not tell how Indian women and children were shot without mercy and how Indians praying to the white man's Christ, on their very knees, were shot to death by white men. History that we study in school says nothing of how Indians were scalped, skinned alive, burned and otherwise tortured by white men or how babies' bodies were brought in for bounty rewards. But all these facts with thousands of instances of heathenish, fiendish savagery committed by white men are on record in documents and books of undisputed authenticity. Why did the heathen rage? Ask the God of nations. (25)[5]

Like Sarah Winnemucca, Parker finds a venue for turning the terms of "savagery" and "civility" on their heads: "heathen rage" is transferred to whites, leaving American Indians with a more justified anger. Sentimentalism and anger converge in the image of mutilated babies, an image to haunt whites and Natives alike. The writer applies the language of savagery to whites in a style not unlike that of earlier Native American activists such as William Apess, who also used the language of Christianity and sentimentality to rewrite American history from an indigenous perspective.

The *American Indian Magazine*'s editorial offered another venue for Native American writers to lay claim to their rightful possessions, a key characteristic of anger as I have described it. In his essay "Certain Important Elements of the Indian Problem," for instance, Parker detailed the list of things that "Americans" had taken from Native peoples. No progress would be made, he argued, until whites acknowledged their appropriation of property, from land to intellectual rights.[6] An editorial from the April–June 1914 issue reclaims the right of Native Americans to represent themselves: "The show Indian is not the real Indian any more than the circus white man is the real white man" (175). The "Editorial Comment" from the October–December issue of 1914 declares in no uncertain terms, "American Indian blood is in America to stay" (262). A January–March 1916 editorial imagines the magazine as a voice for resistance: "*No, the modern Indian cannot live on the bitter pottage of history and eat his heart out thinking how the white man cheated his ancestors.* It is for him to pluck the feathers from his war bonnet and make fountain pens of them" (9–10). Here the images used against Native Americans—the supposedly savage feathers of the war bonnet—become potent weapons as writing instruments. This quotation offers a useful distinction between affect and action. Weeping about persecution is not enough; Native Americans must turn their rage into powerful words.

Such rage is also evident in the narrations of the later American Indian Movement. In their account of the occupation of the Bureau of Indian Affairs building in 1972, Paul Chaat Smith and Robert Allen Warrior describe how each key of a typewriter was carefully twisted beyond repair in an instance of "slow, consuming anger" (167). Here a literal tool of the colonizers' language is literally and symbolically reclaimed by those who have been the subject of documentation and control. An essay from 1964 declares that "to connect young Indian anger to people in local communities was necessary for real social change to occur" (quoted in Smith and Warrior 53). Vine Deloria, Jr. and Clifford M. Lytle claim that the occupation of Wounded Knee in 1973 is "symbolic of the conflict that is raging in Indian hearts everywhere" (*Nations Within* 12). Anger is also a central aspect of pantribalism, linking multiple nations in response to U.S. policies like boarding schools and termination. Alcatraz occupation leader Stella Leach should be understood, Paul Chaat Smith and Robert Allen Warrior claim, in terms of "the anger and resentment fostered during her childhood years in a terrible BIA boarding school"—an anger and resentment that can be multiplied a thousandfold (71). Other protests were products of "pent-up rage—especially among impoverished, underserved Indians in the cities" (Smith and Warrior 93). Whether it is used against American Indians or in their defense, anger remains an important part of this narrative.

In response to such Native narrations of anger, whites produced representations not unlike the phrenology of the 1800s. In his study of NBC coverage of the American Indian Movement protests from 1968 to 1979, for example, Tim Baylor notes, "Social control agents and polity leaders specifically tried to create factionalism to create dissension within AIM's ranks. They understood this would decrease AIM's ability to mount a successful challenge" (248). In other words, representations of internal anger in American Indian resistance movements were used to undermine Native solidarity.[7] Non-Natives imagined an anger not far removed from nineteenth-century stereotypes of "savagery" and "destructiveness,"

Conclusion

"hostiles" and "friendlies." A marshal outside of the Wounded Knee occupation of 1973 told reporters, "They're still roamin' out there, the Injuns. They'd love to get a whitey" (quoted in Smith and Warrior 207).[8] Baylor's study found that "militant" was the frame used in 90 percent of the news segments, even before AIM's major protests had occurred. That is, the movement was described in terms of violence and a lack of law and order—anger out of control—rather than treaty rights, self-defense, or civil disobedience. Charles W. Mills's account of "the racial contract" offers one explanation of this response to AIM: "watchfulness for nonwhite resistance and a corresponding readiness to employ massively disproportionate retaliatory violence are intrinsic to the fabric of the racial polity in a way different from the response to the typical crimes of white citizens" (86). The moral order that the racial contract depends on is one in which whites/persons are distinguished from nonwhites/nonpersons through violence and ideological manipulation. Any challenge to this arrangement, like Custer's defeat or the occupation of Wounded Knee, incites what Mills calls an "*ontological shudder*": the terror that "order" must be restored (86). In this sense, anger is read as savagery that fundamentally challenges the assumptions Anglo-American society is built upon. The anger generated in movements like AIM is further threatening because it, unlike the instances of "playing angry" that I explored in Chapter 1, is not mobilized by or for whites in service of the United States.

But is anger, one might ask, more relevant to Native Americans than to any other disadvantaged group? Wouldn't *any* minority group seeking rights be portrayed by the majority as irrational, dangerous, or neutralized by its own infighting? While I agree that stereotypes of anger have often been mobilized as a hegemonic response to marginal groups, we should be attentive to how anger functions differently for particular groups over time. Certain representations have held import for American Indians; it was against the stereotype of the stoic warrior, for example, that the indigenous newspaper *Warpath* defined a new American Indian during the Civil Rights Movement: "The 'Stoic, Silent Redman' of the past who turned the other cheek to injustice is dead. (He died of frustration and heartbreak.) And in his place is an angry group of Indians. Hate and despair have taken their toll and only action can quiet this smoldering anger that has fused this new Indian movement into being" (quoted in T. Johnson 22).[8] Thus stoicism cannot simply be dismissed as a stereotype applied to Native Americans; it is also a representation against which many indigenous people have understood and constructed their own resistance.

THAT DAZZLING WHIRLWIND

One of the main ways I have theorized anger in this book is in terms of entitlement: the sense that something one owns is unjustly taken away. "Entitlement" is usually a bad word among teachers, referring to students who expect good grades even when they haven't earned them. But I'd like to rescue the word, if only momentarily, considering what it might tell us about productive anger in the American Indian literature classroom. I present here three case studies from my experience at a predominantly white university in which most students work one, two, or even three jobs year-round to pay their way through school. These case studies are just that; I have no intention of capturing the full spectrum of identities or forms of anger that exist in today's college classroom. That said, I'm hoping these examples have some use value beyond my particular context.

Case Study #1

I confess that I often feel angry—or at least irritated—about some students' stereotypes or misconceptions of American Indians. Upon reflection, I've realized that I feel entitled to a classroom in which students share, or are at least willing to entertain, a just, realistic view of Native Americans. I realize this might fly in the face of the educational philosophy that classrooms should be a space of open exchange—the kind of John Stuart Mill milieu I optimistically imagined before I started teaching, in which truth inevitably emerges once all voices are expressed. Indeed, the classroom can never be a kind of "pure" space free from the systematic equalities that exist beyond it. It's more beneficial, then, if instructors are honest about what we feel entitled to, how our anger is tied up in our social identities, and how this translates into our teaching.

I've grown accustomed to (and I'm still irked by) a certain kind of Indian in my travels through student papers: one who is, more often than not, in the past tense. Anticipating this vanished American of student imaginations, I start each semester with a series of questions: (1) How many Native Americans live in the United States today? (The numbers they come up with rarely exceed 500,000.) (2) Name three famous Native Americans no longer living. (I get the usual suspects: Pocahontas, Geronimo, Sitting Bull.) (3) Name three Native Americans living today. (Blank stares.) Then we discuss why people tend to underestimate the

Conclusion

numbers and know far more about (certain) Native Americans from the past than the present. And when they do research on a tribal nation, I require them to include an analysis of the tribe today.[9] All of this is, at least, a first step.

"The Indian" of the past tense isn't the only figure I've come to regard with suspicion, however. I'm also wary of the "white man," who shows up with uncanny persistence in many of the papers I read. The phrase is almost always followed by a note of his atrocities to "the Indian." This invariably leaves me thinking that if we only could track down this "white man" and get rid of him, we'd all be better off. I'm not sure why the phrase bothers me so much; perhaps it makes me think of old westerns. Or maybe it's the maleness—as I usually write in the margins, "man only?," trying to get the writer to think about how white women are involved in colonization as well. But I suspect the phrase is like "mankind"—a term used, also to my dismay, for both sexes. Perhaps then I should be grateful for their inclusion of "white," since whites are taught so well to forget our own racial position. But something tells me that this phrase comes, like the Indian of the past tense, from some reflexive, time-encrusted impulse that isn't entirely thought through. In both cases, my aim is to get them to choose their words more carefully, to realize that neither "the Indian" nor "the white man" is a phrase to use casually.

In trying to take on this casual use of "the white man" who does something bad to "the Indian" of past tense, I spend a good deal of time deconstructing my students' concepts of the real Indian. Wary of the popular images that my students collect like cobwebs in their wanders through mass media, I use a number of techniques to challenge typical notions of authenticity: I distribute images like the advertisement for "Deer Shadow," the Indian of no specific tribe offered for a mere $19.99 monthly installment (satisfaction guaranteed "or your money back"). I've also asked them to bring in positive and negative representations of Native Americans. One student's misinterpretation of "negative representation" as a bad thing that happened to American Indians led to an interesting question: how can we represent an event like Wounded Knee ethically? Many of my students are too hasty to conflate Indianness with despair: as one wrote of *Lost Bird*, a video about a survivor of Wounded Knee, "To me, this is as real as an Indian that you can get. Her whole life was misery and she was never accepted by society." While I hope to steer my students away from any Pollyanna view of American history, this conflation of American Indians and misery is surely not an ideal destination. In choosing the representations that our non-Native students encounter, we must consider what most effectively and ethically counters those images they have come to know so well. How, that is, can we tell a story that includes suffering without making that suffering the only story they remember?

CASE STUDY #2

First, a caveat: I have had a number of non-Native students who express an anger that is more compatible with mine: an indignation about the less palatable parts of American history that they have not been taught before or the stereotypes of Indians they find so easily once their consciousness is raised. I sometimes worry, though, that this anger is characterized by the kind of missionary zeal I've discussed in this book: a non-Native anger *on behalf of* American Indians. So while I try to see this version of student anger as a useful starting point, I would not want to end there. As Deborah Miranda once reminded me, in the classroom my non-Native students and I are privileged in that we can get angry about Indian stereotypes without being read as after our own good, a privilege American Indians aren't typically afforded.[10]

In teaching at higher education institutions in Michigan and West Virginia I have encountered some non-Native students who feel threatened by, and angry about, certain indigenous rights. There was the boy in Michigan, for example, who came from a community close to a Chippewa reservation and who had grown up hearing non-Natives complain about the casino money to which they did not feel the Chippewas were entitled. In response to such student anger, we can provide statistics about the reality of casinos and sovereignty, but we should remember that we are dealing with a deeply sedimented anger that is not likely to go away in a single semester.

Once, during a discussion of Sherman Alexie's novel *Indian Killer*, a student described throwing her copy of the book across the room in disgust at its gruesome images. At the time, I let her stop there, but after more consideration I realize I should have pushed her further. I simply don't buy it: most young people today are so inoculated to graphic violence in film and television that I doubt this in and of itself would provoke anger, especially the kind that inspires one to throw a book across the room. If I could have that moment back, I would ask her to point to a specific "gruesome" scene in the book so that we could identify what I suspect is at the root of this disgust: Native American anger at whites. During our class discussion I pointed to an interview I found with Sherman Alexie that includes the following exchange:

Conclusion

SA: [I wrote *Indian Killer*] because I was sitting at Washington State with frat guys in the back row who I wanted to kill. And I would fantasize about murder.

JF: What were they doing that made you want to kill them?

SA: Just being white. Just drunk on their privilege, essentially. Showing up late, disrupting the class in all sorts of small ways that all added up to my thinking, "I want to kill them." (quoted in Fraser 69–70)

His words drew some raised eyebrows and audible gasps among my students. We do no service to American Indian literature or authors, I believe, when we tiptoe around such anger or pretend it does not exist. In his keynote address at the 2007 Native American Literature Symposium, Alexie called *Indian Killer* a "racist piece of shit"—speaking, presumably, of its indigenous anger.[11] Despite Alexie's characteristic disowning of certain aspects of his work—or at least popular interpretations of it—I still find *Indian Killer* a rich text to include in a Native American literature course. Indeed, Alexie's recent comment makes it all the more important, suggesting how some Native authors might reframe, or even renounce, the anger of their texts. Perhaps part of his response is to society's message that people of color are not entitled to such "messy" anger.

These examples of student anger raise the following question: is there a non-Native anger at Native Americans that is not inherently colonialist or racist, and if so, what might it look like? As Audre Lorde reminds us, not all anger is equal: "For it is not the anger of Black women which is dripping down over this globe like a diseased liquid. It is not my anger that launches rockets ... slaughters children in cities, stockpiles nerve gas and chemical bombs, sodomizes our daughters and our earth" (133). At the same time, it seems possible to acknowledge the different weights that certain forms of anger, and certain individuals, are accorded while still engaging in a healthy dialogue in which all perceived entitlements are on the table. This is the classroom we should work toward.

Case Study #3

A woman of Ojibwe descent who is active in the Native American Studies Program at West Virginia University recently shared how irritated she was with a non-Native professor who insisted on calling American Indian origin stories "myths"—a word he did not use for stories from the Bible. Her comment made me think more self-consciously about the words I use in the classroom, not out of what some call "political correctness," but a commitment to accuracy, reason, and ethics. We have a lot to learn from such anger.

CASE STUDY #4

While teaching *Indian Killer*, I asked students to break into groups to examine particular scenes from the novel. One group was asked to consider a moment in the book when Marie Polatkin, a Native woman, calls her white professor on his professed "expertise" in American Indian literature. I felt most uncomfortable—and, strangely, most satisfied—when a student asked me if I had ever been challenged as Marie challenges her professor. Although this was asked by a non-Native student, it was itself an implicit challenge—one that, I hope, makes me a better teacher. Perhaps most importantly, this circumvents the role of Native American students or teachers as the sole dismantlers of anti-Native racism. Given the right literary texts and contexts, the rest of us might just stumble upon some of the answers ourselves.

I have approached anger with the assumption that while it is not always the best strategy for resistance, it is not by default an "unhealthy" tactic. Philosopher Lynne McFall has argued that even bitterness, which is often thought to be the unhealthiest form of anger, is legitimate as a necessary and ongoing reminder of past (or present) injustice that would otherwise remain unacknowledged. Some may argue that a study of any literature through the lens of a single emotion is reductive, or that an emphasis on anger is inconsistent with American Indian values. Instead of psychoanalyzing or labeling indigenous peoples in particular ways, however, I have attempted to trace the strategies Native authors used to protest oppression when anger was particularly aligned with Indianness.

Some might say that my emphasis on anger and possession is a particularly western one that conflicts with Native collectivity. While I am attentive to what Jace Weaver has called "communitism," I am also wary of the way that non-Natives have emphasized Native collectivism in order to undermine indigenous property rights. In contrast to the stereotype that Native Americans have little sense of property rights—a belief that conveniently works to condone the seizure of Native land and resources—by acknowledging the ways early American Indian women writers laid claim to Native land and rights in their narratives, we challenge this colonialist model. This is not to say that Native American conceptions of property are identical to those of whites, or that they take the same forms across indigenous nations. Rather, to acknowledge these rights as they are articulated in these texts is to acknowledge the rights themselves. And while the first published Native American women are not equally successful in their articulations of indigenous nationhood, their anger—and sentimentality—point toward an activist future in Native American literature. In Harjo's poem, we see a similar invocation of connection across boundaries in order to assert indigenous nationhood. The anger that reverberates so clearly in Joy Harjo's poem finds its roots here.

Notes

INTRODUCTION

1. The *Globe* 11 Feb. 1836. See Scheckel; Bank for further analysis of the play.

2. Since there is no consensus about whether "Native American" or "American Indian" is a preferable term, I use them interchangeably. Like Berkhofer, I tend to use the separate term "Indian" in order to differentiate between the imagined Indian—a product of Anglo fears and fantasies—and actual Native Americans. I refer to "First Nations," the Canadian term, where appropriate.

3. The *Globe* 15 Feb. 1836.

4. While Kilcup notes Nancy Ward's "sentimental appeal to Anglo motherhood" in her analysis of Owen's self-narrative, she places greater emphasis on the matrilocal Cherokee traditions and other genres that Owen employed (6).

5. I should note that these early Native American women writers were preceded by Laah Ceil Manatoi Elaah Tubbee (Delaware-Mohawk), who authored the life story of her husband in 1848.

6. Yet as Canby notes, Marshall's ruling was a "mixed blessing" for American Indians: "Its emphasis on nationhood laid the groundwork for future protection of tribal sovereignty by Marshall and his immediate successors, but the characterization also created an opportunity for later courts to discover limits to tribal sovereignty inherent in domestic dependent status. Marshall's reference to tribes as 'wards' was to have an equally mixed history; it provided a doctrinal basis for protection of the tribes by the federal government, but it also furnished support for those who disagreed with Marshall's view that the tribes were states capable of self-government" (16).

7. Jeffrey Bruner, e-mail to the author, 25 Aug. 2006; Gloria McCarty, personal interview, 25 Aug. 2006. Bruner (Muskogee Creek) is an associate professor of Spanish literature and culture at West Virginia University, and McCarty is an instructor of Creek at the University of Oklahoma.

8. In a compelling illustration of the intimate relationship between anger and grief, anthropologist Renato Rosaldo juxtaposes his study of the Ilongot headhunters with the experience of mourning his wife's sudden death in *Culture and Truth*.

Notes to Introduction

9. See Ruoff, "Justice for Indians and Women: The Protest Fiction of Alice Callahan and Pauline Johnson."

10. Vizenor quotes Cook-Lynn: "That anger is what started me writing. Writing, for me, is an act of defiance born of the need to survive. I am me. I exist. I am a Dakota" (Vizenor *Manifest* 93).

11. For an analysis of Owen's mixed genres, see Kilcup. See Warrior's *The People and the Word* for an extensive discussion of early Native American nonfiction.

12. In more extensive studies of phrenology, a distinction is often made between phrenologists, physiognomists, and craniologists. Morton, for example, is sometimes described as a craniologist whose work was celebrated by the classic phrenologist George Combe. For a comprehensive study of all of the above, including their internal disagreements, see Colbert; M. Stern.

13. See, for example, "The Phrenological Character of George Copway—With a Likeness" in the *American Phrenological Journal* 11 (1849).

14. See Jahoda 133–77 and P. Deloria 106–7 for an examination of this association between the child and the "savage." Slotkin and Drinnon also provide useful commentaries on the construction of the "savage."

15. This emotionality was not always construed in negative terms, however; Lott notes that in a time marked by evangelistic expression, African Americans were often thought of as model Christians for their devout feelings.

16. Mary E. Bennett [Elizabeth Glover], *Family Manners* (New York: Crowell, 1890). Quoted in Kasson 168. An earlier version of this sentiment appears in John Hall's *On the Education of Children* (Hartford, CT: Canfield and Robbins, 1836). He describes the "native" character of children as follows: "It is a truth incontrovertible, and of momentous bearing, that all children, without exception, possess tempers that are irascible; dispositions which are selfish; propensities of various kinds, which tend to evil; that they are impatient of restraint; that they dislike obedience to parental authority . . . and that they prefer the pleasures of the senses to all other gratifications" (14).

17. "Woman, Her Character, Sphere, Influence, and Consequent Duties, and Education," *The American Phrenological Journal* 8 (1846). The last words of this quotation might also refer to the classical figure Columbia, a representation of the United States that was popular at the time. Given that Columbia is a direct descendant of the "Indian Princess," however, the two cannot be easily separated.

18. See, for example, Salaita.

19. See, for example, Washington; Bergstrom; Hales and Hales; Feeney; D. Carpenter; Dahlberg.

20. Kring; Averill; Shields ("Thinking"). Tavris has also shown that these distinctions between men's and women's experience and expression of anger are often overstated.

21. The full title of Harjo's poem is "For Anna Mae Pictou Aquash, Whose Spirit Is Present Here and in the Dappled Stars (for we remember the story and must tell it again so we may all live)." Since the publication of Harjo's poem, in *Mad Love and War*, there have been developments in the investigation of Anna Mae Pictou Aquash's death. In 2004, former American Indian Movement (AIM) member Arlo Looking Cloud was convicted of her murder. Prosecutors argued that AIM leaders ordered her murder because they suspected that she was a spy for the U.S. government. See Mihesuah for a recent commentary on her death.

Notes to Chapter 1

CHAPTER 1

1. After Womack, I refer to this nation as "Muskogee (Creek)." The nation officially spells this "Muscogee." As with many Native nations, the tribe's spelling varies. See Martin for details on these variants.

2. See, for example, Romero; Sollors.

3. See Wald; Karcher; Grasso; Cox for readings of *Hobomok* that consider Mary's rebellion and the title character's compromised role.

4. The most well-known American Indian woman involved in the WNIA was Susan La Flesche Picotte, who served as a medical missionary for the Omaha nation.

5. *14th Annual Report of the WNIA, Nov. 1884* (Philadelphia: WNIA, 1884).

6. Evidence suggests that some women recognized the potential dangers of too much deference. Hagan notes that WNIA leaders explicitly forbade the Indian Rights Association from accepting women for fear that it would decimate the membership of the WNIA. Although the two associations grew increasingly aligned, with the IRA assuming more of the "political" tasks and the WNIA pursuing missionary work and home "improvement" efforts on reservations, Hagan suggests that there was some resistance to a complete merger (33).

7. Hon. H. L. Dawes, *Proceedings on the Occasion of the Presentation of the Petition of the Women's National Indian Association,* 21 Feb. 1882 (Washington, DC: Senate of the United States, 1882).

8. See Mathes 11 for more details of the WNIA's work with the Women's Christian Temperance Union.

9. *Our Brother in Red* 17 Jan. 1891.

10. Methodism had a strong presence in the Creek community by this time; the first principal chief of the Creek Nation after the Civil War, Samuel Checote, was a Methodist minister (M. Green *Creeks* 95). Tatonetti notes that in 1874 "Baptist missionary Rev. John McIntosh went on an expedition to preach to the Native peoples of the Southwest" (29). Callahan's father was the superintendent of Wealaka Boarding School, a Methodist institution, from 1892 to 1894. The obituary of Callahan's mother similarly emphasizes her devotion to Methodism ("Death of Mrs. Callahan," *Muskogee Daily Phoenix* 15 Oct. 1891). Womack is particularly critical of Callahan's choice "to erase Creek contributions to Methodism" (119–20).

11. "Creek Nation Leader Dead," *The Indian School Journal* 6 Apr. 1911.

12. "Capt. Callahan Dies Here Today," *Muskogee Times Democrat* 17 Feb. 1911.

13. See the *Muskogee Phoenix* 17 Nov. 1898, which indicates the degree of animosity that existed within the Creek community about the issue of allotment: "The obstinacy with which some of the old full-bloods hold out against both the treaty and the Curtis bill, is not attributable so much to their own natural inclinations as to bad advice and influence from certain white parties, who have various schemes to promote." Chitto Harjo led this resistance to allotment, establishing a traditional Creek government that held out until he and his followers were jailed. Their sentences were lifted when they promised to accept the allotments, which for most never, in fact, came through (M. Green *Creeks* 105). Harjo continued to speak against allotment before the U.S. Congress. According to Champagne, the governments of the "Five Civilized Tribes" that adopted the principles of the U.S. Constitution but maintained important parts of tribal culture, such as the emphasis on towns, were dismantled by 1907 (74; 90). While Callahan suggests a rather neat divide between "educated mixed-bloods" and "ignorant

full-bloods," whom she claimed would have the most to lose from allotment, reality was, of course, more complicated.

14. Genevieve's response to the dance is notably similar to one found in the papers of Alice Robertson, a missionary among the Creeks. An unidentified speaker writes, "I was glad to hear what has been said on the old heathen ways that so many of our people still cling to. I too think them wrong. It has been said that the busk does no good. This is true. In the early days of our nation before our fore fathers knew there was a God and superstition was their only guide then these customs served to bind the nation more closely together, but now we have a government, we have schools, we have the Bible, our people are fast becoming civilized. Some say that because our fathers went to the busk we should do so too. Should we then wear blankets and war paint because our people used to do so before they knew better . . .?" (10). This statement, which I suspect is from a Creek individual who has been converted, illustrates a version of the position in between white Christians and traditional Creeks that Callahan herself occupied. See the Alice Robertson Collection, McFarlin Library, University of Tulsa (Series I, Box 6, Folder 14:10). For information about the busk in traditional Creek society, see M. Green (*Politics* 15–16). The idea that Native customs are healthier than those of whites has a long literary history; see, for example, Thomas Morton's early account of Narragansetts in *The New Canaan* (1637): "They are indeed not served in dishes of plate with variety of Sauces to procure appetite; that needs not there. The rarity of the aire, begot by the medicinable quality of the sweete herbes of the Country, always procures good stomakes to the inhabitants" (298–99).

15. "Let not your heart be troubled; believe in God, believe also in Me" (*New American Standard Bible*, John 14.1).

16. This refers to the 1889 scandal in which the Creeks were given $10,000 out of a $2,280,857 dollar settlement for their land. As Tatonetti writes, "Tribal reaction was strong and immediate and throughout the summer and fall of that year the *Muskogee Daily Phoenix* carried daily coverage of the issues (Ruoff xxxix). The Muskogee worked through both the tribal and the U.S. government systems to try to reach a solution, and while the truth did not unfold immediately, the barrage of press suggests that most Muskogee, unlike Callahan's Choe, were well aware of the nuances of the situation" (29). See also Debo 348–50; Ruoff, "Editor's Introduction" xxxvii–xxxviii.

17. See, for example, Wright; M. Green (*Politics* 4–16).

Chapter 2

1. See line 40 of Johnson's poem "The Cattle Thief": "For they knew that an Indian woman roused, was a woman to let alone."

2. Quoted in Strong-Boag and Gerson (*Paddling* 13). This unidentified piece, entitled "A Poem to Brantford's Elocutionist," is located in the Trent University Archives.

3. Some have claimed that Howells distanced himself from his cousin because of her marriage to a Mohawk man. The fact that her sons Henry Beverly and Allen stayed with him on occasion suggests, however, that the breach between the two families has been somewhat overstated.

4. Although many indigenous people argue that since the U.S./Canadian bound-

ary was created and enforced by European powers, it is not a legitimate distinction (see, for example, Alfred), for Pauline Johnson this national boundary was crucial to her national and racial/ethnic identity. During the American Revolution, thousands of Loyalists—many of whom were Mohawk—left the New York area to settle in Canada. Their fidelity to the British crown was formally recognized in 1784 when British-Canadian representatives gave them over 650,000 acres of land around the Grand River and the Bay of Quinte (C. M. Johnston iv; 13). Pauline Johnson participated in several ceremonies of Canadian nationalism, and she often expressed displeasure at Americans' failure to acknowledge her Canadian identity: as she once wrote, "The Yankee to the south of us must south of us remain" (quoted in Strong-Boag and Gerson *Paddling* 210). Because of her Canadian nationalism, Strong-Boag and Gerson disagree with her inclusion in anthologies of American literature. I include Johnson alongside Winnemucca and Callahan not as a U.S. resident but as one of the first published indigenous women writers of North America: a category that necessarily challenges any neat definition of "American" literature.

5. See Gerson's essay "Anthologies and the Canon of Early Canadian Women Writers."

6. Anglo-Canadians are not the only individuals who are fascinated by Pauline Johnson. I spoke with a white woman from a Detroit suburb who cherishes a copy of *The White Wampum* that her mother inherited from her own mother and then passed down to her. She still gets tears in her eyes when she reads "The Cattle Thief."

7. *Expositor* 11 March 1961. A copy of this article is in the Pauline Johnson collection at the Brant Museum and Archives, Brantford, Ontario. Two images of her appeared in the stamp: in Joan Whitwill's words, a "Victorian lady and an Indian maid" (quoted in an unidentified article owned by the Brant Museum and Archives). See Gerson and Strong-Boag (*Collected* xxxvi) for a critique of this stamp.

8. The first Wild West Show was performed in the United States in 1883.

9. This distinction between the Mohawks and tribes like the Onondagas is one that George and Pauline often maintained, although not always in a hierarchical sense. In her essay "The Great New Year White Dog: Sacrifice of the Onondagas" (1911), for example, Johnson portrays this ceremony as one that makes Christian devotion pale in comparison. Gerson and Strong-Boag (*Collected* xv) note the divide between people like George and Smoke Johnson and more traditional Onondagas who were skeptical about Anglo-Canadians. A divide persists to this day among the "Longhouse" or traditional Mohawks and the nonconservatives (see S. Weaver).

10. A similar representation of Haudenosaunee anger appears in Mary Jemison's account of her life with the Senecas. In her description of the adoption ceremony, she notes that unless they have only just heard of the loss of a loved one, "and are under the operation of a paroxysm of grief, anger and revenge," they let a prisoner live and "treat him kindly" (quoted in Seaver 22–23). Here Jemison challenges the stereotype of savage avengers by reframing their anger: "It is family, and not national, sacrifices amongst the Indians, that has given them an indelible stamp as barbarians" (quoted in Seaver 23). In other words, it is not racial difference that accounts for their anger; it no difference at all—simply the justified anger and grief of any human who has lost a loved one.

11. This clipping can be found in Box 4, File 9 (1906) of Special Collections, McMaster Mills Memorial Library.

12. This emphasis on emotionality and religious fervor is also evident in whites' rep-

resentations of African Americans; as Lott notes, "'Blackness' was indeed a primary site of the religious appreciation of the emotions that came with the decline of Calvinism" (32).

13. See McClung 35 for her account of this story.

14. The poem may have been inspired by a conversation Johnson had with a Métis woman. See "From the Country of the Cree," which is located in Special Collections, McMaster Mills Memorial Library.

15. Romero notes that the image of the Indian who plunges to his death is a common element of nineteenth-century American literature. See also Fiedler; Sollors.

16. See, for example, Sultan; Bourke; Shreiber. Alexiou's *The Ritual Lament* is considered the classic study of the Greek lament.

17. See also Alfred for an account of a Kahnawake Mohawk Condolence ritual, in which the participants recognize their pain and sorrow and rejoice in their survival. This ritual is the inspiration for his book *Peace, Power, Righteousness: An Indigenous Manifesto*.

18. According to Van Kirk, such intermarriages were common in the Hudson's Bay Company until the 1870s. Whites initially accepted these marriages because there were so few white women in the area and because they found such relationships crucial to the trade economy. With the arrival of white women in the area and shifting trade patterns in the mid-nineteenth century, Anglo-Native marriages were considered less respectable.

19. This image of his "wet lashes" recalls Hendler's account of masculinity and temperance narratives of the 1840s. Through a public display of tears, once-disrespectable men are transformed into models of self-possession, masculinity, and whiteness.

20. According to S. Johnston, "The Avenger" is one of the many poems that have been lost. It was originally printed in the Christmas 1892 edition of *Saturday Night*. A segment of the poem appears in McRaye's *Pauline Johnson and Her Friends*.

21. "Steinway Hall" 16 July 1906. This article is located in Special Collections, McMaster Mills Memorial Library.

22. Ansley to PJ, 10 Apr. 1907: Cook and Ansley. See also Ansley to PJ, 4 Mar. 1907: Cook and Ansley. Both letters can be found in Special Collections, McMaster Mills Memorial Library. In the latter, the editor asks Johnson for another story: "We have a good mothers' story for the Fourth of July; but in the July issue we would like to publish a special story for the Canadian mothers. It must not exceed 3,000 words in length, and may be legendary, historical or humorous as the case may be; but it must be a story for mothers, not women in general."

23. Mrs. U. S. Grant, "The Child's Life and Character Begins in the Youth of the Mother and Father," *Mother's Magazine* Sept. 1908.

24. Johnson further advocated outdoor occupations in *Outing*, a magazine that was also safely removed from the contentious narratives of cross-racial, heterosexual romance. In the series "Outdoor Occupations," the "madness" of the river challenges the character's boating skills in what becomes an exhilarating contest. Here the water—"angry and mad and impetuous"—mirrors her own lively spirit and freedom of movement (40). Anger is imagined in playful, erotic terms of the natural world. In the April 1893 installment of "Outdoor Pastimes for Women," Johnson writes, "But oh! the ecstasy of knowing that her steed is under her control; that the lightest touch of her agile little moccasined foot has the power to swing this whirlwind craft into any

course she chooses; that it obeys every command, every whim, of its imperious young mistress, and never waits for second orders either!" (21). Johnson seems to find greatest erotic freedom when writing outside of an explicitly male/female, Anglo/indigenous divide. Strong-Boag and Gerson note that this sense of nature as a woman's lover is also evident in poems like "The Song My Paddle Sings" (*Paddling* 154).

25. Sceva Stephen, "Housekeeping Responsibilities Outside of Home," *Mother's Magazine* June 1910. These attitudes were a residue of the nineteenth-century moral hygiene movement. For primary examples of the hygiene movement, see Alcott or Graham. For critical analysis see, for example, Smith-Rosenberg's *Disorderly Conduct;* Nissenbaum.

26. Other women in Johnson's family enjoyed a similar status: Johnson's aunt, Margaret Elliott, was described in her obituary as "the mother of the nation." With Elliott's death the ability to nominate chiefs was transferred to her niece, Mary Jocket Hill. See the *Brantford Weekly Expositor* 9 Apr. 1914. The sense that George's position as a salaried interpreter conflicted with his role as a chief resembles the suspicion that Sarah Winnemucca faced from other Northern Paiutes when she interpreted for whites.

27. According to Gerson and Strong-Boag, Johnson's engagement to Charles Drayton ended in the late 1890s (*Collected* xviii). Keller has found evidence for Johnson's subsequent relationship with manager Charles H. Wuerz in 1900. For more on this and her other relationships see Keller 152–67.

CHAPTER 3

1. Although "Hopkins," the name of Winnemucca's last husband, is included in Mann's and C. Fowler's editions, I follow most critics in primarily referring to her as Sarah Winnemucca. "Piutes" is a misspelling in the original edition; the word should include an "a."

2. The most infamous example of Anglo control over Native American self-narratives is the *Life of Ma-ka-tai-me-she-kia-kiak or Black Hawk . . .* (1833). Although J. B. Patterson maintained that he had faithfully transcribed the subject's oral account of his life, he had, in fact, revised Black Hawk's comments to fit predominant literary conventions and constructions of the Indian. For details see Murray (*Forked* 68–69); Krupat (*For Those* 45–53).

3. There is some disagreement about Mann's role as an editor. As Georgi-Findlay notes, a letter that Mann wrote to a friend suggests that she may have made more changes than she admits to in the preface (231). Steward, who is highly suspicious of Winnemucca's narrative, contends that the manuscript was so poorly written that Mann had to rewrite it. I have found no evidence to support this claim. Zanjani notes that a letter by Mary Mann in which she comments on Winnemucca's manuscript "definitively settles the issue" (240).

4. Little is known about Satewaller or the reasons for the marriage's termination. Zanjani speculates that he was either a miner or a cowboy (143–44).

5. See Hermann 49.

6. *Carson Morning Appeal* 29 Feb. 1888; the *Humboldt Record* 19 Mar. 1875. Winnemucca was not the only Paiute woman whose "unwomanly" behavior was

covered in the press; as Knack notes in "The Dynamic of Southern Paiute Women's Roles," similar accounts of Southern Paiute women appeared in local newspapers (153). Winnemucca was defended by some reporters: the 23 Nov. 1879 edition of the *San Francisco Chronicle* assures readers that she "has not lost her womanly qualities."

7. Senier demonstrates, however, that Winnemucca's support of allotment is not altogether clear (*Voices* 74–75; 80).

8. See L. Scott for more details of the rift that developed between the followers of Winnemucca and Captain John. She claims that much of the historical record of the Paiutes is incorrect because historians got their information from the followers of Winnemucca or Natches rather than those of Captain John, another Paiute leader (16). Scott also claims that Chief Winnemucca and Natches once helped soldiers kill several Paiutes who were accused of stealing their horses (32–33) and that Sarah's father, in hopes that she would become an "Indian Princess," sent her to school and tried to limit her time with the Paiutes. As a result, Scott contends, Winnemucca had problems with other Paiutes when she returned (45). It is difficult to verify the family's historical importance since the name "Winnemucca" has become a status symbol in Paiute communities (see L. Scott 136n55). According to Bryant and Bryant, Sarah promoted the image of her father as chief because she realized that the whites wanted to deal with only a few leaders (241), even though leadership in Paiute communities did not tend to be fixed on one particular individual; see Knack and Stewart 27–28; 52–54. It is obviously challenging to disentangle Paiutes' actual leadership from that which the whites understood. The Paiutes likely performed and transformed their leadership in various ways in their negotiations with whites.

9. See Moraga; Alarcón.

10. Elizabeth Peabody had invaluable connections to the publishing industry. She published antislavery tracts, children's literature, and Transcendentalist writing (including the *Dial* for a short period). She and her sister, Mary, had close connections to Henry David Thoreau, Margaret Fuller, Ralph Waldo Emerson, and Nathaniel Hawthorne (their brother-in-law). Mary also published works on educational reform (most famously, a biography and literary collection of the works of her husband, Horace Mann); temperance; and Christianity. For a recent study of the sisters, see Marshall.

11. *Silver State* 9 July 1886.

12. In *Autobiographics*, Gilmore offers a reading of autobiography that also helps bridge these differing accounts of agency: "The autobiographical subject is a representation and its representation is its construction. The autobiographical subject is produced not by experience but by autobiography. This specification does not diminish the autobiographer; rather, it situates her or him as an agent of autobiographical production" (25). Focusing on colonized writers, S. Smith and Watson note that in using conventional forms such as the autobiography, writers can assert their subjecthood: "To enter into language is to press back against total inscription in dominating structures" (xix).

13. In some cases, Brown demonstrates, that "property" is a person; Topsy of *Uncle Tom's Cabin* is represented as an object that should be owned and cherished rather than exchanged. Topsy's own selfhood is never entirely acknowledged.

14. See C. Carpenter; Strange for a discussion of Truckee's reconstruction of the story and its other versions. For another account of similar origin stories that explain the arrival of the whites, see Ruoff, "Reversing the Gaze."

15. *Humboldt Register* 22 June 1872.

16. Indeed, Mann's footnote describes the "refinements and manners" of the Paiutes as "worthy the imitation of the whites" (51).

17. In her discussion of Harriet Jacobs's *Incidents in the Life of a Slave Girl*, Nelson claims that Jacobs asserts her virtue through her affair with a white man (136). One could argue that both Winnemucca and Jacobs affirm their virtue through actions that are typically defined as unwomanly: Jacobs through a sexual liaison, and Winnemucca through violence. In turn, both narratives reveal the hypocrisy of "true womanhood," particularly for women of color.

18. This serves as a corollary to A. Smith's *Conquest*, which describes how white men as perpetrators of sexual violence are ironically figured as Native American women's "protectors" (23).

19. *Silver State* 9 July 1886.

20. *Silver State* 5 Dec. 1883.

21. Unless otherwise indicated, this quotation and those that follow come from Harriet Brady, personal interview, 13 Apr. 2001.

22. Although Winnemucca is frequently referred to as the first American Indian woman to publish a book, she was preceded by Laah Ceil Manatoi Elaah Tubbee (Delaware-Mohawk).

23. Harriet Brady, e-mail to the author, 24 Aug. 2006.

24. Harriet Brady, e-mail to the author, 24 Aug. 2006.

25. Ben Aleck, personal interview, 13 Apr. 2001.

26. Ralph Burns, personal interview, 29 Aug. 2006.

27. Harriet Brady, e-mail to the author, 25 Mar. 2002.

28. Georgia Hedrick, personal interview, 13 Apr. 2001.

29. Harriet Brady, e-mail to the author, 25 Mar. 2002.

30. Harriet Brady, e-mail to the author, 24 Aug. 2006.

31. Louise Tannheimer, personal interview, 22 Apr. 2001.

32. Harriet Brady, e-mail to the author, 25 Aug. 2006.

CONCLUSION

1. Tatonetti cautions us against assuming a cause-effect relationship between the Ghost Dance and Wounded Knee. As she writes, "Historians most often recognize at least two such Ghost Dance religions: the 1870 Ghost Dance and the better-known 1890 Ghost Dance that the Lakotas adopted in the months before the Wounded Knee massacre. Both of these movements originated among the Paiute on the Walker River Reservation in Nevada where two different Paiute healers—Wodziwob (Fish Lake Joe, died c. 1920) in the late 1860s and Wovoka (Jack Wilson, c. 1858–1932) in 1889—had visions in which they were instructed to bring dance ceremonies back to their people. The 1890 Ghost Dance has attracted a great deal more attention than the 1870 movement. While this dearth of critical notice may be due, in part, to the lack of documentation surrounding the 1870 dances, it is also undoubtedly connected to the false melding of the 1890 Ghost Dance and the Wounded Knee massacre" (27).

2. See *Humboldt Register* 22 June 1872.

3. For further analysis of the Society of American Indians, see Warrior (*Tribal Secrets*); Maddox.

4. *American Indian Magazine* 3.2 Apr.–June 1915: 97.

5. Arthur Parker (Gawasa Wanneh), "The American Indian as a Warrior," *American Indian Magazine* 1 Jan.–Mar. 1916: 25–27.

6. Arthur C. Parker, "Certain Important Elements of the Indian Problem," *Quarterly Journal of the Society of American Indians* 2 Jan.–Mar. 1915: 24–38. See Maddox 97–98 for further discussion of this essay.

7. I do not mean to suggest that all American Indians agreed on resistance goals or tactics; scholars like P. Smith and Warrior have shown how organizations like AIM were, and remain, controversial in Native communities. The non-Native constructions of internal frictions, however, tended to be stereotypical accounts of Native Americans that served the status quo rather than accurate assessments of the complex positions that existed in these communities. See also Wilkinson's *Blood Struggle: The Rise of Modern Indian Nations*.

8. In a more current example of Native Americans rendered "hostile," Sergeant Eli Painted Crow (Yaqui) was recently horrified to discover while on service in Iraq that enemy territory is still referred to as "Indian Country." As she says, "Well, they referred to—what they said in the briefing, they called enemy territory 'Indian country.' And I'm standing there, just listening to this briefing, and I'm just in shock that after all this time, after so many Natives have served and are serving and are dying, that we are still the enemy, even if we're wearing the same uniform. That was very shocking for me to hear." See "The Private War of Women Soldiers: Female Vet, Soldier Speak Out on Rising Sexual Assault Within US Military," 8 March 2007, *Democracy Now*, 6 April 2007. http://www.democracynow.org/article.pl?sid=07/03/08/1443232&mode=thread&tid =25>

9. As I've learned, the best teaching ideas are often borrowed. I thank Amelia Katanski and P. Jane Hafen, respectively, for these.

10. Miranda made this comment in the discussion following the roundtable "Generations: A Roundtable Discussion of Teaching American Indian Literatures and American Indian Studies" at the Native American Literature Symposium (Mt. Pleasant, Michigan) in April of 2006. In an e-mail message to the author on 9 May 2007, she added, "I am often glad for 'white anger' about 'red history' as my more resistant white students will often be more responsive to anger that comes from an authoritative non-native source. That kind of anger can be a foot in the door for discussion, whereas my own anger, or Indian anger in general, is often swept aside as either self-serving or otherwise blinded by self-interest."

11. More recently, in comparing it to his new novel *Flight*, Alexie describes *Indian Killer* as a book "about interracial violence and murder.... I got so much into the characters and their justifications for their violence that the book almost becomes a justification for violence. And so that's always disturbed me. So I think *Flight* is much closer to the way I actually feel—my own politics regarding violence and war." Euan Kerr, "Sherman Alexie Takes a Swipe at Violence," Minnesota Public Radio 8 May 2007, 10 May 2007. <http://minnesota.publicradio.org/display/web/2007/05/08/alexie/>

Bibliography

Alarcón, Norma. "Chicana's Feminist Literature: A Re-Vision through Malintzin/or Malintzin: Putting Flesh Back on the Object." *This Bridge Called My Back: Writings by Radical Women of Color*. Ed. Cherríe Moraga and Gloria Anzaldúa. 2nd ed. New York: Kitchen Table, 1983. 182–90.

Alcott, William Andrus. *The Physiology of Marriage*. 1856. Boston: Jewett, 1859.

Alexie, Sherman. *Flight*. New York: Grove/Atlantic, 2007.

———. *Indian Killer*. New York: Warner, 1998.

———. *The Lone Ranger and Tonto Fistfight in Heaven*. 1993. New York: Atlantic Monthly, 1994.

Alexiou, Margaret. *The Ritual Lament in Greek Tradition*. Cambridge, UK: Cambridge University Press, 1974.

Alfred, Taiaiake. *Peace, Power, Righteousness: An Indigenous Manifesto*. New York: Oxford University Press, 1999.

Allen, Paula Gunn. "Angry Women Are Building: Issues and Struggles Facing American Indian Women Today." *Reconstructing Gender: A Multicultural Anthology*. Ed. Estelle Disch. 2nd ed. Mountain View, CA: Mayfield, 1997. 41–45.

The American Lady's Medical Pocket-Book and Nursery-Adviser. Philadelphia: Kay, 1833.

Anzaldúa, Gloria. *Borderlands / La Frontera: The New Mestiza*. 2nd ed. San Francisco: Spinsters/Aunt Lute, 1999.

Apess, William. "Eulogy on King Philip." 1836. *On Our Own Ground: The Complete Writings of William Apess, a Pequot*. Ed. Barry O'Connell. Amherst: University of Massachusetts Press, 1992. 275–310.

Atwood, Margaret, ed. *The New Oxford Book of Canadian Verse in English*. Toronto: Oxford University Press, 1982.

Averill, James R. *Anger and Aggression: An Essay on Emotion*. Ed. Robert F. Kidd. New York: Springer-Verlag, 1982.

Bain, Alexander. *The Emotions and the Will*. London: Parker, 1859.

Bank, Rosemarie K. *Theatre Culture in America, 1825–1860*. Cambridge, UK: Cambridge University Press, 1997.

Bataille, Gretchen M. and Kathleen Mullen Sands. 1984. *American Indian Women, Tell-*

ing Their Lives. Lincoln: University of Nebraska Press, 1987.

Batker, Carol. "'Overcoming All Obstacles': The Assimilation Debate in Native American Women's Journalism of the Dawes Era." *Early Native American Writing: New Critical Essays.* Ed. Helen Jaskoski. Cambridge, UK: Cambridge University Press, 1996. 190–203.

Baylor, Tim. "Media Framing of Movement Protest: The Case of American Indian Protest." *Social Science Journal* 33.3 (July 1996): 241–56.

Bederman, Gail. *Manliness and Civilization: A Cultural History of Gender and Race in the United States, 1880–1917.* Chicago: University of Chicago Press, 1995.

Benhabib, Seyla. *Situating the Self: Gender, Community, and Postmodernism in Contemporary Ethics.* New York: Routledge, 1992.

Bennett, Paula Bernat. *Poets in the Public Sphere: The Emancipatory Project of American Women's Poetry, 1800–1900.* Princeton, NJ: Princeton University Press, 2003.

Bergstrom, Bill. "Nurses Bear Brunt of Hospital Problems." *Ann Arbor News* 7 May 2001: A1.

Berkhofer, Robert F., Jr. *The White Man's Indian: Images of the American Indian, from Columbus to the Present.* 1978. New York: Random, 1979.

Berlant, Lauren Gail. "The Female Complaint." *Social Text* 19–20 (1988): 237–59.

Bernardin, Susan K. "Mixed Messages: Authority and Authorship in Mourning Dove's *Cogewea, The Half-Blood: A Depiction of the Great Montana Cattle Range.*" *American Literature* 67.3 (1995): 487–509.

Bhabha, Homi K. "Of Mimicry and Man: The Ambivalence of Colonial Discourse." *Modern Literary Theory: A Reader.* Ed. Philip Rice and Patricia Waugh. 4th ed. London: Arnold, 1996. 380–87.

Black Hawk: An Autobiography. Ed. Donald Jackson. Urbana: University of Illinois Press, 1964.

Blaeser, Kimberly M. "Native Literature: Seeking a Critical Center." *Looking at the Words of Our People: First Nations Analysis of Literature.* Ed. Jeannette Armstrong. Penticton, BC: Theytus, 1993. 51–62.

Bliss, William White. *Woman, and Her Thirty-Years' Pilgrimage.* New York: American News Company, 1869.

Bolte, Angela. "The Outcast Outlaw: Incorporating Rage into an Account of the Emotions." *APA Newsletter* 98.1 (1998): 1–7. 26 Jan. 2004. <http:///www.apa.udel.edu/apa/archive/newsletter/v98n1/feminism/bolte-asp>

Bomberry, Victoria. "Blood, Rebellion, and Motherhood in the Political Imagination of Indigenous People." *Reading Native American Women: Critical/ Creative Representations.* Ed. Inés Hernández-Avila. Lanham, MD: AltaMira, 2004. 21–38.

Bourke, Angela. "Performing, Not Writing: The Reception of an Irish Woman's Lament." *Dwelling in Possibility: Women Poets and Critics on Poetry.* Ed. Yopie Prins and Maeera Shreiber. Ithaca: Cornell University Press, 1997. 132–46.

Brodhead, Richard H. *Cultures of Letters: Scenes of Reading and Writing in Nineteenth-Century America.* 1993. Chicago: University of Chicago Press, 1994.

Brown, Dee. *Bury My Heart at Wounded Knee.* New York: Holt, 1971.

Brown, Gillian. *Domestic Individualism: Imagining Self in Nineteenth-Century America.* 1990. Berkeley: University of California Press, 1992.

Browning, Elizabeth Barrett. *Aurora Leigh and Other Poems.* 1856. London: Penguin, 1995.

Bibliography

Brumble, David H., III. *American Indian Autobiography*. Berkeley: University of California Press, 1988.
Bryant, Shelle C. Wilson and Patrick W. Bryant. "Sarah Winnemucca Hopkins (1844–1891)." *Nineteenth-Century American Women Writers: A Bio-Bibliographical Critical Sourcebook*. Ed. Denise D. Knight. Westport, CT: Greenwood, 1997. 241–46.
Burack, Cynthia. *The Problem of the Passions: Feminism, Psychoanalysis, and Social Theory*. New York: New York University Press, 1994.
Butler, Judith P. and Joan W. Scott, ed. *Feminists Theorize the Political*. New York: Routledge, 1992.
Callahan, S. Alice. *Wynema: A Child of the Forest*. 1891. Ed. and Introd. A. LaVonne Brown Ruoff. Lincoln: University of Nebraska Press, 1997.
Canby, William C. *American Indian Law in a Nutshell*. 4th ed. St. Paul: West, 1998.
Canfield, Gae Whitney. *Sarah Winnemucca of the Northern Paiutes*. Norman: University of Oklahoma Press, 1983.
Carpenter, Cari M. "Sarah Winnemucca and the Re-Writing of Nation." *Racially Writing the Republic: Racists, Race Rebels, and Transformations of American Identity*. Ed. Bruce Baum and Duchess Harris. Durham, NC: Duke University Press (forthcoming).
Carpenter, Dave. "'Pump Rage' in Full Swing." *Ann Arbor News* 8 May 2001: A1; A12.
Champagne, Duane. *Social Change and Cultural Continuity Among Native Nations*. Lanham, MD: AltaMira Press, 2007.
Chapman, Mary and Glenn Hendler, eds. *Sentimental Men: Masculinity and the Politics of Affect in American Culture*. Berkeley: University of California Press, 1999.
Charlesworth, Hector. *Candid Chronicles*. Toronto: Macmillan, 1925.
Child, Lydia Maria Francis. "An Appeal for the Indians." *Hobomok and Other Writings on Indians*. 1868. Ed. Carolyn L. Karcher. New Brunswick, NJ: Rutgers University Press, 1998. 216–32.
———. *Hobomok and Other Writings on Indians*. 1824. Ed. Carolyn L. Karcher. New Brunswick, NJ: Rutgers University Press, 1998.
Colbert, Charles. *A Measure of Perfection: Phrenology and the Fine Arts in America*. Chapel Hill: University of North Carolina Press, 1997.
Combe, George. *The Constitution of Man Considered in Relation to External Objects*. 1828. New York: Pearson, 1835.
———. *A System of Phrenology*. 4th ed. Edinburgh: Maclachlan and Stewart, 1836.
Cook-Lynn, Elizabeth. *Why I Can't Read Wallace Stegner and Other Essays: A Tribal Voice*. Madison: University of Wisconsin Press, 1996.
Cox, James H. *Muting White Noise: Native American and European American Novel Traditions*. Norman: University of Oklahoma Press, 2006.
Crow Dog, Mary and Richard Erdoes. *Lakota Woman*. 1990. New York: Harper, 1991.
Dahlberg, Tim. "It's All the Rage." *Ann Arbor News* 3 June 2001: D3.
Davitz, Joel Robert. *The Language of Emotion. Personality and Psychopathology*. V. 6. New York: Academic, 1969.
Debo, Angie. *The Road to Disappearance*. Norman: University of Oklahoma Press, 1941.
Deloria, Philip J. *Playing Indian*. New Haven: Yale University Press, 1998.
Deloria, Vine Jr. and Clifford M. Lytle. *American Indians, American Justice*. Austin: University of Texas Press, 1983.

Bibliography

———. *The Nations Within: The Past and Future of American Indian Sovereignty.* 1984. Austin: University of Texas Press, 1998.

Dirlik, Arif. *Postmodernity's Histories: The Past as Legacy and Project.* Lanham, MD: Rowman and Littlefield, 2000.

Douglas, Ann. *The Feminization of American Culture.* New York: Knopf, 1977.

Drake, Francis S. 1884. *Tea Leaves: Being a Collection of Letters and Documents Relating to the Shipment of Tea to the American Colonies in the Year 1773, by the East India Tea Company.* Detroit: Singing Tree, 1970.

Drinnon, Richard. *Facing West: The Metaphysics of Indian-Hating and Empire-Building.* 1980. Norman: University of Oklahoma Press, 1997.

Eastman, Charles (Ohiyesa). *From the Deep Woods to Civilization.* 1916. Mineola, NY: Dover, 2003.

The Etiquette for Ladies; with Hints on the Preservation, Improvement, and Display of Female Beauty. Philadelphia: Lea and Blanchard, 1841.

Evans, Chad. *Frontier Theatre: A History of Nineteenth-Century Theatrical Entertainment in the Canadian Far West and Alaska.* Victoria, BC: Sono Nis, 1983.

Feeney, Mary K. "Venting Online: The Angry Weave a Web of Rage." *Ann Arbor News* 20 Aug. 2000: C1–C2.

Fiedler, Leslie A. *The Return of the Vanishing American.* New York: Stein and Day, 1968.

Fisher, Philip A. *Hard Facts: Setting and Form in the American Novel.* New York: Oxford University Press, 1985.

Fliegelman, Jay. *Prodigals and Pilgrims: The American Revolution against Patriarchal Authority, 1750–1800.* Cambridge, UK: Cambridge University Press, 1982.

Foreman, Grant. *Muscogee: The Biography of an Oklahoma Town.* St. Louis: n.p., 1945.

Foster, Mrs. W. Garland. *The Mohawk Princess: Being Some Account of the Life of Tekahionwake (E. Pauline Johnson).* Vancouver: Lions' Gate, 1931.

Fowler, Catherine S. "Foreword." *Life Among the Piutes: Their Wrongs and Claims.* 1883. Vintage West. Reno: University of Nevada Press, 1994. 3–4.

———. "Sarah Winnemucca, Northern Paiute, ca. 1844–1891." *American Indian Intellectuals of the Nineteenth and Early Twentieth Centuries.* 1976. Ed. Margot Liberty. Norman: Red River/University of Oklahoma Press, 2002. 38–50.

Fowler, O. S. *Practical Phrenology.* New York: Fowlers and Wells, 1849.

Fowler, O. S. and L. N. *Phrenological Almanac and Physiological Guide for the Year of Our Lord 1845: Self-Knowledge is the Summary of All Knowledge.* New York: O.S. Fowler, 1845.

Fraser, Joelle. "An Interview with Sherman Alexie." *The Iowa Review* 30.3 (2000): 59–70.

Frye, Marilyn. *The Politics of Reality: Essays in Feminist Theory.* Berkeley: Crossing, 1983.

Georgi-Findlay, Brigitte. "The Frontiers of Native American Women's Writing: Sarah Winnemucca's *Life Among the Piutes.*" *New Voices in Native American Literary Criticism.* Ed. Arnold Krupat. Smithsonian, 1993. 222–52.

Gerson, Carole. "Anthologies and the Canon of Early Canadian Women Writers." *Re(Dis)covering Our Foremothers: Nineteenth-Century Canadian Women Writers.* Ed. Lorraine McMullen. Ottawa: University of Ottawa Press, 1989. 55–76.

Gerson, Carole and Veronica Strong-Boag. *E. Pauline Johnson, Tekahionwake: Collected*

Bibliography

Poems and Selected Prose. Toronto: University of Toronto Press, 2002.

Gilbert, Sandra M., and Susan Gubar. *The Madwoman in the Attic: The Woman Writer and the Nineteenth-Century Literary Imagination.* New Haven: Yale University Press, 1979.

Gilmore, Leigh. *Autobiographics: A Feminist Theory of Women's Self-Representation.* Ithaca: Cornell University Press, 1994.

Ginzberg, Lori D. *Women and the Work of Benevolence: Morality, Politics, and Class in the Nineteenth-Century United States.* New Haven: Yale University Press, 1990.

Graham, Sylvester. *Lectures on the Science of Human Life.* London: Horsell, 1854.

Grasso, Linda M. *The Artistry of Anger: Black and White Women's Literature in America, 1820–1860.* Chapel Hill: University of North Carolina Press, 2002.

Green, Michael D. *The Creeks.* Indians of North America. General ed. Frank W. Porter. New York: Chelsea, 1990.

———. *The Politics of Indian Removal: Creek Government and Society in Crisis.* Lincoln: University of Nebraska Press, 1982.

Green, Rayna. "The Tribe Called Wannabee: Playing Indian in America and Europe." *Folklore* 99.1 (1988): 30–55.

Gustafson, Sandra M. *Eloquence is Power: Oratory and Performance in Early America.* Chapel Hill: University of North Carolina Press, 2000.

Hagan, William T. *The Indian Rights Association: The Herbert Welsh Years, 1882–1904.* Tucson: University of Arizona Press, 1985.

Hale, Horatio. "Chief George H.M. Johnson—Onwanonsyshon: His Life and Work Among the Six Nations." *Magazine of American History* February 1885: 131–42.

Hales, Dianne and Robert E. Hales. "Is Work Driving You Mad?" *Parade Magazine* 18 March 2001: 8–9.

Hardy, J. P., ed. *The Political Writings of Dr. Johnson; a Selection.* New York: Barnes and Noble, 1968.

Harjo, Joy. *In Mad Love and War.* Middletown, CT: Wesleyan University Press, 1990.

Harnar, Nellie Shaw. *The History of the Pyramid Lake Indians, 1843–1959, and Early Tribal History, 1825–1834.* Sparks, Nevada: Dave's Printing and Publishing, 1974.

Heilbrun, Carolyn G. *Writing a Woman's Life.* New York: Norton, 1988.

Hendler, Glenn. "Bloated Body and Sober Sentiments: Masculinity in 1840s Temperance Narratives." *Sentimental Men: Masculinity and the Politics of Affect in American Culture.* Ed. Mary Chapman and Glenn Hendler. Berkeley: University of California Press, 1999. 125–48.

Hermann, Ruth. *The Paiutes of Pyramid Lake: A Narrative Concerning a Western Nevada Indian Tribe.* San Jose, CA: Harlan-Young, 1972.

Hewitt, Barnard Wolcott. *Theatre U.S.A., 1665 to 1957.* New York: McGraw-Hill, 1959.

Hopkins, Sarah Winnemucca. *Life Among the Piutes: Their Wrongs and Claims.* 1883. Reno: University of Nevada Press, 1994.

Howard, June. *Publishing the Family.* Durham, NC: Duke University Press, 2001.

Howard, Oliver Otis. *Famous Indian Chiefs I Have Known.* New York: Century, 1912.

Hubbard, William and Samuel Gardner Drake. *The History of the Indian Wars in New England from the First Settlement to the Termination of the War with King Philip, in 1677.* 1677. Roxbury, MA: Woodward, 1865.

Bibliography

Huhndorf, Shari M. *Going Native: Indians in the American Cultural Imagination*. Ithaca: Cornell University Press, 2001.

Hutcheon, Linda. *Irony's Edge: The Theory and Politics of Irony*. London: Routledge, 1994.

Inter-Tribal Council of Nevada. *Numa: A Northern Paiute History*. Salt Lake City: University of Utah Printing Service, 1976.

Jack, Dana Crowley. *Behind the Mask: Destruction and Creativity in Women's Aggression*. Cambridge: Harvard University Press, 1999.

Jacobs, Harriet A. *Incidents in the Life of a Slave Girl*. 1860. Ed. Jean Fagan Yellin. Cambridge: Harvard University Press, 1987.

Jaggar, Alison M. "Love and Knowledge: Emotion in Feminist Epistemology." *Gender/Body/Knowledge: Feminist Reconstructions of Being and Knowing*. Ed. Alison M. Jaggar and Susan R. Bordo. New Brunswick, NJ: Rutgers University Press, 1989. 145–71.

Jahoda, Gustav. *Images of Savages: Ancient Roots of Modern Prejudice in Western Culture*. London: Routledge, 1999.

James, Edward T., Janet Wilson James, and Paul Boyer, ed. *Notable American Women, 1607–1950: a Biographical Dictionary*. V. 3 (P–Z). Cambridge: Harvard University Press, 1971.

Johnson, E. Pauline. "As It Was in the Beginning." *The Moccasin Maker*. 1913. Ed. A. LaVonne Brown Ruoff. Tucson: University of Arizona Press, 1987. 144–56.

———. "The Avenger." *Saturday Night* Christmas no. 1892: 15.

———. *Canadian Born*. Toronto: Morang, 1903.

———. "The Cattle Thief." 1894. *Flint and Feather*. Toronto: Musson, 1931. 12–16.

———. "A Cry From an Indian Wife." *Flint and Feather*. Toronto: Musson, 1931. 17–19.

———. *Flint and Feather*. 1912. Toronto: Musson, 1931.

———. "From the Child's Viewpoint." *Mother's Magazine* May; June 1910: 30–31; 60–62.

———. "From the Country of the Cree." *Our Animal Friends* Sept. 1895: 14.

———. "The Great New Year White Dog: Sacrifice of the Onondagas." *Daily Province Magazine* 14 Jan. 1911: 16.

———. "Her Dominion—A Story of 1867, and Canada's Confederation." *Mother's Magazine* July 1907: 10–11; 40.

———. "Heroic Indian Mothers." *Mother's Magazine* Sept. 1908: 23–24.

———. "The Legend of Lillooet Falls." *Mother's Magazine* January 1912: 19; 45.

———. *Legends of Vancouver*. Toronto: McClelland, 1911.

———. "The Lodge of the Law-Makers." *Daily Express* 14 Aug. 1906: 4.

———. *The Moccasin Maker*. 1913. Ed. A. LaVonne Brown Ruoff. Tucson: University of Arizona Press, 1987.

———. "Ojistoh." *Flint and Feather*. 1912. Toronto: Musson, 1931. 3–5.

———. "Outdoor Occupations of the Indian Mother and Her Children." *Mother's Magazine* July 1908: 22–23.

———. "Outdoor Pastimes for Women." *Outing* May 1892: 40.

———. "Outdoor Pastimes for Women." *Outing* Apr. 1893: 21.

———. "A Red Girl's Reasoning." 1893. *The Moccasin Maker*. 1913. Ed. A. LaVonne Brown Ruoff. Tucson: University of Arizona Press, 1987. 102–26.

———. *The Shagganappi*. Toronto: Briggs, 1913.

Bibliography

———. "The Six Nations." *Brantford Expositor* 1895: souvenir number.
———. "A Strong Race Opinion: On the Indian Girl in Modern Fiction." *Sunday Globe* 22 May 1892: 1.
———. *"When George Was King" and Other Poems*. Brockville, Ont.: Brockville Times, 1908.
———. *The White Wampum*. London: Lane, 1895.
———. "Winter Indoor Life of the Indian Mother and Children." *Mother's Magazine* Feb. 1908: 5; 42.
Johnson, Troy R., Joane Nagel, and Duane Champagne. *American Indian Activism: Alcatraz to the Longest Walk*. Urbana: University of Illinois Press, 1997.
Johnston, C. M. *Brant County: A History 1784–1945*. Toronto: Oxford University Press, 1967.
Johnston, Sheila M. F. *Buckskin & Broadcloth: A Celebration of E. Pauline Johnson—Tekahionwake 1861–1913*. Toronto: Natural Heritage, 1997.
Juno, Andrea et al. *Angry Women*. San Francisco: RE/Search, 1991.
Justice, Daniel. *Our Fire Survives the Storm: A Cherokee Literary History*. Minneapolis: University of Minnesota Press, 2006.
Kaplan, Amy. "Manifest Domesticity." *American Literature* 70.3 (1998): 581–606.
Karcher, Carolyn L. *A Lydia Maria Child Reader*. Durham, NC: Duke University Press, 1997.
Kasson, John F. *Rudeness and Civility: Manners in Nineteenth-Century Urban America*. New York: Hill and Wang, 1990.
Keller, Betty. *Pauline: A Biography of Pauline Johnson*. Vancouver: Douglas and McIntyre, 1981.
Kelsey, Penelope. "Natives, Nation, Narration: Reading Roanoke in the American Renaissance." *ESQ* 49.1–3 (2003): 149–60.
Kilcup, Karen L. *A Cherokee Woman's America: Memoirs of Narcissa Owen, 1831–1907*. Gainesville: University Press of Florida, 2005.
Klages, Mary. *Woeful Afflictions: Disability and Sentimentality in Victorian America*. Philadelphia: University of Pennsylvania Press, 1999.
Knack, Martha C. "The Dynamics of Southern Paiute Women's Roles." *Women and Power in Native North America*. Ed. Laura F. Klein and Lillian A. Ackerman. Norman: University of Oklahoma Press, 1995. 146–58.
Knack, Martha C. and Omer Call Stewart. *As Long as the River Shall Run: An Ethnohistory of Pyramid Lake Indian Reservation*. Berkeley: University of California Press, 1984.
Konkle, Maureen. *Writing Indian Nations: Native Intellectuals and the Politics of Historiography, 1827–1863*. Chapel Hill: University of North Carolina Press, 2004.
Kring, Ann M. "Gender and Anger." *Gender and Emotion: Social Psychological Perspectives*. Ed. Agneta H. Fischer. Cambridge, UK: Cambridge University Press, 2000. 211–31.
Krupat, Arnold. *For Those Who Come After: A Study of Native American Autobiography*. Berkeley: University of California Press, 1985.
———, ed. *Native American Autobiography: An Anthology*. Madison: University of Wisconsin Press, 1994.
Lape, Noreen Groover. "'I would rather be with my people, but not to live with them as they live': Cultural Liminality and Double Consciousness in Sarah Winnemucca

Bibliography

Hopkins's *Life Among the Piutes: Their Wrongs and Claims*." *American Indian Quarterly* 22.3 (1998): 259–79.

———. *West of the Border: The Multicultural Literature of the Western American Frontiers*. Athens: Ohio University Press, 2000.

Lashgari, Deirdre. *Violence, Silence, and Anger: Women's Writing as Transgression*. Charlottesville: University Press of Virginia, 1995.

Leslie, Eliza. *Miss Leslie's Behaviour Book: A Guide and Manual for Ladies*. 1853. Philadelphia: Peterson, 1859.

Lighthall, W. D. *Songs of the Great Dominion: Voices from the Forests and Waters, the Settlements and Cities of Canada*. London: Scott, 1889.

de l'Isère, Colombat. *A Treatise on the Diseases and Special Hygiene of Females*. 1845. Philadelphia: Lea and Blanchard, 1849.

Lorde, Audre. *Sister Outsider: Essays and Speeches*. Berkeley: Crossing, 1984.

Lott, Eric. *Love and Theft: Blackface Minstrelsy and the American Working Class*. New York: Oxford University Press, 1993.

Lutz, Catherine. *Unnatural Emotions: Everyday Sentiments on a Micronesian Atoll and Their Challenge to Western Theory*. Chicago: University of Chicago Press, 1988.

MacEwan, Grant. *. . . And Mighty Women Too: Stories of Notable Western Canadian Women*. Saskatoon, Saskatchewan: Western Producer Prairie, 1975.

Macpherson, C. B. *The Political Theory of Possessive Individualism: Hobbes to Locke*. Oxford: Clarendon, 1962.

Maddox, Lucy. *Citizen Indians: Native American Intellectuals, Race, and Reform*. Ithaca: Cornell University Press, 2005.

"Madness." *Oxford English Dictionary*. Ed. J.A. Simpson and E.S.C. Weiner. 2nd ed. Vol. 9. Oxford: Clarendon, 1989. 177.

Mair, Charles. "An Appreciation." *The Moccasin Maker*. Toronto: Briggs, 1913. 9–19.

Mann, Mary Elizabeth. Preface. *Life Among the Piutes: Their Wrongs and Claims*. By Sarah Winnemucca Hopkins. 1883. Reno: University of Nevada Press, 1994. 2.

Mardock, Robert Winston. *The Reformers and the American Indian*. Columbia: University of Missouri Press, 1971.

Marshall, Megan. *The Peabody Sisters: Three Women Who Ignited American Romanticism*. New York: Houghton, 2005.

Martin, Joel W. *Sacred Revolt: The Muskogees' Struggle for a New World*. Boston: Beacon, 1991.

Mathes, Valerie Sherer. "Nineteenth Century Women and Reform: The Women's National Indian Association." *American Indian Quarterly* 14.1 (1990): 1–18.

McClung, Nellie L. *The Stream Runs Fast; My Own Story*. 1945. Toronto: Allen, 1965.

McFall, Lynne. "What's Wrong with Bitterness?" *Feminist Ethics*. Ed. Claudia Card. Lawrence: University Press of Kansas, 1991. 146–60.

McRaye, Walter. *Pauline Johnson and Her Friends*. Toronto: Ryerson, 1947.

Merish, Lori. *Sentimental Materialism: Gender, Commodity Culture, and Nineteenth-Century American Literature*. Durham: Duke University Press, 2000.

Meyers, Diana Tietjens. "Emotion and Heterodox Emotional Perception: An Essay in Moral Social Psychology." *Feminists Rethink the Self*. Ed. Diana Tietjens Meyers. Boulder, CO: Westview, 1997. 197–218.

Mihesuah, Devon Abbott. *Indigenous American Women: Decolonization, Empowerment, Activism*. Lincoln: University of Nebraska Press, 2003.

Bibliography

Mills, Charles W. *The Racial Contract*. Ithaca: Cornell University Press, 1997.
Moody, Joycelyn. *Sentimental Confessions: Spiritual Narratives of Nineteenth-Century African American Women*. Athens: University of Georgia Press, 2001.
Moraga, Cherríe. "From a Long Line of Vendidas: Chicanas and Feminism." 1986. *Theorizing Feminism: Parallel Trends in the Humanities and Social Sciences*. Ed. Anne C. Herrmann and Abigail J. Stewart. 2nd ed. Boulder: Westview, 2001. 38–55.
Morgan, Lewis Henry. *League of the Iroquois*. 1851. Secaucus, NJ: Citadel, 1996.
Morton, Samuel George and George Combe. *Crania Americana; or, a Comparative View of the Skulls of Various Aboriginal Nations of North and South America*. Philadelphia: Dobson, 1839.
Morton, Thomas. *New English Canaan*. 1637. *The Heath Anthology of American Literature*. Ed. Paul Lauter. 5th ed. Vol. A. Boston: Houghton, 2006. 296–307.
Murray, David. *Forked Tongues: Speech, Writing and Representation in North American Indian Texts*. London: Pinter, 1991.
Nelson, Dana D. *The Word in Black and White: Reading "Race" in American Literature, 1638–1867*. New York: Oxford University Press, 1992.
New American Standard Bible. Nashville, TN: Thomas Nelson, 1977.
Newman, Louise Michele. *White Women's Rights: The Racial Origins of Feminism in the United States*. New York: Oxford University Press, 1999.
Nissenbaum, Stephen. *Sex, Diet, and Debility in Jacksonian America: Sylvester Graham and Health Reform*. Westport, CT: Greenwood, 1980.
Owens, Louis. *Other Destinies: Understanding the American Indian Novel*. Norman: University of Oklahoma Press, 1992.
Parker, Gilbert. *The Translation of a Savage*. New York: Appleton, 1893.
Parkes, Mrs. William. *Domestic Duties; or, Instructions to Young Married Ladies, on the Management of Their Households, and the Regulation of Their Conduct in the Various Relations and Duties of Married Life*. New York: Harper, 1828.
The Passionate Child. Mother's Series. New York: McLoughlin, n.d.
Peabody, Elizabeth P. *Sarah Winnemucca's Practical Solution of the Indian Problem*. Cambridge, MA: Wilson, 1886.
———. *Second Report of the Model School of Sarah Winnemucca, 1886–87*. Cambridge, MA: Wilson, 1887.
Pearce, Roy Harvey. *Savagism and Civilization: A Study of the Indian and the American Mind*. 1965. Berkeley: University of California Press, 1988.
Pickering, Michael. *Stereotyping: The Politics of Representation*. New York: Palgrave, 2001.
Pinch, Adela. *Strange Fits of Passion: Epistemologies of Emotion, Hume to Austin*. Stanford: Stanford University Press, 1996.
Powell, Malea. "Rhetorics of Survivance: How American Indians Use Writing." *College Composition and Communication* 53.3 (2002): 396–434.
Prucha, Francis Paul. *The Great Father: The United States Government and the American Indians*. Vol. II. Lincoln: University of Nebraska Press, 1984.
Richardson, Kenneth D. "The Disadvantages of Anger." Letter. *The Chronicle of Higher Education* 26 Apr. 2002. 30 July 2003. <http://chronicle.com/weekly/v48/i33/33b02102.htm>
Roediger, David R. *The Wages of Whiteness: Race and the Making of the American Working Class*. Rev. ed. New York: Verso, 2000.

Bibliography

Romero, Lora. "Vanishing Americans: Gender, Empire, and New Historicism." *The Culture of Sentiment.* Ed. Shirley Samuels. Oxford: Oxford University Press, 1995. 115–27.

Rosaldo, Renato. *Culture and Truth: The Remaking of Social Analysis.* Boston: Beacon, 1989.

Ruoff, A. LaVonne Brown. Editor's Introduction. *Wynema: A Child of the Forest.* By S. Alice Callahan. 1891. Ed. A. LaVonne Brown Ruoff. Lincoln: University of Nebraska Press, 1997. xiii–xlviii.

———. "Justice for Indians and Women: The Protest Fiction of Alice Callahan and Pauline Johnson." *World Literature Today* 66.2 (1992): 249–55.

———. "Reversing the Gaze: Early Native American Images of Europeans and Euro-Americans." *Native American Representations: First Encounters, Distorted Images, and Literary Appropriations.* Ed. Gretchen M. Bataille. Lincoln: University of Nebraska Press, 2001. 198–221.

Saddlemyer, Ann. *Early Stages: Essays on the Theatre in Ontario, 1800–1914.* Toronto: University of Toronto Press, 1990.

Salaita, Steven. "Ethnic Identity and Imperative Patriotism: Arab Americans Before and After 9/11." *College Literature* 32.2 (2005): 146–68.

Samuels, Shirley. Introduction. *The Culture of Sentiment: Race, Gender, and Sentimentality in Nineteenth-Century America.* Ed. Shirley Samuels. New York: Oxford University Press, 1992. 3–8.

Sánchez-Eppler, Karen. "Raising Empires like Children: Race, Nation, and Religious Education. *American Literary History* 8.3 (1996): 399–425.

———. *Touching Liberty: Abolition, Feminism, and the Politics of the Body.* 1993. Berkeley: University of California Press, 1997.

Sands, Kathleen M. "Indian Women's Personal Narrative: Voices Past and Present." *American Women's Autobiography: Fea(s)ts of Memory.* Ed. Margo Culley. Madison: University of Wisconsin Press, 1992. 268–94.

Sarah Winnemucca: The Dream Fulfilled. VHS and DVD. Nevada: Department of Cultural Affairs, 2005.

Sarris, Greg. *Keeping Slug Woman Alive: A Holistic Approach to American Indian Texts.* Berkeley: University of California Press, 1993.

Sartre, Jean-Paul. Preface. Trans. Constance Farrington. *The Wretched of the Earth.* By Frantz Fanon. New York: Grove, 1968. 7–31.

Saville-Troike, Muriel. *The Ethnography of Communication: An Introduction.* 1982. 3rd ed. Malden, MA: Blackwell, 2003.

Scheckel, Susan. *The Insistence of the Indian: Race and Nationalism in Nineteenth-Century American Culture.* Princeton, NJ: Princeton University Press, 1998.

Scheman, Naomi. *Engenderings: Constructions of Knowledge, Authority, and Privilege.* New York: Routledge, 1993.

Scott, Jack. "The Passionate Princess." *Maclean's Magazine* 1 Apr. 1952: 12–13; 54–5; 57.

Scott, Lalla. *Karnee: A Paiute Narrative.* Reno: University of Nevada Press, 1966.

Seaver, James E. *A Narrative of the Life of Mrs. Mary Jemison.* 1824. Syracuse: Syracuse University Press, 1990.

Senier, Siobhan. "Allotment Protest and Tribal Discourse: Reading *Wynema*'s Successes and Shortcomings." *American Indian Quarterly* 24.3 (2000): 420–40.

Bibliography

———. *Voices of American Indian Assimilation and Resistance: Helen Hunt Jackson, Sarah Winnemucca, and Victoria Howard*. Norman: University of Oklahoma Press, 2001.

Shields, Stephanie A. *Speaking from the Heart: Gender and the Social Meaning of Emotion*. Cambridge, UK: Cambridge University Press, 2002.

———. "Thinking About Gender, Thinking About Theory: Gender and Emotional Experience." *Gender and Emotion: Social Psychological Perspectives*. Ed. Agneta H. Fischer. Cambridge, UK: Cambridge University Press, 2000. 3–23.

Showalter, Elaine. *The Female Malady: Women, Madness, and English Culture, 1830–1980*. 1985. New York: Penguin, 1987.

Shreiber, Maeera. "'Where Are We Moored?': Adrienne Rich, Women's Mourning, and the Limits of Lament." *Dwelling in Possibility: Women Poets and Critics on Poetry*. Ed. Yopie Prins and Maeera Shreiber. Ithaca, NY: Cornell University Press, 1997. 301–17.

Simpson, Audra. "Paths Toward a Mohawk Nation: Narratives of Citizenship and Nationhood in Kahnawake." *Political Theory and the Rights of Indigenous Peoples*. Ed. Duncan Ivison, Paul Patton, and Will Sanders. Cambridge, UK: Cambridge University Press, 2000. 113–36.

Slotkin, Richard. *Regeneration Through Violence: The Mythology of the American Frontier, 1600–1860*. Middletown, CT: Wesleyan, 1973.

Smith, Andrea. *Conquest: Sexual Violence and American Indian Genocide*. Cambridge, MA: South End, 2005.

Smith, Paul Chaat and Robert Allen Warrior. *Like a Hurricane: The Indian Movement from Alcatraz to Wounded Knee*. New York: New, 1996.

Smith, Sidonie and Julia Watson, eds. *De/Colonizing the Subject: The Politics of Gender in Women's Autobiography*. Minneapolis: University of Minnesota Press, 1992.

Smith-Rosenberg, Carroll. *Disorderly Conduct: Visions of Gender in Victorian America*. 1985. New York: Oxford University Press, 1986.

Sollors, Werner. *Beyond Ethnicity: Consent and Descent in American Culture*. New York: Oxford University Press, 1986.

Sorisio, Carolyn. "'The Reverse of a Mirage': Sarah Winnemucca's Negotiation of Spectacle in the Northeastern United States, 1883–1884." SSAWW Conference. Fort Worth, Texas. 25 Sept. 2003.

Spivak, Gayatri Chakravorty. *In Other Worlds: Essays in Cultural Politics*. New York: Methuen, 1987.

Stearns, Carol Zisowitz and Peter N. Stearns. *Anger: The Struggle for Emotional Control in America's History*. Chicago: University of Chicago Press, 1986.

Stern, Julia A. *The Plight of Feeling: Sympathy and Dissent in the Early American Novel*. Chicago: University of Chicago Press, 1997.

Stern, Madeleine B. *Heads & Headlines: The Phrenological Fowlers*. Norman: University of Oklahoma Press, 1971.

Stevenson, O. J. *A People's Best*. Toronto: Musson, 1927.

Steward, Julian H. and Erminie Wheeler-Voegelin. *The Northern Paiute Indians*. New York: Garland, 1974.

Stowe, Harriet Beecher. *Uncle Tom's Cabin*. 1852. New York: Washington Square, 1964.

Strange, William C. "Story, Take Me Home: Instances of Resonance in Sarah

Bibliography

Winnemucca Hopkins' *Life Among the Piutes.*" *Entering the 90s: The North American Experience: Proceedings from the Native American Studies Conference at Lake Superior State University, October 27–28, 1989.* Ed. Thomas E. Schirer. Sault Ste. Marie, MI: Lake Superior State University Press, 1991. 184–94.

Strong-Boag, Veronica Jane. "'Ever a Crusader': Nellie McClung, First-Wave Feminist." *Rethinking Canada: The Promise of Women's History.* Ed. Veronica Jane Strong-Boag and Anita Clair Fellman. 2nd ed. New Canadian Readings. Toronto: Copp Clark Pitman, 1991. 308–21.

Strong-Boag, Veronica Jane, and Carole Gerson. *Paddling Her Own Canoe: The Times and Texts of E. Pauline Johnson (Tekahionwake).* Toronto: University of Toronto Press, 2000.

Sultan, Nancy. "Private Speech, Public Pain: The Power of Women's Laments in Ancient Greek Poetry and Tragedy." *Rediscovering the Muses: Women's Musical Traditions.* Ed. Kimberly Marshall. Boston: Northeastern University Press, 1993. 92–110.

Takaki, Ronald T. *Violence in the Black Imagination: Essays and Documents.* New York: Putnam, 1972.

Tate, Claudia. *Domestic Allegories of Political Desire: The Black Heroine's Text at the Turn of the Century.* New York: Oxford University Press, 1992.

Tatonetti, Lisa. "Behind the Shadows of Wounded Knee: The Slippage of Imagination in *Wynema: A Child of the Forest. Studies in American Indian Literatures* 16.1 (2004): 1–31.

Tavris, Carol. *Anger: The Misunderstood Emotion.* 1982. Rev. ed. New York: Simon, 1989.

Tompkins, Jane. *Sensational Designs: The Cultural Work of American Fiction, 1790–1860.* New York: Oxford University Press, 1985.

Tracy, Stephen. *The Mother and Her Offspring.* 1853. New York: Harper, 1860.

Tubbee, Okah. *The Life of Okah Tubbee.* Ed. Daniel F. Littlefield. Lincoln: University of Nebraska Press, 1988.

Van Kirk, Sylvia. "The Role of Native Women in the Fur Trade Society of Western Canada, 1670–1830." *Rethinking Canada: The Promise of Women's History.* Ed. Veronica Jane Strong-Boag and Anita Clair Fellman. 2nd ed. Toronto: Copp, 1991. 73–80.

Venuti, Lawrence, ed. *Rethinking Translation: Discourse, Subjectivity, Ideology.* London: Routledge, 1992.

———. *The Translator's Invisibility: A History of Translation.* 1995. London: Routledge, 2002.

Vizenor, Gerald. "Almost Browne." *Landfill Meditations: Crossblood Stories.* Hanover, NH: University Press of New England, 1991. 1–10.

———. *Manifest Manners: Postindian Warriors of Survivance.* Hanover, NH: University Press of New England, 1994.

Wald, Priscilla. *Constituting Americans: Cultural Anxiety and Narrative Form.* Durham: Duke University Press, 1995.

Warrior, Robert. *The People and the Word: Reading Native Nonfiction.* Minneapolis: University of Minnesota Press, 2005.

———. *Tribal Secrets: Recovering American Indian Intellectual Traditions.* 3rd ed. Minneapolis: University of Minnesota Press, 2001.

Washington, Adrienne T. "Look in Rearview Mirror as You Curse Road Rage." *Wash-

ington Times 13 April 2007: B02.
Watts-Dunton, Theodore. Rev. of Pauline Johnson's Poetry. *The Athenaeum* 28 Sept. 1889: 412.
Weaver, Jace. *That the People Might Live: Native American Literatures and Native American Community.* New York: Oxford University Press, 1997.
Weaver, Jace, Craig S. Womack, and Robert Warrior. *American Indian Literary Nationalism.* Albuquerque: University of New Mexico Press, 2006.
Weaver, Sally M. *Medicine and Politics among the Grand River Iroquois: A Study of the Non-Conservatives.* Ottawa: National Museums of Canada, 1972.
Wexler, Laura. "Tender Violence: Literary Eavesdropping, Domestic Fiction, and Educational Reform." *The Culture of Sentiment.* 1991. Ed. Shirley Samuels. Oxford: Oxford University Press, 1995. 9–38.
Whitlock, Gillian. "Have You Read the One About the Angry Woman Who Laughed?" *A Double Colonization: Colonial and Post-Colonial Women's Writing.* Ed. Kirsten Holst Petersen and Anna Rutherford. Mundelstrup, Denmark: Dangaroo, 1986. 123–31.
Wierzbicka, Anna. *Semantics, Culture, and Cognition: Universal Human Concepts in Culture-Specific Configurations.* New York: Oxford University Press, 1992.
Wilkinson, Charles. *Blood Struggle: The Rise of Modern Indian Nations.* New York: Norton, 2005.
Williams, Robert A. *Linking Arms Together: American Indian Treaty Visions of Law and Peace, 1600–1800.* New York: Routledge, 1999.
Winn, Colette H. "Early Modern Women and the Poetics of Lamentation: Mourning, Revenge, and Art." *Mediaevalia: An Interdisciplinary Journal of Medieval Studies Worldwide* 22 (1999): 127–55.
Womack, Craig S. *Red on Red: Native American Literary Separatism.* Minneapolis: University of Minnesota Press, 1999.
Wright, J. Leitch, Jr. *Creeks and Seminoles: The Destruction and Regeneration of the Muscogulge People.* Lincoln: University of Nebraska Press, 1986.
Yamada, Mitsuye. "Invisibility Is an Unnatural Disaster: Reflections of an Asian American Woman." *This Bridge Called My Back: Writings by Radical Women of Color.* Ed. Cherríe Moraga and Gloria Anzaldúa. New York: Kitchen Table, 1983. 35–40.
Zanjani, Sally. *Sarah Winnemucca.* Lincoln: University of Nebraska Press, 2001.
Zitkala-Ša. *American Indian Stories.* 1921. Ed. Susan Rose Dominguez. Lincoln: University of Nebraska Press, 2003.
———. "The Indian's Awakening." *American Indian Magazine* 4 (1916): 57–59. *Native American Women's Writing: An Anthology, c. 1800–1924.* Ed. Karen L. Kilcup. Oxford, UK: Blackwell, 2000. 296–98.
———. "What It Means to Be an Indian Today." *Friends Intelligencer* 19 March 1929: 46–47.

Index

abolition, 34
African Americans, 20, 111, 113, 142n15, 146n12. *See also* women, African American
agency: and autobiography, 148n12; and language, 94–98, 113, 114; and narrative, 98–100
Alcatraz occupation, 133
Aleck, Ben, 119, 121
Alexander, George, 72
Alexie, Sherman, 11, 137–39, 150n11
Alfred, Taiaiake, 146n17
Allen, Paula Gunn, 11
Allotment and Assimilation (1887–1928) period, 2
"Almost Browne" (Vizenor), 10
"The American Indian as a Warrior" (Parker), 132
American Indian Literary Nationalism, 129
American Indian Magazine, 130, 132–33
American Indian Movement (AIM), 11, 133–34, 142n21, 150n7
American Indian Stories (Zitkala-Ša), 5, 74, 131
The American Lady's Medical Pocketbook, 21
American Phrenological Journal, 19, 22–23, 66
American Revolution, 56, 145n4
anger: about indigenous rights, 137; case studies, 135–40; definition, 7–15; over honoring of Winnemucca, 122–25; physical attributes of, 18–19, 21–22; power of, 8, 27, 100, 133; provocations and consequences of, 25–26; and sentimentality, 4–5, 10, 24, 52, 85–86, 132, 140; stereotype of Native American, 2, 3, 9–12, 110–11, 133–34; toward whites, 43–44, 49–51, 68–71, 132–34, 137–38; types of, 138. *See also* madness; "playing angry"
Anglo-Canadians, 60, 83–84, 145n9
"Angry Women are Building" (Allen), 11
Ansley, Elizabeth, 82
Apess, William, 12, 13, 132
"An Appeal for the Indians" (Child), 33
Aquash, Anna Mae Pictou, 26–27, 126, 142n21
Arapaho Indians, 33
Asian Americans, 14
"As It Was in the Beginning" (Johnson), 24, 74–77, 80, 86, 111, 128
"As Red Men Die" (Johnson), 58
assimilation, 93, 113. *See also* civility; colonialism; reformers
The Athenaeum, 57
Atwood, Margaret, 72
authenticity, 10–11, 89, 136–37, 147n3
Autobiographics (Gilmore), 148n12
autobiography, 94–95, 116, 148n12
"The Avenger" (Johnson), 76, 146n20

Index

Bain, Alexander, 20
Bannock Indians, 95, 106
Bartlett, Edward, 91
Bataille, Gretchen, 93
Batker, Carol, 12
Baylor, Tim, 133–34
Bederman, Gail, 22, 128
Benhabib, Seyla, 96–97
Bennett, Paula, 57
Berlant, Lauren, 85
Bernardin, Susan K., 3
Bhabha, Homi, 116
biblical references, 19, 44, 49–50, 75, 103, 138–39
Big Foot, 126
bitterness, 13, 139
Black Hawk, 19, 147n2
Black, Lewis, 26
Blaeser, Kimberly, 12, 115
Bliss, William White, 21, 22
boarding schools, 4, 118, 130–31, 133. *See also* education
Bolte, Angela, 8
Bomberry, Victoria, 14
Bonney, Mary, 33
Boston, 110
Boston Indian Citizenship Association, 33
Boston Tea Party, 31–32
Boudinot, Elias, 12, 18
Boys' World, 56
Brady, Harriet, 117–18, 121–24
Brantford Collegiate, 56
Brantford, Ontario, 62
Brodhead, Richard, 4
Brown, Dee, 118
Brown, Gillian, 38, 99, 113, 148n13
Brumble, David H., 12, 106
Bryant, Patrick W., 148n8
Bryant, Shelle C. Wilson, 148n8
Buffalo Bill's Wild West Shows, 50, 59, 145n8
Burack, Cynthia, 13
Bureau of American Indian Affairs, 110, 133
Bury My Heart at Wounded Knee (Brown), 118
busk, 40, 144n14

Butler, Judith, 96–97

California, 106
Callahan, S. Alice: anger, sentimentality, and nationhood connection, 3, 5–7, 17, 24, 49–51, 88, 127; comparison to Johnson, 47, 50, 57, 63, 73–75, 77–78, 80; comparison to Winnemucca, 42, 43, 46, 49, 50, 104, 105, 108, 110; comparison to Zitkala-Ša, 130; context of writing, 2, 18, 36–37; death, 37; feminist critique by, 45–46; gender roles in, 128; on land allotment, 144n13; portrayal of Native Americans, 39–41, 47, 129; as reformer, 35–39; relationship with Creek Indians, 35–36, 51; on self-possession, 24, 48
Callahan, Samuel, 35–36, 143n10
Canada: Johnson's family in, 55–57, 83, 145n4; Johnson's performances in, 58; literature of, 72; Métis rebellions in, 3. *See also* Anglo-Canadians
Canadian Born (Johnson), 56
Canadian Literature Evening, 58
Canfield, Gae Whitney, 91
Captain John, 148n8
Carberry News, 65
Carson City, NV, 121
casinos, 137
"The Cattle Thief" (Johnson), 8, 50, 67–72, 79, 105, 130, 145n6
"Certain Important Elements of the Indian Problem" (Parker), 132
Chambers, Ross, 109
Champagne, Duane, 143n13
Charlotte Temple (Rowson), 13–14
Checote, Samuel, 143n10
Cherokee Indians, 1–2, 6, 18, 19, 26
Cheyenne Indians, 33
Chicago Tribune, 67
Chiefswood, 57
Chikena (character in *Wynema*), 29, 30, 49–52, 128. See also *Hobomok* (Child)
Child, Lydia Maria, 29–30, 33. See also *Hobomok* (Child)
children: and anger, 9–10, 14; and emotions, 20–21, 142n16; Native Ameri-

Index

cans seen as, 37, 39–41, 43, 46, 113–14; and sentimentality, 4; Winnemucca's references to, 100–105
"The Child's Life and Character Begins in the Youth of the Mother and Father" (Grant), 82
"la chingada," 93
Chinook Indians, 83
Chippewa Indians, 137
Christianity: in American historical description, 132; and Creeks, 144n14; and Delawares, 59; and emotionality, 142n15; and Johnson, 62; and Winnemucca, 93, 103, 108, 112
civility: and emotional control, 20; and gender, 22–23; Johnson on, 68, 82; and sarcasm, 13, 103, 108, 130; Winnemucca on, 103, 105, 108, 111, 113, 130. See also reformers; savagery
Civil Rights Movement, 3, 134
Cleveland, H. I., 81
collectivity: manipulation of Native American, 139–40; and power of anger, 27, 133; and reformers, 37, 130–31; Winnemucca on, 95–96, 100–104, 113. See also nationhood
colonialism: and autobiography, 148n12; and dispossession, 139–40; and gender, 136; at Indian schools, 118; language of, 132–33; and nationhood, 16, 17, 18, 129; and sentimentality, 4, 7, 105; and translation, 97, 98
"colonial mimicry," 116
Colorado, 33
Columbia (classical figure), 142n17
Columbia Exposition of 1893, 2
Combe, George, 19, 142n12
"communitism," 95, 139. See also collectivity
Confederate Congress, 35
Conquest (A. Smith), 149n18
The Constitution of Man (Combe), 19
Cook-Lynn, Elizabeth, 3, 11, 16
Copway, George, 19
Cortés, Hernán, 93
The Council Fire and Arbitrator, 110, 117
courtship, 60
Cox, James H., 12

Crania Americana (Morton), 19
Crannell, Mrs., 33–34
Cree Indians, 67–71, 74–78
Creek Council, 36
Creek Indians: and 1889 scandal, 44, 144n16; and allotment policies, 37, 143n13; and busk, 144n14; Callahan's relationship with, 35–36, 51; definition of anger, 9; gender roles, 128; and Methodism, 143n10; and naming, 51; temperance activities of, 35; in *Wynema*, 30, 32, 40, 41–44, 46, 51–52, 129
crimes, 2, 33
cross-racial relationships, 72–80, 85–86, 115, 128–29, 146n18. See also mixed-blood Indians
Crow Dog, Mary, 123
"A Cry from an Indian Wife" (Johnson), 58, 70
cultural authority, 128, 129, 131
Curtis Bill, 143n13
Curtis, George, 1–2
Custer, George A., 134

Dawes Act. See General Allotment (Dawes) Act (1887)
Debo, Angie, 36
Delaware Indians, 59
Deloria, Philip J., 10, 31, 32
Deloria, Vine, Jr., 2, 133
destructiveness, 4, 19–20, 31, 134
Diné (Navajo) language, 9
Dirlik, Arif, 18, 52
discipline, 4
dispossession: era of, 2–3; in Johnson, 69, 70, 76, 78–79; of land, 2, 8, 139–40; and sentimentality, 5, 7
Dodge, Frederick, 93
domesticity: and anger, 21–23; and nationhood, 17; and Winnemucca, 91, 92, 112–14; in *Wynema*, 41, 46–48; in Zitkala-Ša, 131
Dominion Illustrated, 72
Douglas, Ann, 4
Douglass, Frederick, 16
Drayton, Charles, 147n27

Index

"The Dynamics of Southern Paiute Women's Roles" (Knack), 148n6

Eastman, Charles (Ohiyesa), 7, 126–27
Edison, Thomas, 58
editors, 94, 95
education, 20, 42, 91, 104, 105, 113. *See also* boarding schools
Egan (Ehegante), 103
elders, 4, 68
Elliott, Margaret, 147n26
elocution, 58
Ely, Dorothy, 122
Emerson, Ralph Waldo, 148n10
emotions: and African Americans, 20, 142n15, 146n12; and children, 20–21, 142n16; and gender, 21–24; of Haudenosaunee (Iroquois), 62; and phrenology, 18; and reformers, 33
Emotions and the Will (Bain), 20
England, 58, 62
English language: and agency, 94–98, 113, 114; definition of anger, 9; Johnson's use of, 68–70; Winnemucca's use of, 88–90, 94–95, 98–99, 107–8, 112–13, 127. *See also* language
entitlement, 7–8, 75, 76, 135, 138
Esther (character in "As It Was in the Beginning"), 74, 77, 78, 80, 129
The Etiquette for Ladies, 21
"Eulogy on King Philip" (Apess), 13
Evans, Chad, 58

family. *See* collectivity; maternalism; nationhood; paternalism
Fanon, Frantz, 16
Farleigh, Malcolm, 84
FBI (Federal Bureau of Investigation), 26
"female complaint," 85
femininity: and Indianness, 29–30, 57–67, 77, 81–84, 110–11; Johnson on, 74–75, 85–86, 128–29; of Northern Paiute women, 120, 122–23; in *Wynema*, 41. *See also* gender
feminism, 13–15, 35, 45–46, 96
Feminists Theorize the Political (Butler), 96
Festival of Flowers, 105

Finley, Karen, 85
First Nations, 55, 57, 58, 76, 77, 80, 141n2. *See also* Cree Indians; Mohawk Indians
Fisher, Philip A., 4–5
Five Civilized Tribes, 36, 143n13
Flight (Alexie), 150n11
Flint and Feather (Johnson), 56, 75
Fort Yuma Tribal Council, 121
Foster, Mrs. Garland W., 56
Fowler, C. S., 93–94
Fowler, Lorenzo, 19
Fowler, Orson, 19
Freeland, Jessie M., 79, 80
Frémont, John C., 98, 120
"From the Child's Viewpoint" (Johnson), 60
Frontier Theatre (Evans), 58
Frye, Marilyn, 8, 45
Fuller, Margaret, 148n10

Gems of Poetry (Johnson), 56
gender: and anger, 9–10, 17–19, 24–27, 34–35, 37, 45–47, 55, 85–86, 128–29, 142n20; and colonialism, 136; and emotions, 21–24; in "Ojistoh," 71–72; power of, 106–7; and temperance, 146n19; and violence, 44–45, 76–77. *See also* femininity; maternalism; paternalism
General Allotment (Dawes) Act (1887), 2, 37, 93, 114. *See also* land, allotment policies
Genevieve (character in *Wynema*), 39, 40–47, 124, 128, 144n14
Genoa, NV, 88
Georgi-Findlay, Brigitte, 147n3
Gerald (character in *Wynema*), 40–44, 46, 48–49
Gerson, Carole: on Johnson in American literature, 145n4; on Johnson's appearance, 66; on Johnson's engagement, 147n27; on Johnson's writing, 67, 72, 80; on nature, 147n24; on tribal distinctions, 145n9
Ghost Dance, 126, 127, 149n1
Gilbert, Sandra, 13, 14
Gilmore, Leigh, 148n12

Index

Ginzberg, Lori D., 60
Globe, 1
Grasso, Linda M., 14, 17, 27, 33
Great Awakening, 62
Great Basin, 88
"Great Father," 101. *See also* Hayes, Rutherford B.
"The Great New Year White Dog: Sacrifice of the Onondagas" (Johnson), 145n9
Green, Rayna, 10, 34, 51
grief: and anger, 9, 13–14, 52, 141n8, 145n10; in Johnson's poetry, 70; in *Wynema*, 44. *See also* weeping
Gubar, Susan, 13, 14
Gustafson, Sandra, 61

Hadjo, Masse, 48
Hagan, William T., 143n6
Hale, Horatio, 58, 59
"half-breeds," 98. *See also* cross-racial relationships; mixed-blood Indians
Hall, John, 142n16
Harjo, Chitto, 143n13
Harjo, Choe (character in *Wynema*), 43, 144n16
Harjo, Joy, 26–27, 126, 127, 129, 140, 142n21
Harnar, Nellie Shaw, 93
Harrell Institute, 35, 36
Haudenosaunee (Iroquois), 59, 62, 129, 145n10
"Have You Read the One About the Angry Woman Who Laughed?" (Whitlock), 13
Hawthorne, Nathaniel, 148n10
Hayes, Rutherford B., 100–102, 108, 114–16
Hedrick, Georgia, 120, 122, 123, 124, 127–28
Heilbrun, Carolyn G., 8, 13
Hendler, Glenn, 146n19
"Her Dominion—A Story of 1867, and Canada's Confederation" (Johnson), 84
"Heroic Indian Mothers" (Johnson), 82
heterosexual relationships, 72–80, 85–86, 91–92, 104, 128–29
Hill, Mary Jocket, 147n26

Hobbes, Thomas, 19, 20
Hobomok (Child), 29–30, 32, 33, 51–53. *See also* Chikena
Hopkins, Lewis H., 91
"Housekeeping Responsibilities Outside of Home" (Stephen), 82
Howard, June, 10
Howard, Oliver, 92, 110
Howells, Emily. *See* Johnson, Emily Howells
Howells, William Dean, 55, 144n3
Hudson's Bay Company, 146n18
Huhndorf, Shari M., 2, 10, 15–16
Humboldt Register, 110
Huron Indians, 71–72
Hutcheon, Linda, 109
Hutchinson, Thomas, 31

Icelandic language, 9
idolatry, 59, 77–78
Ifaluk culture, 8
Incidents in the Life of a Slave Girl (Jacobs), 39, 109, 149n17
"Indian," 141n2
Indian Act of 1869, 58
"Indian Country," 150n8
Indian Journal, 35
Indian Killer (Alexie), 137–39, 150n11
Indian Mission Conference, 35
Indianness: and gender, 23, 29–30, 43–44, 57–67, 77, 81–84, 110–11; Johnson's use of word, 80; and nationhood, 30–32, 43–44, 51; and physical appearance, 19, 89–90; search for authentic, 10–11, 136–37
"Indian poetry" (Sigourney), 32–33
Indian Rights Association, 43, 143n6
"The Indian's Awakening" (Zitkala-Ša), 130–31
individualism. *See* collectivity; self-possession
intellect, 18, 20
Iraq, 150n8
irony: and anger, 13; Callahan's use of, 24, 43, 49, 127; Johnson's use of, 57, 127; and sentimentality, 5–6; Winnemucca's use of, 108–9, 111, 127; Zitkala-Ša's use of, 131

Index

Iroquois Indians. *See* Haudenosaunee (Iroquois)
Isparhecher (Creek), 36

Jack, Dana, 14
Jackson, Helen Hunt, 33
Jacobs, Harriet, 39, 81, 94, 109, 149n17
Jaggar, Alison, 13
Jane Eyre (Brontë), 13, 14
Jemison, Mary, 70, 145n10
Johnson, Allen, 144n3
Johnson, Emily Howells, 55–56, 58, 60, 81, 144n3
Johnson, E. Pauline, *64, 65;* admirers of, 124; anger, sentimentality, and nationhood connection, 3, 5, 8, 12–13, 17, 24, 88, 127; authority of, 128; background, 55; comparison to Callahan, 47, 50, 57, 63, 73–75, 77–78, 80; comparison to Winnemucca, 57, 66, 67, 82, 86, 91, 104, 105, 110–12, 128; comparison to Zitkala-Ša, 130; context of writing, 2; engagement, 86; English heritage, 55–56, 67, 145n4; as Englishwoman, 64–66; essays of, 78–84; expressions of anger, 55, 57–67, 69–75, 78–80, 83, 88, 146n24; as "fiery Indian maiden," 8, 10, 55, 59; genres of, 24, 53, 55; goals of, 79; on justified anger, 23–24, 78; literary career, 56–57; and maternalism, 55, 76–77, 81–84, 129; performances, 58–67, 85–86; physical appearance, 64–67; poetry of, 54, 67–72; on race and femininity, 74–75, 85–86, 128–29; short stories of, 72–80; on tribal distinctions, 145n9
Johnson, George Martin (Onwanonsyshon), 55, 56, 59, 60, 83, 145n9, 147n26
Johnson, Henry Beverly, 144n3
Johnson, John Smoke (Sakayengwaraton), 56, 145n9
Johnson, Samuel, 31
Johnston, C. M., 62
Johnston, S., 146n20
Justice, Daniel, 6

Kahnawake Indians, 118

Kahnawake Mohawk Condolence ritual, 146n17
Kaplan, Amy, 17
Karnee (Scott), 118
Keller, Betty, 147n27
Kelsey, Penelope, 12
Ki Na Sumoowakwatu, 120
Kiotseaeton (Mohawk), 12
Klages, Mary, 4
Knack, Martha C., 148n6
Konkle, Maureen, 18, 52
Krupat, Arnold, 95, 131
Ku-yui Dicutta. *See* Northern Paiute Indians
Kuyuidika-a (Eaters of the Cui-ui), 88

Lakota Indians, 24, 47–50, 52, 126, 128, 149n1
land: allotment policies, 2, 36, 37, 44, 46–47, 93, 114, 143n13, 144n16, 148n7; Canadian, 145n4; dispossession of, 2, 8, 139–40
language: and agency, 94–98, 113, 114; bias in, 138–39; of colonialism, 132–33; power of, 106, 133; and race, 102–3, 136. *See also* English language
Lape, Noreen Groover, 94–95, 116
Lashgari, Deirdre, 13
Laurence (character in "As It Was in the Beginning"), 74–76, 128
Lawson, Frank, 70–71
Leach, Stella, 133
League of the Iroquois (Morgan), 62
"The Legend of Lillooet Falls" (Johnson), 83
Legends of Vancouver (Johnson), 56
The Life and Adventures of Joaquin Murieta (Ridge), 40
Life Among the Piutes (Winnemucca): authenticity of, 89; comparison to Callahan, 49, 50; criticism of, 93; Hedrick on, 120; implications for modern relationships, 124, 131; language and agency in, 96; letters from white men in, 92, 114; modern attitudes toward, 25, 116–18, 127–28; "outrage" in, 109–10; preface to, 87; shaming in, 107–8

Index

Life of Ma-ka-tai-me-she-kai-kiak or Black Hawk ... (Patterson), 147n2
Lighthall, William Douw, 57, 66
l'Isère, Colombat de, 23
Little Fox (character in *Wynema*), 48
"The Lodge of the Law-Makers" (Johnson), 62
The London News, 70–71
The Lone Ranger and Tonto Fistfight in Heaven (Alexie), 11
Longfellow, Henry Wadsworth, 67
"Longhouse" Mohawk Indians, 145n9
Looking Cloud, Arlo, 142n21
Lorde, Audre, 15, 125, 138
Lost Bird, 136
Lott, Eric, 20
Love and Theft (Lott), 20
Lutz, Catherine, 7, 8
Lytle, Clifford M., 2; on social change, 133

Maddox, Lucy, 7
madness, 13–14, 23, 31, 52
The Madwoman in the Attic (Gilbert and Gubar), 13
Maine, 31
Mair, Charles, 80
Major Crimes Act (1885), 2
Malheur Reservation, 98, 101, 102, 119
Mann, Horace, 148n10
Mann, Mary Elizabeth, 87, 89, 95, 128, 147n3, 148n10
marriage. *See* cross-racial relationships; heterosexual relationships
Marshall, John, 6, 141n6
maternalism: in Johnson, 55, 76–77, 81–84, 129, 146n22; and sentimentality, 4, 141n4; of Winnemucca, 101, 102, 112–14; in *Wynema*, 42, 46, 49–50, 128
Maurice (character in *Wynema*), 45–47
McDonald, Charlie, 73–74, 76–78
McDonald, Christie, 73–74, 76–78, 80, 129
McFall, Lynne, 13, 139
McIntosh, Rev. John, 143n10
McIntosh, William, 44
McRaye, Walter, 76, 146n20
McTavish, Rose, 79
medicine men, 104, 112

Merish, Lori, 113
Methodism, 35, 36, 62, 112, 143n10
Métis rebellions (1869–70), 3, 56
Metropolitan Theatre, 89
Mexican-American War, 98–99, 119
Meyers, Diana Tietjens, 13
Michigan, 137
Mills, Charles W., 19, 20, 134
Miniconjou Sioux Indians, 126
Minnehaha, 67
minstrelsy, 67
Miranda, Deborah, 137, 150n10
Miscona (character in *Wynema*), 48, 49
missionaries. *See* reformers
Miss Leslie's Behaviour Book (Leslie), 22
mixed-blood Indians, 30, 36, 40, 98, 144n13. *See also* cross-racial relationships
The Moccasin Maker (Johnson), 56
Mohawk Indians: anger of, 59–60, 145n9; eloquence of, 62; and Johnson's heritage, 55–56, 59, 67, 81–84, 145n4; in "Ojistoh," 71–72
Moody, Jocelyn, 6
moral hygiene movement, 82, 147n25
morality: Johnson on, 59, 60–61, 81, 82; and phrenology, 18; and reformers, 33, 35, 44–47, 124; and theater, 58; Winnemucca on, 91, 103, 104, 108, 111, 149n16
Morgan, Lewis Henry, 62
Morton, Samuel George, 19, 142n12
The Mother and her Offspring (Tracy), 21
"Mothers of a Great Red Race" (Johnson), 81, 83
Mother's Magazine, 24, 56, 81, 84
Mourning Dove (Christine Quintasket), 3
Murray, David, 94
Muskogee (Creek), 143n1. *See also* Creek Indians
Muskogee Daily Phoenix, 44, 144n16
Muskogee House of Kings, 35
Muskogee Supreme Court, 35
"My Little Jean" (Johnson), 56
"My Mother" (Johnson), 55

naming, 51

Index

Napoleon, 56
National Council of American Indians (NCAI), 130
National Theater, Washington, DC, 1, 26
nationhood: of Americans, 15–17, 25–26; anger and sentimentality connection, 3–8, 12–13, 17, 24–25, 49–53, 88, 90–92, 100–114, 116, 118, 127, 140; definition, 15–18; and Johnson, 55, 57, 72, 74, 78–80, 83–84, 128; in literature, 129; Marshall on, 141n6; and "playing Indian," 30–32, 43–44, 51; and Winnemucca, 86, 99–100, 113, 115, 116. *See also* Indianness
Native American Literature Symposium (2007), 138
Native Americans: activism, 3, 130–34; alliances with whites, 24–25; anger at whites, 43–44, 49–51, 132–34, 137–38; authority to speak for, 139; diminishment of anger, 33–34; eloquence of, 62; image of death in American literature, 68, 146n15; modern knowledge about, 135–36; modern rights of, 137, 139–40; as objects, 77–78; origin stories, 138–39; protection of, 37–39, 43–49, 51, 109–10; as protectors, 49–50; sexism and racism toward, 123; stereotypes, 1–3, 7–12, 23, 41, 50, 63, 66–70, 76, 79, 80, 111–12, 126–27, 133–37, 145n10, 150nn7–8; terminology for, 141n2; theatrical performances of, 58–59; tribalism of, 129; "vanishing," 29–30, 32, 50–51, 97, 105, 135–36. *See also* mixed-blood Indians; *specific tribes;* women, Native American
Nelson, Dana D., 149n17
Nevada, 88, 112, 117, 120–21
Nevada Women's History Project, 120–22, 124
Newman, Louise Michele, 37
Northern Paiute Indians: attitudes toward Winnemucca, 25, 93, 114–25, 127–28; collectivity of, 95–96, 100–104; comparison to whites, 104–5; creation story, 100–102, 107–8; early encounters with whites, 88–89; and Ghost Dance, 149n1; modern identity of, 118, 119, 120; origin story, 12, 116; political structure of, 46, 104, 120, 129, 148n8; weeping of, 90–91; whites' mistreatment of women, 108–12, 149n18; Winnemucca as speaker for, 87–89, 94–98, 106, 114–16, 124, 147n26; women's behavior, 92, 148n6

objectification. *See* idolatry; "other"
objects, 99, 148n13. *See also* dispossession
O'Brien, Arthur Henry (Harry), 59
Occom, Samson (Mohegan), 62
Ojibwe Indians, 59
"Ojistoh" (Johnson), 67, 71–72, 76, 80
On the Education of Children (Hall), 142n16
Onondaga Indians, 145n9
Ontario, Canada, 55
"ontological shudder," 134
Ormsby, William, 88, 119
Ortiz, Simon, 18
Osceola, 19
"other," 4, 63, 94, 103
Our Brother in Red, 35
Our Nig (Wilson), 14
"Outdoor Occupations of the Indian Mother and Her Children" (Johnson), 82, 146n24
Outing, 146n24
"outrage," 33, 109–12. *See also* rage
Owen, Narcissa, 3, 12, 141n4
Owens, Louis, 40
Oytes, 103

Painted Crow, Sergeant Eli (Yaqui), 150n8
Paiute Indians. *See* Northern Paiute Indians
Pancho (Northern Paiute), 119
Parker, Arthur (Gawasa Wanneh), 130, 132, 150n5
Parker, Gilbert, 61, 63
Parrish, Samuel, 101, 103
The Passionate Child, 21
"The Passionate Princess" (Scott), 62–63
paternalism: and "female complaint," 85; in *Hobomok,* 29; and nationhood, 84; rage against, 13, 31–32; of U.S. government, 101, 102; and white women, 27, 34; in

172

Index

Wynema, 39–40, 43. *See also* gender
Patterson, J. B., 147n2
Pauline Johnson and Her Friends (McRaye), 146n20
Peabody, Elizabeth, 89, 91, 112–14, 115, 148n10
Peace, Power, Righteousness: An Indigenous Manifesto (Alfred), 146n17
Pearce, Roy Harvey, 20
Pennsylvania, 31
"pericolonialism," 16
Peterson, Carl (character in *Wynema*), 49
"The Petition of an African Slave, to the Legislature of Massachusetts" (Moody), 6
Philadelphia, PA, 33–34
Phoenix Indian School, 122
Phrenological Almanac (Fowler and Fowler), 19
phrenology, 18–19, 23, 58, 133–34, 142n12
Pickering, Michael, 63
Picotte, Susan La Flesche, 143n4
The Pilgrim's Progress (Bunyan), 19
"playing angry," 29–33, 43–44, 47–48, 127, 134, 137
"playing Indian," 10, 30, 34, 47, 51. *See also* Indianness
Pocahontas, 58, 90, 93, 129
Pocahontas, or The Settlers of Virginia, A National Drama, 1–2, 26
Polatkin, Marie (character in *Indian Killer*), 139
politics: in Johnson, 72, 83–85, 147n26; and Native American sovereignty, 6; and Northern Paiute women, 46, 104, 120, 129
Pomo culture, 11
possession. *See* dispossession; self-possession
Powell, Malea, 3, 33, 97, 111
Pratt, Colonel Richard H., 130–31
property. *See* land; objects
prostitution, 60–61
Pyramid Lake Battles, 119
Pyramid Lake Paiute Tribal Council, 120
Pyramid Lake Reservation: attitudes toward Winnemucca at, 25, 116–25, 127–28; and Northern Paiute culture, 88; teaching of *Life Among the Piutes* at, 117–18; visitor center, 119–20
Pyramid Lake War of 1860, 119

Quarterly Journal. *See American Indian Magazine*
Quinton, Amelia, 33

race: and anger, 10–11, 14–15, 18–27, 122, 123, 126–29; and emotional control, 20–23; and Johnson, 67, 85–86; and language, 102–3, 136; and nationhood, 17, 25; and violence, 44–45, 76–77, 134. *See also* cross-racial relationships
The Racial Contract (Mills), 19
rage: distinction from anger, 8; in feminist studies, 13, 15, 85; Native American use of, 133; against patriarchy, 13, 31–32; use of term, 26; of whites, 132. *See also* "outrage"
"Raising Empires Like Children" (Sánchez-Eppler), 17
"A Red Girl's Reasoning" (Johnson), 23–24, 72–78, 104, 128
Red on Red (Womack), 80
Red Stick War of 1813–14, 32
reformers: in Johnson's short story, 74–75; limits of, 41; and "playing angry," 32–33, 43–44, 127; as protectors, 37–39, 43–49, 51, 109–10; right to express anger, 44–46; Zitkala-Ša on, 130–31. *See also* whites; Women's National Indian Association (WNIA); women, white
religion, 59, 103, 112, 146n12. *See also* Christianity; Methodism
removal, 2, 32–33
Removal and Relocation (1828–87) period, 2
Reno, NV, 121
resistance: and anger, 8, 10, 13–14, 55, 139; to Indianness, 11; of indigenous writers, 57, 130–31, 133–34, 150n7; and nationhood, 18, 32; and Winnemucca, 88–89, 91, 97, 99, 115–16
revenge: desire for, 20, 70; Jemison on ste-

Index

reotype, 145n10; in Johnson, 73, 74, 76, 80; and Native Americans, 23, 111; in Zitkala-Ša, 131
"rhetorics of survivance," 3
Rinehart, William, 92, 98, 103, 107
"Rizpah," 49–50
Robertson, Alice, 144n14
Robin (character in *Wynema*), 46, 47, 77
Roediger, David, 67
Romero, Lora, 146n15
Rosaldo, Renato, 141n8
Ross, John, 1–2, 26
Rowson, Susanna, 13
Ruoff, A. LaVonne Brown, 10, 38, 41

"Sally," 110
Samuels, Shirley, 17
Sánchez-Eppler, Karen, 17, 52, 90
Sand Creek Massacre, 33
Sands, Kathleen Mullen, 93
San Francisco, CA, 89
San Francisco Chronicle, 148n6
Santee Dakota Indians, 126–27
Sarah Winnemucca Day, 120
Sarah Winnemucca: The Dream Fulfilled, 121
Sarah Winnemucca's Practical Solutions of the Indian Problem (Peabody), 114
sarcasm: Callahan's use of, 24, 43, 49, 127, 130; of "civilized," 13; Johnson's use of, 77, 79, 80, 127, 130; and sentimentality, 5–6, 127; Winnemucca's use of, 25, 43, 49, 86, 88, 103, 104, 108–9, 127, 130; Zitkala-Ša's use of, 130
Sarris, Greg, 11
Sartre, Jean-Paul, 16
Satewaller, Joseph, 91, 147n4
Saturday Night, 64, 74, 146n20
"savagery": in American Revolution, 31; and anger, 10; and gender, 22–23; Jemison on stereotype, 145n10; in Johnson, 59, 66, 68, 70, 72, 75, 76, 82; and sentimentality, 108, 111–13; theories of Native American, 19–20, 25, 132–34; in *Wynema*, 39–41, 43, 48. *See also* civility

Saville-Troike, Muriel, 9
scalping, 1
Scheman, Naomi, 13, 14
schools, 42. *See also* boarding schools; education
Scott, Jack, 62–63
Scott, Lalla, 93, 118, 148n8
Second Report of the Model School of Sarah Winnemucca (Peabody), 112
self-defense, 110–11
self-development, 30, 45–47, 124
self-possession: and anger, 8, 73–74; Callahan on, 24, 48; of indigenous writers, 57, 132–33; Johnson on, 79; and nationhood, 16–18, 53, 102; and Winnemucca, 89, 95–98, 113–14, 116, 127, 147n2. *See also* autobiography
Seminole War, 19
Seneca Indians, 70, 145n10
Senier, Siobhan, 47, 95–96, 148n7
sentimentality: and anger, 4–5, 10, 24, 52, 85–86, 132, 140; Callahan's use of, 38–45, 49–51, 80; costs of, 128; definition, 3–7; Johnson's use of, 57, 68, 71, 73–75, 79–81; as literary tactic, 3, 13, 15, 25, 85, 88, 127; and nationhood, 17, 100–114, 140; and possession, 99, 113; Winnemucca's use of, 90–92, 107–8, 110–14, 115; of Zitkala-Ša, 3, 5, 131–32
September 11 terrorist attacks, 25
sexual assault, 109–11, 149n18. *See also* violence
The Shagganappi (Johnson), 56
shaming, 107–8
Shields, Stephanie, 7–8, 14
Shoshone Indians, 117
Showalter, Elaine, 23
Sigourney, Lydia, 32–33
Silver State, 91, 113
Simpson, Audra, 16, 118
Sisseton Reservation, 49
Sister Outsider (Lorde), 15
"The Six Nations" (Johnson), 59
Six Nations Reserve, 55
slavery, 4, 6, 113
Smith, Andrea, 45, 149n18
Smith, Paul Chaat, 133, 150n7
Smith-Rosenberg, Carroll, 60
Smith, Sidonie, 148n12

Index

The Snakes, 36
snakes, 75, 76
social class, 9, 10, 22, 60–61. *See also* women, white
Society of American Indians (SAI), 130
Sollors, Werner, 31
"The Song My Paddle Sings" (Johnson), 147n24
Songs of the Great Dominion (Lighthall), 57
Sorisio, Carolyn, 91
sovereignty, 6, 99, 137, 141n6
Spirit Father, 95, 109, 111
Spivak, Gayatri, 14
"squaw," 73
Standing Bear (Ponca), 33
Stanley Park, Vancouver, 57
Stearns, Carol Zisowitz, 9–10, 35, 60
Stearns, Peter N., 9–10, 35, 60
Steinway Hall, 63, 80
Stephen, Sceva, 82
Stern, Julia A., 13
Stevenson, O. J., 63
Steward, Julian H., 147n3
stoicism, 134
Stowe, Harriet Beecher. *See Uncle Tom's Cabin* (Stowe)
Strong-Boag, Veronica Jane, 66, 67, 72, 80, 145n4, 145n9, 147n24, 147n27
"A Strong Race Opinion: On the Indian Girl in Modern Fiction" (Johnson), 78–80, 85–86, 128, 129
suicide, 78–79
Sunday Globe, 78
survivance, 57
A System of Phrenology (Combe), 19

Takaki, Ronald T., 16–17, 76
Tannheimer, Louise, 121–23
Tate, Claudia, 6
Tatonetti, Lisa, 44, 143n10, 144n16, 149n1
Tavris, Carol, 13
"Taxation Not Tyranny" (S. Johnson), 31
tears. *See* weeping
Tedlock, Dennis, 115
"Tekahionwake," 82
temperance, 32, 34, 35, 146n19
"tepees," 41, 129

theater, 58
Thoreau, Henry David, 148n10
Tompkins, Jane, 4
Toronto, 58, 63
Tracy, Stephen, 21
translation, 42, 97–100, 114–16, 124. *See also* Winnemucca, Sarah
treaties, 12
Treaty of Indian Springs (1825), 44
Truckee John (Northern Paiute), 109
Truckee (Northern Paiute): to California, 106; creation story, 100–102, 107–8; in Mexican-American War, 98–99, 119; on possession, 113; weeping of, 90; and whites, 93, 98–99, 111
Tubbee, Laah Ceil Manatoi Elaah (Delaware-Mohawk), 141n5, 149n22
Tuboitony. *See* Winnemucca, Tuboitony

Uncle Tom's Cabin (Stowe), 4, 10, 38, 85, 148n13
United States: aggression against Indians, 33; allotment policies, 36; anger in, 9–10, 25–26; and Canadian boundary, 145n4; Johnson's performances in, 58; and nationhood, 15–17, 25–26, 29–32, 52–53, 55; Winnemucca's criticism of, 107–8; Winnemucca's work with, 25, 88–89, 99–101, 115
University of Nevada at Reno, 123
U.S. Capitol, 120–21
U.S. Congress, 2, 19, 102, 143n13
U.S. Constitution, 143n13
U.S. military, 33

Van Kirk, Sylvia, 146n18
la vendida, 93
ventriloquism, 96–97, 116
Venuti, Lawrence, 97, 115
violence: Alexie on, 150n11; and gender, 44–45, 76–77; against Northern Paiute women, 109–11; and race, 44–45, 76–77, 134; and sentimentality, 4; and translation, 97; weeping over, 91; white cultural, 105
Violence, Silence, and Anger (Lashgari), 13
Virginia City, NV, 89

Index

Vizenor, Gerald, 10, 57
Voorhees, Alex, 118

Wahpeton Reservation, 49
Wald, Priscilla, 30
Walker River Reservation, 149n1
Wanneh, Gawasa. *See* Arthur Parker
war dances, 1
Ward, Nancy, 141n4
Warpath, 134
Warrior, Robert Allen, 2, 7, 16, 129, 133, 150n7
Washoe Indians, 91, 117
Watson, Julia, 148n12
Watts-Dunton, Theodore, 57
Wealaka Boarding School, 143n10
Weaver, Jace, 16, 95, 129, 131, 139
The Week, 67
weeping, 90–91, 131, 133. *See also* grief
West Virginia, 137
West Virginia University, Native American Studies, 138
"wet lashes," 73, 146n19
Wexler, Laura, 4–5, 131
"What It Means to be an Indian Today" (Zitkala-Ša), 130
"When George Was King" and Other Poems (Johnson), 56
Whiskey Rebellion, 31
whites: alliances with Native Americans, 24–25; as audience of Native American autobiographies, 95; as authors, 78–79; comparison to Northern Paiutes, 104–5; conception of as "man," 136; early encounters with Northern Paiutes, 88–89, 119; and emotional control, 20; on Ghost Dance, 126; as Johnson's audience, 57–67, 70, 71, 72, 81, 85–86; language of, 98–99, 102–3; Native American anger toward, 43–44, 49–51, 68–71, 132–34, 137–38; in Northern Paiute creation story, 100–102, 107–8; perceptions of Native American anger, 133–34; and "playing angry," 29–33, 48, 137; as protectors, 37–39, 43–49, 51, 109–10; violence against women, 108–12, 149n18; and Winnemucca,

87–88, 90–94, 97, 98, 101–6, 108, 109, 111, 112, 114–16, 123. *See also* Anglo-Canadians; cross-racial relationships; reformers; women, white
The White Wampum (Johnson), 56, 71, 145n6
Whitlock, Gillian, 13
Why Can't I Read Wallace Stegner and Other Essays: A Tribal Voice (Cook-Lynn), 3
Wierzbicka, Anna, 8
William, Robert A., 12
Wilson, Harriet, 14
Winn, Colette H., 70
Winnemucca, Chief, 88–91, 93, 100, 106, 148n8
Winnemucca, Elma (Mrs. John Smith), 89–90
Winnemucca, Natches (Natches Overton), 119, 148n8
Winnemucca, Sarah: anger of, 86, 90–92, 94, 100, 106–9, 111; anger, sentimentality, and nationhood connection, 3, 5, 12, 16, 17, 24–25, 90–92, 100–114, 127; authenticity of narrative, 89, 147n3; authority of, 87–88, 106–7, 110, 128, 129, 131; comparison to Callahan, 42, 43, 46, 49, 50, 104, 105, 108, 110; comparison to Hadjo, 48; comparison to Johnson, 57, 66, 67, 82, 86, 91, 104, 105, 110–12, 128; comparison to Johnson's father, 147n26; comparison to Zitkala-Ša, 130, 131; context of writing, 2; critics of, 93–94, 98, 114–19, 122, 148n8; decision to lecture, 99–100; name, 147n1, 148n8; personal life, 88–92, 117, 148n6, 149n17; physical appearance, 89–90; stage career, 89–90; statue, 120–21; supporters of, 92–94, 120–24, 148n8; tribalism of, 129; visibility as translator, 97–98; Voorhees as, 118
Winnemucca, Tuboitony, 88, 91, 93, 106, 111, 113
Winnipeg Free Press, 66
"Winona's Tryst" (Freeland), 79
"Winter Indoor Life of the Indian Mother and Children" (Johnson), 82–83

Index

WNIA. *See* Women's National Indian Association (WNIA)

Wodziwob (Fish Lake Joe), 149n1

Womack, Craig: on Creek Methodism, 143n10; critique of *Wynema*, 32, 41–43, 49, 51–52; on indigenous literature and tradition, 12, 129; and Johnson, 80; on nationhood, 16, 129; on sentimentality, 7; terminology of, 143n1

Woman, and her Thirty Years' Pilgrimage (Bliss), 21, 22

Woman's Christian Temperance Union (WCTU), 35

women, African American, 6, 14, 34, 109–11. *See also* African Americans

women, Native American: anger toward men, 123; dignity of, 73–74; and emotional control, 22–24; honor of Northern Paiute, 120; literary expressions of anger, 2–3, 7–15, 21, 88, 139–40; and reformers, 36; right to express anger, 26–27, 139–40; sentimentality of, 5–7; sexuality of, 62–63, 66, 79, 85, 92; stereotypes, 79, 80, 85–86

women, white: anger of, 14, 27, 128; limits as reformers, 41; morality of, 111, 149n16; as mothers, 81–82, 84, 113, 114; self-development of, 30, 45–47, 124; sentimentality of, 4–5; on Winnemucca, 122, 124; Winnemucca's lecture to, 91. *See also* reformers

Women's National Indian Association (WNIA), 33–37, 45, 143n4, 143n6

Wounded Knee Occupation: Crow Dog on, 123; description of, 134, 136; and dispossession, 2; and Ghost Dance, 149n1; Harjo's poem about, 26, 126–27; rage over, 133; in *Wynema*, 49, 108

Wovoka (Jack Wilson), 149n1

Wretched of the Earth (Fanon), 16

Writing a Woman's Life (Heilbrun), 8, 13

Wuerz, Charles H., 147n27

Wynema (Callahan): anger, sentimentality, and nationhood connection in, 24; characters, 39–41, 129; comparison to *Hobomok*, 29–30, 52–53; comparison to Johnson, 63, 73–75, 77–78; comparison to Winnemucca, 105, 108; context of writing, 36–37; "playing angry" in, 32, 43–44, 47–48, 127; sentimentality of, 5–7, 38–45; and temperance, 35; Womack's critique of, 32, 41–43, 49, 51–52

Wynema (character): childishness of, 39–41; domesticity of, 47–48; and expression of anger, 46, 128; as interpreter, 42; as stereotype, 79, 80

Yakima Reservation, 102

Yamada, Mitsuye, 14

Yeigh, Frank, 63

Zanjani, Sally, 117, 122, 147n3, 147n4

Zitkala-Ša (Gertrude Bonnin), 3, 5, 74, 129, 130–32

Lightning Source UK Ltd.
Milton Keynes UK
UKHW010858071020
371168UK00001B/33